Robert E. Watkins is Associate Professor of Politics and Cultural Studies at Columbia College, Chicago. He has published in, among others, the journals *Political Theory*, *History of the Human Sciences* and *Perspectives on Politics*.

'What can cinema offer political theory? And what can political theory contribute to the experience of film? Through a series of transformative readings of recent Hollywood films, American political thought, and contemporary cultural theory, Watkins discerns the threads of a new political film genre that organizes itself around the representations of precarious lives. In doing so, Watkins challenges us to rethink not only the terms of what a cultural politics may be, but also its reach, sensibilities, and limits. What one discovers in the pages of *Freedom and Vengeance on Film* is the centrality of spectatorship for a radical democratic politics that isn't easily persuaded by the fragile myth of American individualism and autonomous choice. More than this, Watkins's book is an exemplary instance of an ethics of paying attention to the world of appearances that imbues and surrounds our contemporary condition.'

Davide Panagia, Associate Professor of Political Science, University of California, Los Angeles

'Arguing that we are not sovereign, isolated individuals, but dependent, precarious subjects, Robert E. Watkins aims his critical sights on the hollow idea of individualism that hovers near the heart of American liberalism. But this is not yet another abstract critique of liberal political philosophy; instead, in doing *cultural politics* by reading recent American film, Watkins offers a deft analysis of the powerful and abiding notions of freedom and vengeance. He thereby reveals to his readers the tangible reality of liberal practices of freedom, showing not just *that* sovereign individualism is a myth, but *how* that myth sustains itself and with what effects.'

Samuel A. Chambers, Associate Professor of Political Science, Johns Hopkins University

'The myth of the self-reliant individual saturates US cinema, and Robert E. Watkins offers an incisive analysis of its effects. He shows how filmic visions of individualism ignore social dependence while legitimating domination and vengeance. Yet Watkins also reveals an alternative cinema that rejects the violence of individualism by emphasizing "unchosen" experiences of political vulnerability. This astute and timely book should be read by political theorists, film scholars, and anyone interested in investigating the US political imaginary.'

Elisabeth Anker, Associate Professor of American Studies and Political Science, The George Washington University

FREEDOM AND VENGEANCE ON FILM
Precarious Lives and the Politics of Subjectivity

ROBERT E. WATKINS

BLOOMSBURY ACADEMIC
LONDON • NEW YORK • OXFORD • NEW DELHI • SYDNEY

BLOOMSBURY ACADEMIC
Bloomsbury Publishing Plc
50 Bedford Square, London, WC1B 3DP, UK
1385 Broadway, New York, NY 10018, USA
29 Earlsfort Terrace, Dublin 2, Ireland

BLOOMSBURY, BLOOMSBURY ACADEMIC and the Diana logo
are trademarks of Bloomsbury Publishing Plc

First published in Great Britain 2016 by I. B. Tauris
This paperback edition published in 2021

Copyright © Robert E. Watkins, 2016

Robert E. Watkins has asserted his right under the Copyright,
Designs and Patents Act, 1988, to be identified as Author of this work.

For legal purposes the Acknowledgements on p. ix constitute
an extension of this copyright page.

All rights reserved. No part of this publication may be reproduced or
transmitted in any form or by any means, electronic or mechanical,
including photocopying, recording, or any information storage or retrieval
system, without prior permission in writing from the publishers.

Bloomsbury Publishing Plc does not have any control over, or responsibility for,
any third-party websites referred to or in this book. All internet addresses given
in this book were correct at the time of going to press. The author and publisher
regret any inconvenience caused if addresses have changed or sites have
ceased to exist, but can accept no responsibility for any such changes.

A catalogue record for this book is available from the British Library.

A catalog record for this book is available from the Library of Congress.

ISBN: HB: 978 1 78453 010 5
PB: 978 1 3502 4234 0
ePDF: 978 0 85772 737 4
eBook: 978 0 85772 941 5

To find out more about our authors and books visit
www.bloomsbury.com and sign up for our newsletters.

Table of Contents

	Acknowledgements	ix
	Introduction: Freedom and Vengeance at the Movies	1
Chapter 1	Opting Out: *Into the Wild* and the Fantasy of Liberal Independence	24
Chapter 2	Avenging Dependence: *Mystic River* and the Political Ontology of Vulnerability	49
Chapter 3	Grieving Identity Politics: *The Three Burials of Melquiades Estrada* and the Question of Grievability	65
Chapter 4	A Predicament of Precarity: *Wendy and Lucy* and the Impossibility of Neoliberal Self-Care	84
Chapter 5	Familial Subjectivity and *Winter's Bone*	105
	Conclusion: The Unchosen and the Politics of Subjectivity	130
	Notes	138
	Bibliography	154
	Index	161

For Smita –
We built something…

Acknowledgements

My having written this book is a very concrete illustration of the very idea at the heart of this book: that I am not autonomous but rather dependent, in this case on many colleagues, institutions, friends, and family. To my mind, one especially familiar and compelling way to capture that essential dependence is through the idea, the practice, and the language of family, because of the way it can account for the chosen and the unchosen, the made and the inherited. I am blessed to have been a part of many supportive families, both academic and personal, and I am very grateful to them all for their companionship and assistance along my journey to become the thinker and writer that I am today.

I was fortunate to have had not one but two academic families during my time in graduate school, benefitting immensely from two communities of political scientists and theorists, one at the University of Pennsylvania and the other at Johns Hopkins University. I chose to attend Penn because of Anne Norton's understanding of the way that politics and culture are mutually implicated and constituted, and her guidance to me always been true that insight. At Penn, Anne was more than understanding as an advisor—she was easygoing, yet incisive, tolerant yet critical. She allowed me the freedom to chart my own course, and then helped me reorient when necessary. I was incredibly fortunate to cross paths with Uday Mehta while at Penn. Any student would be blessed to have a professor much less a mentor like Uday, for he combines a fearless intelligence with a delicacy of spirit that continues to inspire me as a thinker, a writer, and an advisor. To this day, I cannot imagine my own thinking absent Uday having re-introduced me to Burke. While I was at Penn, many folks were very valuable to me as sharp interlocutors in the classroom and generous friends beyond it, including Bobbi Adams, Amel Ahmed, Graham Dodds, Michael Janson, Thomas Lee, Joe Mink, Mia Stillman, and Justin Wert.

At Johns Hopkins, I was welcomed and embraced by a vibrant group of theorists and friends. Though I did not take courses with these friends at Hopkins, I have nonetheless found them to be not only smart academics but welcoming and generous friends: Erin Ackerman, Libby Anker, Blake Etheridge, Simon Glezos, Matt Moore, George Oppel, Sacramento Rosello, Andrew Ross, Matt Scherer, Mina Suk, Lars Toender, and Nick Tampio. When I first ventured into political

Acknowledgements

theory and film just after graduate school, I am grateful that Jane Bennett saw something in the work and encouraged me to develop it and connect with other political theorists doing work on visual culture, including Sam Chambers. Sam, who has since come to reside academically at Hopkins, has been the most generous of counsellors and colleagues. In particular with regard to this book, I am exceedingly thankful for his help in cultivating this book project at its early stages as well his comments on many chapters herein.

For the past five years while writing this book, I have frequently taught a hybrid political science/cultural studies course at Columbia College Chicago called "Power and Freedom on Screen" based on this book project as it evolved through many stages. I want to thank my many perceptive students for their thoughtful engagements with the course and with my ideas, however strange or muddled they may have been at the time: Mitch Arnold, Ariel Atkins, Sarah Barnett, Caroline Browne, Kayla Christofferson, Miranda Coffeldt, Megan Coronado, Nicole Erhardt, Raven Feagins, Amy Gooch, Brandon Howard, Leif Janzen, Chris Metzger, Nadezh Mulholland, Matt Ohlson, Lydia Raabe, Matt Real, Shelby Rothman, Heath Rumble, Janine Shoots, Lana Slaby, Tricia Van Gessel, and Rian Wilson. This book owes much to the many conversations and class discussions in which these and other students questioned and probed deeply as we dissected all of the films and the texts addressed here.

As an arts and media college with a liberal arts core, Columbia College Chicago has been a very hospitable place for me to work on the intersection of politics and film. I was fortunate to have a sabbatical leave to work on this book. Many valuable colleagues and mentors at Columbia College have also been supportive to me throughout the process of writing this book. The Humanities, History, and Social Sciences department has been my academic family for many years now, providing much friendship and intellectual sustenance. I would like to acknowledge the assistance and encouragement from many of these colleagues, including Joan Erdman, Andrew Causey, Steve Asma, Teresa Prados-Torreira, Erin McCarthy, Kim McCarthy, Rami Gabriel, Ann Hetzel-Gunkel, Bill Hayashi, Michelle Yates, Zack Furness, Jaafar Aksikas, and Sean Johnson-Andrews. Two department chairs were essential to the genesis and completion of this book as well: Lisa Brock at the very start encouraged me to think big and write a book, and Steve Corey provided important support at the very end. Finally, among my Columbia colleagues, I have special gratitude for Carmelo Esterrich: thank you for your shared love of movies and innumerable conversations about them, and thank you also for your attentive, perceptive listening, your subtle insights, and your generosity of spirit.

Acknowledgements

I have presented parts of this book ay many conferences where I have been fortunate to have insightful comments and conversations with many political theorists. I would like to thank them as well: Terrell Carver, Steve Johnston, and Davide Panagia, among them. Additionally, the assistance of many people at I.B.Tauris has made this possible. I would like to thank Philippa Brewster, Anna Coatman, Baillie Card, and Lisa Goodrum.

Of course, I owe an astonishing debt to my personal families as well, both the one I was born to and the one I have made, the unchosen and the chosen. My parents Jimmy Ray and Marvenia Watkins have long been supportive and have counselled me with much wisdom. Above all, they taught me the value of hard work and integrity. I owe my love of movies to my father, with whom I have spent countless afternoons in front of a screen in a darkened theatre. My most significant early movie memories are set in those theatre, and he is always by my side.

My final and most extraordinary debts are to Kai and Smita. Becoming Kai's father has been, and still is, a transformative personal process for which I am spectacularly thankful. Kai's tenacious spirit and fearless curiosity are continually humbling and inspiring. And Smita, I cannot conceive of having made it this far into not just an academic career but also a phenomenal family life without your tireless encouragement, your patient counsel, your lightning-fast smarts, and your emotional acuity. We set out to build something many years ago, and we have been through agony and euphoria together to do it. Your friendship and love mean everything to me, and this book, among many good things in my life, owes much to you.

An earlier version of chapter 2 was published as "Vulnerability, Vengeance, and Community: Butler's Political Thought and Eastwood's *Mystic River*" in Judith Butler's *Precarious Politics: Critical Encounters*, edited by Terrell Carver and Samuel A. Chambers.

Introduction: Freedom and Vengeance at the Movies

> I am already up against a world I never chose when I exercise my agency.
>
> (Judith Butler, "Interview with Judith Butler")[1]

From the cowboy and the pioneer to the road-tripper and the rogue cop, the free and independent individual has long been one of America's most compelling cultural and political icons. This storied figure is the embodiment of a sturdy vision of personal freedom that fortifies an American myth of individualism, a shared social theory that privileges the personal over the social and the chosen over the unchosen. As a central feature of the liberalism that suffuses American politics and culture, this strain of individualism forms a key part of common sense in the US.[2] Indeed, the identification of freedom with individualism has only grown with the extension of the market to more and more facets of cultural life.

Freedom, long a cornerstone principle of Western political thought, is among the most captivating and seductive ideas today. One hesitates to even qualify it as a specifically political concept given the efforts that politicians, businesses, and universities, among others throughout contemporary culture, expend in order to present themselves as bearers, protectors, or enablers of freedom. Freedom – specifically individual freedom (for there is virtually no other kind, it would seem) – is apparently so universally admirable and desirable that dissent from or even qualification of the very principle is rarely heard. In the United States in particular, as political theorist Mark Lilla has noted, freedom owes a great deal of its contemporary dominance to the successful sedimentation of two great revolutions of the last 50 years: the revolution in "private autonomy (sex, divorce, casual drug use)" associated with the cultural and counter-cultural changes of the 1960s, and the revolution in "economic autonomy (individual initiative, free markets, deregulation)" associated with the Reagan admininstration and the rise of neoliberalism in the 1980s.[3]

Among the ordinary, recurring tropes of the free individuality characteristic of the American myth of individualism are, for instance, the practice (or even just the desire) of casting off the past and starting a new life from scratch and the act of taking justice into one's own hands. The myth of self-reliant individualism underpins these ideals of freedom and vengeance, two recurrent and powerful political ideas that animate many of the familiar representations of American individualism. These two ideas stand out, finding near continual validation and reinforcement in the cultural mainstream with movie after movie, year after year. The desire for freedom, whether from the past or from the constraints of family or tradition, is a familiar and (to many) comforting trope in a variety of US movie genres, from romantic comedies to animated features. Similarly, presumptions about the legitimacy of vengeance inform so many action–adventure movies and dramatic films that it can be difficult for filmmakers and moviegoers alike to avoid the revenge narrative – particularly in certain genres, such as Westerns and action movies. As freedom and vengeance are among the most familiar of character motivations in American movies, audiences may be forgiven for thinking that these motivations and their related principles are inscribed in the natural order of things. But of course images of freedom and vengeance are cultural constructions, that (re-)circulate throughout the film industry as well as the broader cultural atmosphere. What is at stake politically when it comes to freedom and vengeance on screen is a cherished but misleading understanding of the individual's relation to society, politics, and culture.

One of the more troubling expressions of license informed by the ideal of individual freedom is vengeance. The all-too-prevalent theme of vengeance in American film also betrays a seductive but impossible assertion of individual sovereignty. The avenger presumes himself or herself justified in not only extinguishing the life of another but also in thinking (in true Lockean fashion) that he or she is upholding the social order rather than undermining it. Still, when we experience the loss of someone dear to us, the ideological fiction of our self-sufficient individualism is breached, and the dependence necessarily entailed in our subjectivity can come more fully into view. Movies that narratively deploy loss as an opportunity to explore the ways in which we are inescapably connected and vulnerable to others are few and far between. Instead, the vengeance ritually invoked in movies as a naturalized response to loss amounts to an effort to deny subjectivity, dependency, and vulnerability and reassert sovereignty and control over the unruly world

Introduction

of social relations. One of the films examined here, *Mystic River*,[4] offers a slightly different perspective on this tendency.

The vision of sovereign individualism underlying the depictions of freedom and revenge in many contemporary movies is often so pure that it becomes compelling precisely because it is a fantasy of decontextualization and depoliticization. "The American cultural emphasis on the importance of individual belief and behavior, and of individual heroism and failure," according to political theorist Wendy Brown, "is relentlessly depoliticizing."[5] Feature films that focus on individual characters and leave the social, economic, political, and/or historical context only barely sketched or suggested play a large role in reinforcing the naturalness of this individualistic emphasis. Most movies only lightly suggest the structuring social and political context in which characters find themselves and must act, thereby leaving the impression that characters, especially heroic protagonists, are free agents, that all their action is inner-directed and self-reliant. Leaving the context out of focus results in depoliticization insofar as conditions necessary for enabling action and sustaining life are not acknowledged, and thus cannot become the subject of political deliberation. Two films examined here, *Wendy and Lucy*[6] and *Winter's Bone*,[7] reject the normal decontextualization and instead manage to give a strong sense of the challenging economic context of contemporary neoliberal capitalism.

The familiar but fantastic construction of the sovereign individual has the effect of abstracting from the troubling realities of unchosen powers, relations, and determinations that not only restrict but also enable our lives. In other words, the freedom and revenge so often sought in contemporary film ignores and erases the unchosen relations and circumstances that cannot ordinarily be overlooked or willed away but must instead be negotiated. The work of such negotiation is too often left off the screen, or is actively excluded by the on-screen action. At the heart of this vision, in turn, is a character familiar to movie audiences: the sovereign individual who is master of his or her world, whether casting off old traditions in the name of freedom or avenging loss through acts of vigilantism in the name of justice. This attention to character over context meshes seamlessly with the individualism of America's liberal common sense. "Liberal ideology at its most generic," Brown notes, "always already eschews power and history in its articulation and comprehension of the social and the subject."[8] Subjectivity as I use the term here is another way of signifying the idea of the individual person, and rather than emphasizing freedom of choice, independence, and uniqueness, it puts the emphasis on those elements of culture, context, and condition that shape and influence individuals, making them in some sense subject to forces beyond individual control. In other words, whereas individualism connotes choice, subjectivity suggests an accounting for the unchosen – those influences that despite being not chosen, are still active and influential.

The practice of individual freedom in America has, of course, a longer history that stretches well beyond its representation in Hollywood film. Writing in the nineteenth century, Alexis de Tocqueville noted long ago that in the American mind freedom is understood as a property of individuals more than of collectives.[9] He was also attuned to the interconnections between politics and culture, captured in his focus on mores, or "habits of the heart," including "the different notions possessed by men, the various opinions current among them, and the sum of ideas that shape mental habits."[10] One of the mental habits among Americans most striking to Tocqueville was individualism, whereby proverbial self-made men "form the habit of thinking of themselves in isolation and imagine their whole destiny is in their hands."[11] Such individualistic habits of mind are still very powerful today, and find sustenance through a variety of cultural representations and forms, including films, wherein heroes/heroines appear as sovereign masters of their own destinies.

The connection between singular individuals and pure freedom also has a long history, for throughout much of the Western tradition of political thought freedom has been identified with sovereignty, for the individual subject as well as the State.[12] This identification has of late produced a seductive, all-too-compelling vision of freedom as choice. This is a freedom *from* all that would be considered unchosen: all that would inhibit, even influence, the full realization of the individual, thereby compromising the sovereign individual. Yet to be a subject and to be subject to unchosen influences and relations, as we all are, is to be essentially non-sovereign and inescapably dependent. When the unchosen inevitably impinges on sovereign individuals in many movies, these would-be "masters of the universe" often react with resentment and vengeance, fighting against the condition of subjectivity in an attempt to preserve their sense of invulnerability. As a recurring trope, for instance, many popular movies often present only a single scene of grieving the loss of a loved one before the hero/heroine musters the will to seek and the tools to achieve vengeance.

Whereas tradition and custom are often understood to be polar opposites of freedom and liberty, especially in the context of individualistic liberalism,[13] flattering representations of individualistic freedom have become customary and traditional in American culture, having found expression in classic literature such as Ralph Waldo Emerson's "Self-Reliance" and Henry David Thoreau's *Walden* as well as archetypal films like *High Noon* and *Superman*, or basically any superhero movie. This independent individual is roundly celebrated for saying and doing whatever he or she wants to regardless of custom, constraint, or even law.[14] What the American myth of individualism obscures, however, are the ways in which individuals are always already subjects, seeking independence in a world inescapably built on dependence and thus perpetually exercising their free choice in circumstances not of their own choosing. Despite the liberal common sense, which is reinforced by a movie culture that overwhelmingly focuses on decontextualized individual characters, persons are always already subject rather than sovereign, living precarious lives never fully under their control.

Freedom is rarely as free, unencumbered, or frictionless as our liberal common sense tells us it is, or as many movies suggest that it is through their focus on individual heroic or villainous characters. Since freedom is always exercised in a specific time and place, there is always friction and subjection interwoven with it. That is, freedom is always braided together with a certain given – you might say "unfree" or "unchosen" – context that is itself constituted by those elements of culture including history, language, institutions, and identity that precede and exceed us. It is within these multiply determined contexts that we pursue and exercise our freedom. Given that freedom is today popularly understood as choice (not unproblematically, but still popularly), we might call this given context "the unchosen," the unchosen that sets the stage for choosing. Not only understanding but representing this inescapable amalgam of freedom and unfreedom, the twinned ideas of the chosen and the unchosen lead to a better appreciation of the nature of agency as more a conditioned negotiation than that of purely "free agency."

Like the proverbial image of the "glass half full," the familar talk of freedom and choice is but one optimistic way of framing our perception of contemporary social life, leaving out of the frame questions about freedom's opposite and the conditions that make freedom possible. (Proverbially, the glass is simply half-full or half-empty, as no one ever asks about the quality of the water or the provenance of the glass). Philosopher and cultural theorist Slavoj Žižek addressed the apparent hegemony of the language of freedom when, in the context of the Occupy Wall Street protests from 2011 onwards, he frequently voiced the sentiment that "we feel free because we lack the very language to articulate our unfreedom."[15] For Žižek, not only are we unfree, we also lack the language with which to grasp that unfreedom. Thus Žižek raises the often elided question of freedom's relationship to its opposite unfreedom both at the level of language and in terms of social ontology. (When I say often elided, I mean that the social and cultural dimensions of our unfreedom receive short shrift. Conservatives, however, never tire of demonizing the government as a source of unfreedom.) Though Žižek speaks to contemporary conditions specifically, the idea behind unfreedom is perennial and has assumed many forms in literature and philosophy, from fate and fortune to structure and nature. Niccolò Machiavelli, in the penultimate chapter of *The Prince*, asserts that while fortune controls half of our actions, we are left to control the other half. In contrast, the myth of individualism paints a picture that over-inflates the portion in our control and severely underestimates that which is beyond our control.

Elaborating her conception of precarious life, theorist Judith Butler has also problematized the ontological view associated with liberal individualism, even echoing the linguistic–ontological connection evoked by Žižek. "[L]iberal norms presupposing an ontology of discrete identity," Butler writes, "cannot yield the kinds of analytic vocabularies we need for thinking about global interdependency and the interlocking networks of power and position in contemporary life."[16] Thus, we might say that our ideas of about the reality of independent individuals are at odds with the fact of interdependent subjects situated within matrices of power. Further, as a matter of politics, both colloquial and theoretical, there is a need for language with which to apprehend the unfreedom and interdependence with which we live continually but which we have difficulty naming and taking seriously. What I am calling the unchosen invokes those elements of our social ontology that condition our choices and are not fully in our control. These include social relations, relations of power, forces of history, and cultural representations and tropes. These things not only precede us they also exceed us – i.e. they exceed our (individual) grasp. In order to de-centre the language and ontology of individualism, I will throughout this book employ instead the language of subjectivity in order to suggest a more contextual view of individuals that takes better account of the unchosen factors that make identity less than discrete. Put slightly differently, behind liberalism's familiar idea of the free individual is an oppositional, zero-sum supposition about the relationship between freedom and power. According to this view, where power is, freedom is not, and vice versa, such that one is free when and where power does not interfere. In short, power can only be a threat to freedom. This view underpins the great mainstream of American politics and betrays the extent of America's liberal lineage. (In addition, on this view, the only, or at least the most significant, source of threatening power is government; social structure and/or culture are perceived as threatening. John Stuart Mill in *On Liberty* is exemplary in this respect.) By contrast, the view of subjectivity that I am elaborating here draws on Michel Foucault's understanding that freedom and power are coeval and overlapping, such that both power and freedom are always there. Speaking against the very assumption that power is only negative and the antithesis of freedom,

Introduction

Foucault says that although power is always there, "We cannot jump *outside* the situation, and there is no point where you are free from all power relations. But you can always change it. So what I've said does not mean that we are always trapped, but that we are always free" (emphasis original).[17] Subjectivity as opposed to individualism, then, indicates freedom and power; freedom and unfreedom are always imbricated together.

Scholars of political theory and cultural studies have in recent years worked to reveal the limits of sovereign individualism and the ways in which subjects are constituted by, and dependent upon, powers and conditions that precede and exceed them.[18] Among the more compelling of these efforts is Judith Butler's explication of the idea of "precarious life." Against the ontology of the liberal individual, Butler affirms that "we are, as it were, social beings from the start, dependent on what is outside ourselves, on others, on sustained and sustainable environments, and so are, in this sense, precarious."[19] In contrast to the predominant emphasis on independence and self-reliance so characteristic of American culture, Butler underlines the essential fact of our social dependence, insisting that we (as bodies especially) rely on social conditions and structures of various shapes and scales for our very existence. Furthermore, precisely because each of our lives is not entirely self-sufficient but sustained by norms, organizations, and institutions, we are dependent and precarious in fundamental and inescapable ways. This precariousness is not as celebrated, popularly and discursively, as independence, and thus too often it escapes our attention because of the dominance of the myth of the free individual. A cultural politics of subjectivity, however, can undercut the habitual power of that myth.

The term "individual" generally connotes freedom and chosen features of identity and action, whereas "subject" (as in subjectivity) suggests unfreedom and unchosen features of identity and action.[20] While "radical individualism" is often a target of communitarian, republican, and conservative criticism because it connotes a withdrawal from the commons and from public duties, my use of the term is differently inflected. My concern is not that a celebration or normalization of individualism produces selfishness and withdrawal but that it promotes a misunderstanding of the powers that produce individual subjects and structure their social contexts. While, for instance, withdrawal was in part Tocqueville's concern, he also recognized that in the American context "individualism is based on misguided judgment rather than depraved feeling."[21] Critics often disapprove of radical individualism for excessively celebrating choice to the neglect of given communities and/or moral orders.[22] While I share the concern with the overestimation of choice associated with liberal individualism, I have a very different reason and a different understanding of the unchosen context within which choice is exercised. Whereas communitarian conservatives are often concerned to protect and promote respect for the unchosen context of traditional morality, my interest is in highlighting the unchosen social, structural, and cultural contexts that shape not only individual choice but also individual subjects themselves.

The conceptual shift from viewing persons as individuals to seeing them as subjects, captured in the discursive move from "individual" to "subject," necessitates a perspectival shift away from spotlighting personal independence to investigating social dependence. Such an account of the necessary relations between subjectivity and power yields a chastened vision of freedom as something other than sovereign. On this view, freedom is itself situated and precarious, demanding attention to conditions and social relations and requiring negotiation with powers that cannot simply be willed away. Yet because the ideology of liberal individualism remains so dominant and compelling in the popular imagination – and since this ideology continues as well to be sustained by so many movies – the struggle to grasp subjectivity continues. This effort finds surprising nourishment in the heart of popular culture: a select few mainstream feature films that dare to question and rework the inherited figures of freedom and vengeance.

A critical analysis of individualism and the associated sovereignty of choice intimates the need to not merely better appreciate the unchosen, structural context in which agency takes place but also to rethink agency itself as less free, more negotiated, and subject to some external determination. Agency is hardly as free as it is often imagined, but is instead situated and conditioned by social, political, historical, and cultural circumstances. Such conditioning means that agency can be better understood as a form of negotiation with the given, and that subjects can be better understood as acting *in medias res* than as having *carte blanche*.[23] That is to say, the idea of starting over, free of determinations of any kind, is simply a fantasy because we are always already subject to contexts and determinations that constructively shape our identities and actions. To put it directly: I do not have *carte blanche*, but must instead negotiate with the given, the unchosen that precedes and exceeds me. We cannot but be in the middle of things when it comes to culture and politics. Liberalism's common-sense vision of freedom and individuality can be critiqued through an examination of freedom and vengeance, subjectivity and vulnerability in a select few contemporary films in order not only to make visible their individualistic assumptions but also to explore alternative frames.

Through an analysis of the cultural politics of radical individualism in film, I seek to contribute to the effort to re-politicize the individual whom liberalism and neoliberalism have depoliticized through their privileging of choice and

Introduction

de-emphasizing of unchosen contexts, relations, and structures. Though the individual in contemporary liberal capitalist society in some ways seems always already political insofar as he or she bears rights and enjoys social, economic, and political freedoms, this individual subject less often appears politicized, or apprehended as a political problem requiring naming and addressing. Common-sense liberalism depoliticizes the subject – situated in specific cultural contexts and norms as well as concrete relations of power – and presents instead a seductive picture of the individual – free, equal, rational, and able to consume. Such an image is a significant cultural achievement, a construction that naturalizes or ontologizes the free individual as independent of constraint. A cultural politics of subjectivity, by contrast, can defamiliarized and denaturalize the individualist ontology that informs/underpins reductive representations of freedom and vengeance on screen. The rights-based individualism of liberalism as well as the consumerist freedom of neoliberalism both contribute to the dominant representation of the free and independent individual, capable and worthy of the ultimate feature of dignity in today's world – choice. And yet, individual agents are always formed and acting in and among unchosen structures over which they do not have full control. A cultural politics of subjectivity can use cultural texts to bring into view our dependence and the precarious character of life.

Analysing the cultural politics of the sovereign individual's filmic representation helps to re-contextualize and re-politicize the way in which we understand the pursuit of freedom and vengeance. "Reading" films that not only contribute to this figure but also call it into question, this book seeks to make visible and challenge two all-too-familiar tropes: firstly, facile representations of freedom that do not account for the ways in which individual subjects are the products of unchosen powers; and secondly, the familiarity of murderous vengeance as motive for characters who ignore or seek dominance over the social relations in and through which we craft our lives. Through the lenses of political theory and cultural politics, we will examine how these contemporary films contribute to the writing and rewriting of these political concepts in public discourse, complicating the ordinary understanding of freedom, vengeance, and the sovereign individualism that too often informs them.

This book focuses on a group of contemporary US feature films that illuminate precarious lives – that is, films that shed light on the ways in which individual subjects are always already non-sovereign, dependent upon and acting in contexts not of their own choosing (whether they know it or not). In particular, we will look at two different kinds of film. On the one hand, we will consider *Into the Wild*[24] and *Mystic River*, films in which protagonists infused with sovereign individualism's common-sense vision of freedom and invulnerability struggle for independence and vengeance with devastating consequences. On the other hand, we will analyse *The Three Burials of Melquiades Estrada*,[25] *Wendy and Lucy*, and *Winter's Bone* – films in which protagonists, well aware of their own precarious subjectivity, respond to circumstantial predicaments (the murder of a friend, the loss of economic security, threatened loss of the homestead) in ways that acknowledge the inescapability of subjectivity and precarious vulnerability, or the fact that the unchosen always impinges upon us.

Given that subjects are too often seeking independence in a world inescapably built on dependence, we will examine both the dangerous and depoliticizing effects of the aspiration to sovereign individual independence in recent cinema. At the same time, we will explore films that examine the situated negotiations of those subjects who acknowledge the unconquerable conditions on which they depend. Building upon recent work in both political theory and cultural studies that has expanded our understanding of the political beyond government and public opinion, this book makes a significant contribution to understanding in concrete visual terms what Wendy Brown calls "the varieties of social, economic, and political powers producing subjects and conditioning their thinking and actions."[26] The precarious lives on film examined here illuminate some of the various in which subjects either deny or negotiate the unchosen powers constitutive of the world in which we live.

Approaching the Cultural Politics of Film

> If you pay attention to the movies they will tell you what people desire and fear.
> (Roger Ebert, "Reflections After 25 Years At the Movies")[27]

In the broadest sense, this book is about politics and movies. But note that it is not about political movies, at least not in the most ordinary sense of the word "political." Films such as Frank Capra's *Mr. Smith Goes to Washington* or Steven Spielberg's *Lincoln* are prototypical "political movies" insofar as their subject matter directly concerns politics and political institutions in the most commonplace sense of what politics is and where it takes place. They are, however, in a sense too easily recognizable as "political," and as such they reinforce a restricted idea of politics and of how power circulates and functions in contemporary society. To be more precise, then, I am concerned here with politics and movies as situated in the matrix of culture – that is, what we will call the cultural politics of movies.

Introduction

The approach to movies and politics employed here is rooted in the intersection of cultural studies and political theory. From these two fields of study, I derive two guiding insights: one, that politics is not confined to the halls of government and ordinary political debate; and two, that movies can do important cultural work to politicize and/or depoliticize issues and ideas, identities, and discourses. These two insights are fundamentally related, two sides of the same coin if you will: the cultural character of politics and the political character of culture.

One pillar of misleading conventional wisdom about politics concerns the very basic sense of what politics is and where it happens. There exists a long-standing tendency among citizens and scholars of politics alike easily and rigorously to demarcate politics as specific to political campaigns and government, even though such delimitation misunderstands the fluidity and porousness of politics and its embeddedness in culture – particularly in democratic societies. While scholars working in the field of cultural studies have long recognized popular culture as a political space, many political scientists and political theorists have been surprisingly reluctant to affirm and attend to the cultural character of politics, instead treating culture as a variable, either "independent" or "dependent," abstracted from the rich texture of social context and endowed with explanatory power.[28] Such scholars seem to want to hold fast to the notion that politics is autonomous rather than situated in, and affected by, culture.

Consider, by contrast, the way in which ideas, idioms, and images employed in political debate do not necessarily originate there, but can travel and filter in from culture at large, carrying many layers of meaning and harboring multiple avenues for connection. One of the more memorable examples of this kind of migration in American politics is the figure of a former Hollywood actor later elected president, Ronald Reagan. He himself was remarkable evidence of the mutually constitutive relationship of politics and culture.[29] Reagan used his actor training to good effect throughout his political career. Recall, for instance, his rhetorical appropriation of the motto of one of the most famous movie vigilantes. Speaking at the White House to members of the American Business Conference, Reagan said, "I have only one thing to say to the tax-raisers, go ahead – make my day."[30] Reagan's use of a popular movie hero's signature phrase highlights the porous border between politics and culture. Like many political statements before and after, such a performance activates a whole complex of images, meanings, and associations, from the masculine toughness of Westerns to the urban vigilantism of 1970s exploitation films. Reagan's appropriation was politically efficacious not only in working directly to demonstrate his resolve to keep taxes low, but also in reinforcing indirectly the legitimacy of rogue-cop vigilantism as well as the racism and sexism that fuelled it. Political scientist Michael Rogin, recalling the context in which Clint Eastwood's character "Dirty" Harry Callahan utters the famous line, notes that the effect of the line is that Dirty Harry is "daring a black man to murder a woman, in other words, so that Dirty Harry can kill the black." In short, Reagan appropriates a performance of masculinity in which "the lives he proves his toughness by endangering are female and black, not his own."[31]

The rhetoric, ideas, and discourses that we use every day to describe ourselves, the world, and our place in it are not isolated from what we ordinarily understand as politics. Rather, they are always circulating in and across domains, crossing over from one to another and back again. The conventional and narrow idea of politics – again, held by many ordinary citizens as well as political scientists – separates politics not only conceptually but actually from culture,[32] narrowing it to mere electioneering and governing without attending to the cultural environment that not only is constituted by the subjects and institutions doing the work of electioneering and governing but also in fact constitutes those very subjects and institutions. Understanding politics as always situated within culture opens up politics beyond governing to encompass a much broader set of activities and ideas, practices and discourses, and policies and meanings that impact subjects in and out of the spheres of government and campaigns.

While many political scientists have at best downplayed the role of culture in political life and at worst ignored the necessary and constitutive relationship between politics and culture, others, particularly political theorists, have illuminated the close relationship of culture and politics and worked against the perceived autonomy of politics in order to bring about an expanded understanding of the political and its necessary relationship to culture. They have worked to reshape the meanings associated with phrases such as "political culture" and "cultural politics." Contrary to the received wisdom in political science, political theorist Anne Norton argues for "understanding the political as an aspect of culture, and culture as the field in which politics is conceived and enacted."[33] Given that culture and politics are inescapably interrelated, politics cannot but take place in culture, and culture is itself always political and has the potential to become contested.

In this view, culture is understood not in the familiar but limited sense as the arts or even as a particular set of customs, but rather in the larger, yet still ordinary, sense of a "whole way of life"[34] or as a matrix of meanings and practices, as well as texts.[35] Apprehending culture as a matrix aids in expanding our view of politics and power by grasping their constitution in culture. "The idea of culture as a matrix," writes Norton, "directs us to look at culture not only as a field or as a network but also as a medium – the medium in which we are cultured."[36] The

Introduction

approach to film that I employ here starts simply from the idea that movies are part of the matrix of culture that includes politics as well. When we understand this relationship between politics and culture, we can see that other films may be just as political as familiar "political movies," but differently so. The question for political analysis then becomes what kind of intervention in cultural politics can this or that film be interpreted as making, and in what context(s). "Cultural politics, like democratic politics more generally," argues political theorist Samuel Chambers, "emerges in unexpected, unpredictable, and uncontrollable ways. The job of those who study politics ought not be the vain effort to predict those occurrences, but the attempt to read and perhaps rewrite"[37] the cultural meanings, tropes, images, and discourses that arise in the medium of culture. To a greater or lesser extent, films contribute to either reinforcing or undermining (sometimes both, in different ways) the common sense of our times as constituted through the words and images that we use to talk about and represent the world that we hold in common.

As the boundaries of the political are more permeable than is usually understood, Chambers argues that "[t]here can never be a thing called culture that is hermetically sealed off from a thing called politics. *Cultural politics* is all there is"[38] (emphasis in original). If politics is necessarily in and of culture, then in studying cultural politics we investigate, among other things, (a) the role that cultural texts and practices play in (re)producing and circulating the stuff of politics – the ideas, the opinions, the issues, the biases, the interests, and so forth; and (b) the role that political ideas and political language play in culture, too, as they make their way explicitly or implicitly into film, television, novels, and other arts. Therefore, I want to examine movies as a site of cultural politics where images, ideas, and discourses circulate and compete for attention as they work to define and redefine our sense of how the world works and of our capacities within the world. Thus for me, investigating movies as a space of cultural politics means analysing how movies participate in the reproduction or interruption of social and political ideas and possibilities – specifically freedom, vengeance, subjectivity, and precariousness.

From this perspective, examining political movies through the lens of cultural politics presents an opportunity to abandon the sequestration of politics and to expand our sense of power, the public, and the political in order to better make sense of political stakes and connections throughout culture. As Chambers, again, argues, "to theorize cultural politics is to change the meaning of politics, to show that there is no such thing as 'politics itself.'"[39] I theorize the cultural politics of freedom and vengeance through movies. Reading certain films effectively as texts of political theory, my argument is that these films have something significant to say about the central political concepts of freedom and vengeance, theorizing as they do the individualist subject of liberalism through the deployment of ideas and tropes of freedom and vengeance.

Many scholars working in the area of cultural studies over the last few decades have brought critical political attention to the whole expanse of contemporary culture, showing us that images and ideas collide, that discourses circulate, and that power is exercised throughout culture in ways large and small that contribute to how we make sense of the world. Movies are, of course, part of the broader cultural matrix, a matrix whose political dimensions leave it fluid and open to revision. While my approach takes its bearings from the work of political theorists who have unsettled the boundaries of the political in order to foreground the relationship between politics and culture, it also finds support in the work of cultural studies scholars who have helped to bring to light the ways in which movies and visual culture can be politically significant. Thus, I also want to push beyond limited views of movies, seeing them as "neither merely vehicles of a dominant ideology, nor pure and innocent entertainment," as Douglas Kellner argues, but instead seeing them as "complex artifacts that embody social and political discourses"[40] reflective of the time. In particular, the subject here concerns the discourses of freedom and vengeance understood in light of the reality of precariousness and the limits of individualism. My analysis takes movies seriously as political interventions in these discourses, reading them through the lens of cultural politics in order to understand how they reflect and construct political desires, fears, and needs for and around freedom and vengeance. More than merely political ideas, or even ideals, freedom and vengeance circulate promiscuously through politics, culture, and society via images, representations, discourses, and practices.

If politics concerns our common life, then culture, including film, participates in the (re)production of our common sense – but this production is contested. "Film is the site of a contest of representations over what social reality will be perceived as being and indeed will be," as Kellner and Michael Ryan claim in their outstanding study of politics and ideas in movies *Camera Politica*.[41] The approach deployed here starts from that same premise and concentrates on how films can either fortify conventional, accepted ideas about the social and political world or undermine familiar notions about what is socially commendable and politically possible, thus either buttressing or eroding common sense. Films do this work through many avenues, including the stories they tell, the characters they set forth, their formal choices, and the modes of perception that they elicit. While formal politics stages the struggle over the government and legal ordering of our common life, movies feed into formal politics by accentuating or ridiculing, sanctioning or validating particular ideas, metaphors, and images about our common life. For example, from John Wayne's Ethan Edwards of *The Searchers* and Clint Eastwood's *Dirty Harry* to Liam Neeson's Bryan Mills in the *Taken* series, Hollywood feature films routinely deploy murderous vengeance as an overriding character motivation, thereby repeatedly presenting violent retribution as the natural, accepted response to violent trauma. These characters participate in a long-running constellation of aspirations and agitations that brings together individualistic ideas about vengeance and freedom to inform the justice system itself.[42] In the following chapters, I analyse some of those political ideas, images, and associations related to freedom and vengeance that work on our common sense.

Beyond the notion of apprehending film as a space of contested social representation, scholars working in cultural studies have also drawn attention to the way that movies bridge the personal and the political, thus influencing and shaping subjectivity. In particular, Henry Giroux has formulated an instructive approach to the cultural politics of film that resonates in many ways with my own approach. Giroux and I share an interest in bringing movies into broader public conversations about the world we live in today, especially through an attention to the politics of subjectivity as engaged by film. Investigating how movies participate in their social and political contexts in order to "both mirror and construct the interests, fears, longings, and anxieties" of their times,[43] Giroux appreciates that films are a cultural force in the dissemination and circulation of images, ideas, and identities that can have either interruptive or reproductive effects on subjects and discourses. Film, according to Giroux, "offers up subject positions, mobilizes desires, influences us unconsciously, and helps to construct the landscape of American culture."[44] Bridging the personal, the social, and the political, movies exercise power in ways that demand critical analysis like any explicitly political or governmental power does, regardless of any formal distinction between civil society and government, or public and private power. Analysing and theorizing the cultural politics of film, as I do here, involves investigating how the "meanings that film produces align, reproduce, and interrupt broader sets of ideas, discourses, and social configurations at work in the larger society."[45] Finally then, this book brings movies into conversation with political theory and cultural studies in order to open both the films and the theory up to broader public engagement around questions of freedom, vengeance, subjectivity, and precariousness.

JFK and Cultural Politics

Before bringing this introduction to a close, I would like to briefly discuss a "political film" that exhibits the double movement that characterizes my approach to the cultural politics of film – the double movement, that is, of situating politics in culture and of articulating movies to politics. While a film about the assassination of the 35th US president is obviously a political film in the most familiar sense, Oliver Stone's *JFK* is an uncommonly political film. To be sure, it makes a political argument – indeed, a challenging, even radical, one about who killed the President – but *JFK* is and does more than this, not only because of its status as a film addressing politics but also because of the relationship of its form to its content. The way the film clothed its critical and historical politics in the narrative trappings of an investigative procedural and courtroom thriller was out of the ordinary for both movies and politics, as was the aestheticized form of political argument. *JFK* is thrilling and entertaining, even as it brings up for consideration the relationship between aesthetics and politics through its innovative aesthetic choices in cinematography and editing. The film's seamless blending of actual and simulated/recreated historical footage with classical Hollywood film-making was new and distinctive, and for many journalists and critics responding at the time it represented a controversial and dangerous blurring of supposed partitions between "fact" and "fiction," or "journalism" and "entertainment." The debate around the film, as dominated by those determined to delegitimize or at least question the filmmaker and his work, was as fascinating and instructive as the film's content, and an exemplary instance of the cultural politics of film.

In December of 1991, after months of negative press coverage, *JFK* was released in theatres across the United States and quickly began to accumulate box-office receipts that would eventually reach nearly $100 million in the US. As the number of *JFK* viewers grew, so did the controversy over the movie, its director, its/his politics, its content, and its form. The movie was the target of strong media condemnation for months before and for months after its release. Indeed, the news media constructed this particular movie as an event meriting intense public discussion by making the film's consumption and production the subject of public attention for months. That is to say, before the movie was even released, and hence before there was any reaction to it from the public at large, a number of articles had appeared warning of and/or condemning the movie's conspiracy-theory aspects and historical revisionism.[46] As one scholar has noted, "[m]ajor newspapers approached *JFK* as front-page news," such that the *New York Times*, for example, "deemed the [motion] picture worthy of editorials, a run of op-ed pieces, political columns, cartoons, dozens of letters to the editor, and two lengthy reviews."[47]

Although movies are not generally considered to be politically significant or even "political speech," especially in the popular press, *JFK* became a political matter, and not merely because of the political character of its content (its argument

Introduction

for a conspiracy behind the death of the President). What was striking at the time was the development of an intensely fraught public discourse around the film, including an immense amount of scorn aimed at director Oliver Stone for questioning the received history of John Kennedy's assassination. While Stone was able to make his historical and political argument with the film, many other voices in the media "tribunal" passed judgment as well, and their efforts to marginalize and discredit the film ended up framing many people's perception of it. Crossing borders between politics and movies, this episode of cultural politics offered a glimpse of the politics of not just the sayable and the unsayable, but also of who can intervene in political and historical discourses.

By merely addressing the film and its director, the *news* media (not simply the movie reviewers and entertainment press) accorded Oliver Stone and his film a certain degree of political status not ordinarily given to movie directors and motion pictures. From the moment the first damning article appeared, Stone shot back at his critics, defending *JFK* against the charges. Nevertheless, the media commentators set the terms of the debate before the film was even released, and as a result Stone appeared always to be on the defensive, having to reply on terms he had not set. As the debate wore on for months and as a number of commentators began to question why the media reacted to *JFK* in the way it did, Stone received insightful support from critics on the left, but they were writing in publications, such as *Z Magazine* and the *Nation*, with much smaller circulations than the *New York Times* and *Newsweek*.

If we look at the issue through the lens of cultural politics, the very fact that the film became a matter of politics suggests the power of its challenge to received ideas about political speech and political speakers. The film's provocation, as evidenced by the popular debate that it generated, illuminates the interrelated character of culture and politics, as the boundaries between fact and fiction, journalism and entertainment were alternately contested and defended. Troubling some of the conventional borders between news and entertainment, politics and movies, journalism and history via its form as well as its content, the film unsettled perceptions of the boundaries between politics and culture in ways that make apparent the ineluctable imbrication of politics and culture.

The debate around the film might be read simply as a question of content, of what happened in Dallas in November 1963, such that Stone's challenge is the challenge of conspiracy against the official narrative of the Warren Commission, otherwise known as the "lone gunman" theory. Though the content as conveyed through the film's formal structure is politically significant, I read the debate elicited by the film differently, for it reveals more than just a dispute over the "facts" of the event. It was in actuality a dispute over who can address politics and political history in a publicly prominent way. The film, and many responses to it from many quarters within the media and the academy, ended up raising questions of who can intervene in politics and how different media are constituted as legitimate political speakers. One scholar remarked that *JFK*, like the novel and the newspaper before it, "recognizes the media as a terrain" of political and cultural struggle.[48] In other words, *JFK* and the debate that grew up around it are indicative of a kind of cultural politics that has only become more prominent over the ensuing years. For that reason, it bears scrutiny as we begin this book's exploration of movies and cultural politics.

JFK helps to make visible the way in which politics is situated in culture, for the discourse spawned by the film attests to the contestation over which institutions and agents are the proper custodians of national history and arbiters of political discourse. On the one hand, a Hollywood director of a major motion picture intervened in the cultural and historical politics of the assassination and made a claim on power, while on the other hand, established figures in traditional journalism interpreted *JFK* as a threat to their authority as the "gatekeepers" of political debate and national history. Media scholar Barbie Zelizer writes in her book *Covering the Body: The Kennedy Assassination, the Media and the Shaping of Collective Memory* that *JFK* "gave rise to extensive public discussion that made the workings of cultural authority an explicit topic of popular discourse and popular culture."[49] Indeed, the whole episode was remarkable precisely because of the cultural contest over legitimacy of political speakers and speech. The fact that the film came to be positioned at the centre of a large public debate that carried on before, during, and after its release attests to the discursive character of cultural politics. "Cultural politics does not exist *simpliciter*," as Samuel Chambers argues. "Rather, it is produced through a set of discontinuous discursive practices. This is certainly not to say that cultural politics somehow turns out to be a solely academic exercise. Activists, artists, and 'ordinary' people practise cultural politics every day."[50] The range of political and cultural actors involved in this episode of cultural politics elicited by *JFK* bears out the film's challenge to, and the journalists' defence of, the notion that films are not legitimate interlocutors in political debate. The film and the debate around it, then, serve to corroborate the notion that politics is not carried out separately from culture and aesthetics but rather is contested in and constituted of culture and aesthetics. The very existence of the debate around the film argues for the cultural character of politics.

In addition to the cultural character of politics, *JFK* also proves valuable for illustrating the political character of culture, or how film as an aesthetic experience in itself can also be political and politicized. In addition to the way in which it contests cultural and political authority, as manifest in the debate, *JFK* as a filmic text also intervenes politically in two important and related ways. Firstly, it de-centres a traditionally singular and individual visual and narrative perspective, and instead offers multiple, unconventional subject positions for its audience; and secondly, it contests familiar ideas and representations of American politics around individualism and conspiracy.

The debate around *JFK* reveals that it was challenged and criticized because of its origin and status as a feature film, traditionally the preserve of "fiction" films (i.e. "entertainment"), and the implication was that this film was intruding on the terrain of political journalism. In the same vein, it was also criticized by journalists because of its distinctive mixture of form and content, specifically its jump-cut editing and continual juxtaposition of many different film stocks (not to mention its conspiracy-at-the-heart-of-American-government thesis). Criticisms of these aspects help, in turn, to reveal the political potential of film generally, as well as the political character of this film in particular.

JFK's combination of conspiracy content and fractured imagery and editing worked together as a provocation to the conventional idea of political speech as reasoned, true, and primarily linguistic. Historiographical and literary theorist Hayden White summed up what seems to have troubled many traditional political journalists about this particular film's intrusion into the political discourse: "Stone's film seemed to blur the distinction between fact and fiction by treating an historical event as if there were no limits to what could legitimately be said about it, thereby bringing under question the very principle of objectivity as the basis for which one might discriminate between truth on the one side and myth, ideology, illusion, and lie on the other."[51] Clearly a film that does this would be threatening to a journalistic profession premised on impartiality and fidelity to "the facts," and yet White situates the film's provocation within the larger cultural dissolution of "the taboo against mixing fact with fiction, except in manifestly 'imaginative' discourse."[52] White's assessment alludes as much to the film's visual form and structure as to its content. One of the most distinctive and potent features of *JFK*'s politics is its look – whether it is thought to be politically troubling or aesthetically thrilling, or both.

Such a taboo has only further weakened in the years since *JFK*'s release, particularly with the rise of the internet, the ubiquity of video, and the growing prevalence of remix culture. On the occasion of the 50th anniversary of the Kennedy assassination in 2013, film critic Bilge Ebiri argued that the movie still holds up over 20 years after its first release, particularly with respect to its form:

> The real attraction in *JFK* was the film's densely packed, kaleidoscopic whirr of mixed-media imagery – golden-hued cinematography cut with newsreel cut with fake newsreel cut with still shots cut with flashbacks cut with re-creations. Here was a stylistic breakthrough and a historical document all in one, a movie that wanted to change both cinema and the world.[53]

Indeed, its style was part of the film's political intervention, as the debate over it confirms. These and other cinematic techniques are part of the film's effort to self-consciously style itself as political intervention. In a sense, it worked – for it ignited a startlingly large and intense public debate over many, many issues, including not only social and cultural questions about the relationships between (and among) movies and politics, movies and journalism, and movies and history, but also artistic and cinematic questions about spectatorship as well as the relationship between truth, fact and fiction, art and truth, and politics and myth making.

A central feature of many arguments against Stone's *JFK* was the assertion of the manipulative power of motion pictures and the corresponding assumption of the vulnerability of younger audiences – an assumption that sees audience members (other than the purveyor of such an argument, of course) as passive receptors and empty containers into which images and ideas flow unimpeded, rather than as the engaged citizens and discerning jurors that the film tries to construct as its audience. Still, in such arguments, critics use this stance to justify their concern that the younger generation will be led by this movie to believe that there was a conspiratorial plot behind the assassination of President Kennedy.[54] In order to demonstrate this point, one journalist even went so far as to interview a number of youths who had seen the movie and believed that there was a conspiracy.[55]

The troubling of the borders between journalism and fiction cited in the debate over Stone's movie derives in large part from the film's formal techniques. *JFK*'s distinctive mixture of visual imagery deprives viewers of the ability to take the film's "grammar" for granted, as is usual in Hollywood fare. Instead, their viewing experience is unsettled with unconventional editing and multiple, shifting film formats that make up this protean visual form of political argument. The shuffling of footages and filmstocks in *JFK* not only fractures the look of the film but also has the effect of fracturing and de-centring the traditional movie-viewing subject, multiplying the subject positions and encouraging the audience to watch themselves as they watch the film. Beyond their vantage points as consumers of a political thriller and a courtroom drama, viewers of *JFK* are also positioned variously

Introduction

as citizens evaluating political speech, as protestors against the government and its official explanation, as television viewers of historical events, and finally as jurors in the conspiracy case brought by New Orleans District Attorney Jim Garrison. The film thus gives visual expression to the theoretical insight that identity is multiple, and this is a notion crucial to the very idea of the subject as distinguished from the notion of a unified individual. For whereas "subjects are manifold, containing constellations of identities," as Anne Norton reminds us, "the concept of the individual, like the word itself, argues for a notion of the subject as indivisible, a single being."[56] Though *JFK* has political aspirations, it does not limit itself to imagining its audience only as citizens. Rather, the many subject positions that the film invites its viewers to occupy serve as an argument for the multiplicity of the subject and the necessary intertwining of politics and culture in the matrix.

Finally, the film's de-centring of the traditional movie-viewing subject and multiplication of subject positions also serve as an echo and amplification of the film's narrative political argument for conspiracy. In addition to the contestation of a familiar idea about the unified individual via the film's form, its story also contests familiar, explanatory representations of social and political life using the figure of conspiracy. Like the conspiracy films from the 1970s that "reverse[d] the polarities of earlier political thrillers, which generally affirmed American institutions, by suggesting that the source of evil was those very institutions,"[57] *JFK* targets a particular nexus of institutions at the centre of American life as the source of danger. From its very first frames, the movie takes aim at "the military-industrial complex." The phrase is, of course, a durable piece of American political discourse, coined by President Eisenhower in his 1961 farewell address, and *JFK* itself begins with video of Eisenhower's televised address delivering his warning against this very complex: "We must guard against the acquisition of unwarranted influence, whether sought or unsought, by the military-industrial complex [...] We must never let the weight of this combination endanger our liberties or democratic processes." Viewers of the film see Eisenhower caution them, for they are positioned as members of the American polity and viewing public. The video clip of the historic, televised address appears during the film's opening credits and directly after an epigraph from Ella Wheeler Wilcox that states, "To sin by silence when we should protest makes cowards out of men." The unusual combination, at least in terms of Hollywood classical style,[58] of an exhortatory epigraph with President Eisenhower's grave admonition at the very outset of the film positions the audience as engaged readers and critical citizens, rather than simply passive moviegoers, and primes them to shift their thinking to the institutional and structural level of the complex and away from individual actors. That is to say, *JFK* frames itself in an unusual way.

There has long been a popular suspicion regarding the official "myth" of the Kennedy assassination that there was no conspiracy, predating not only *JFK* but even the Warren Commission's report itself and its infamous "single bullet" and "lone gunman" theories regarding Lee Harvey Oswald. Since the release of the Warren Commission report, the number of distrustful Americans has only grown.[59] Much of the general populace continued to believe that there was a conspiracy behind the death of President Kennedy; polls before and after the release of *JFK* showed a significant measure of conspiracy suspicion. Consider, for example, these two, one taken before and one after the release of the film: (1) "A *Washington Post* survey in May 1991 revealed that 56 percent of the population believed in a conspiracy; only 19 percent agreed with the Warren Commission's thesis"; (2) a February 1992 NBC poll reported that a mere 6 percent of those surveyed believed the Warren Commission.[60] The high-box office gross garnered by *JFK* may also be read as a sign of conspiracy's "thinkable-ness" among the American public, if not a confirmation of their belief in it. When Stone's movie was released in December 1991, it entered a public sphere where serious doubts about the notion of the absence of conspiracy in explanations of the assassination of President Kennedy had long been features of the terrain. These doubts are symptomatic of a widespread cynicism that has followed in the wake of the recent history of American political scandal, corruption, and conspiracy at the highest levels of government.

Given the contours of debate into which it intervenes, what is most striking to me politically and theoretically about *JFK* is the collision that it stages between two radically different perspectives on social reality: a familiar, individualistic apprehension of social and political reality as epitomized by the so-called "lone gunman theory" (as well as the "magic bullet theory" for that matter) and a more challenging, institutional-structural understanding of social and political reality as represented in the film's central argument that the military-industrial complex was behind the murder of the President.

With respect to its explicitly political content, on one familiar reading, the film's political force lies in the charge of conspiracy as a challenge to the "lone gunman theory." But when the content is grasped in its connection with the introductory frame, the fractured visual form, and the de-centring of the subject, the charge of conspiracy takes on a different valence. The conspiracy critique begins to point toward the social and political forces that shape and influence persons, making them situated subjects rather than voluntaristic individuals. Reading the conspiracy in this film metaphorically – or more precisely, reading it as a synecdoche for the social and political structures within which subjects necessarily act, we can see that the opposition the film stages between the lone gunman theory and a conspiracy charge in a sense maps onto distinction between two different ways of understanding social and political phenomena or events: a reductivist, individualist explanation versus a complex, structural account of forces. In turn, this distinction echoes conceptually the distinction between the individual and the subject.

Beyond the political ordinary, then, what a look at *JFK* offers to a study of cultural politics is a revealing example of the intertwining of the political character of culture (film in particular) and the cultural character of politics. On the one hand, an examination of this particular film shows how movies are capable of political work – contesting representations of social reality and politicizing issues, institutions, and subject positions. On the other hand, the film and the debate that surrounded it afford us a view of how politics extends beyond the halls of government and the ordinary circuit of political debate, contesting presumptions about the mode and agency of "political speech." *JFK*, together with the discourse spawned around it, testifies to the multi-layered character of cultural politics.

1

Opting Out: *Into the Wild* and the Fantasy of Liberal Independence

> Society, you're a crazy breed, I hope you're not lonely without me.
> (Eddie Vedder, "Society," from *Into the Wild* soundtrack)

The ideal of liberal individualism still exerts a powerful hold on the American political and cultural imagination. That influence is evident in the popularity of continued academic debates in and around liberalism as well as neo-*Walden*-esque representations of liberal individuals such as *Into the Wild*, both the book by Jon Krakauer and the film by Sean Penn. There are a multitude of theories, representations, and practices that contribute to the (re)production and circulation of ideas of what liberal subjectivity is as well as the possibilities open to it in contemporary America. Yet there is a particularly persistent strain of critical liberal individualism found not only in *Into the Wild* but also in other contemporary works such as Elizabeth Gilbert's book *The Last American Man*, Werner Herzog's film *Grizzly Man*, and most recently Cheryl Strayed's memoir *Wild* and the film based upon it.[1] The heroes and heroines of these stories are held up for their courage in transgressing the norms of existing society in order to "return" to nature and achieve a purer, more authentic freedom.

The roots of this strain of critical individualism extend back at least to the middle of the nineteenth century, to the key works of Henry David Thoreau's *Walden* (1854) and John Stuart Mill's famous essay *On Liberty* (1859). The latter is particularly influential for the way that it draws inspiration from Romanticism to paint a vivid and inspiring, yet radically individual, picture of liberty. Mill's intoxicating, romanticized liberalism offers a dazzling representation of sovereign individuality, one opposed not only to conformity but to what he refers to as "the despotism of custom."[2] Fuelled by the rejection of customary society limned by Mill, popular stories such as *Into the Wild* participate in a long-running cultural and political imaginary that, under the aegis of liberal freedom, directs social and political

Into the Wild and the Fantasy of Liberal Independence

critique not only into the cultivation of a non-conformist individualism but often into a radical refusal of existing society and custom.

As enthralling and popular as these expressions of liberal individuality may be, such texts can, however, work to re-inscribe a seductively misleading representation of freedom and individuality, bearing more than a trace of an impossible autonomy. Such representations portray the liberal individual as starkly de-contextualized and free of power insofar as they downplay the necessary links between individual and community and urge escape over negotiation, refusal over amendment. By contrast, a less atomistic representation of individual liberty might acknowledge that individuals are always exercising freedom within unchosen contexts. Such is the view captured in Karl Marx's famous lines from the *Eighteenth Brumaire of Louis Bonaparte*: "Men make their own history, but they do not make it just as they please; they do not make it under circumstances chosen by themselves, but under circumstances directly found, given, and transmitted from the past."[3] Like later post-structuralist thinkers such as Michel Foucault, Marx here draws our attention to the unchosen context(s) within which individual choices are made, recognizing the reality of situated subjectivity and interdependence rather than indulging in an atomistic fantasy of independence. A further implication of Marx's formulation is that a simple and radical refusal of circumstances (social, political, cultural, historical, discursive, and so on) is not possible either, meaning that our actions are always situated – or circumstanced, if you will. Yet, *Into the Wild*, the film especially, offers a dramatic and misleading glorification of refusal, as if circumstance and power can simply be willed away.

In this chapter, I will bring the post-structural critique of the subject and the insights of productive power to bear on this popular representation of American individualism in order to reveal the limits of liberal individualism – specifically, tracking both the confirmation and subversion of liberal ideals in the film *Into the Wild*. What this simultaneous confirming subversion amounts to is a forceful, if unintended, critique of liberal individualism. Through a close reading of the film together with key texts in liberal theory and post-structuralist theory, this chapter reveals the extent to which the liberal individual – even the most atomistic one who seems most free, living in the woods alone and apart from society – is still a part of society and thus a subject, like others, who is always already acting in unchosen contexts that precede and exceed him or her.

Why, from the perspective of political theory, study popular culture in general, and this story in particular? For at least a couple of reasons drawn from the emergent discipline of cultural studies. Firstly, work at the interface of political theory and cultural studies can serve to contextualize political questions generally and issues of liberal individuality in particular. As Jodi Dean has noted, "Importantly for politics in the information age, contextualization enables political and cultural analyses to take de-politicization seriously, to address the means through which spaces, issues, identities, and events are taken out of political circulation or are blocked from the agenda."[4] The critical issue of de-politiciziation is particularly important with *Into the Wild*, for its story offers what many see as an admirable representation of critical individuality in the figure of Chris McCandless, but it is one that sanctions depoliticizing practices in the name of a radical Romantic individualism. Secondly, popular culture constitutes a significant field of power relations, within which subjectivity is forged. Scholars Jeffrey Nealon and Susan Searls Giroux summarize the methodological insights of politically informed cultural studies when they write that "one of the most crucial reasons to study popular culture is not so much to *learn* from it but to examine how it *teaches* us certain things." We learn much from popular culture in ways both conscious and unconscious. Specifically, for instance, we learn "how to be subjects, or how to be certain types of subjects" (emphasis original).[5] That is to say, we learn what kinds of subjectivities and identities are acceptable and unacceptable, normative and transgressive. *Into the Wild* is no exception to this learning process, for it makes certain kinds of pedagogical claims about how to be a subject in liberal society and about the expectations of, and possibilities open to, the liberal subject. In other words, situating *Into the Wild* in these larger discursive formations reminds us what the film itself seems to forget – namely, that freedom of choice itself is exercised in an unchosen context, such that "the choices we appear to make have already been made for us."[6]

Freedom and Power: Complicating the Liberal Subject

Before turning to a closer examination of *Into the Wild*'s representation of liberal individuality, let us first consider how liberalism has traditionally understood the individual and how key developments from Friedrich Nietzsche to Michel Foucault have complicated that understanding in light of unchosen contexts and productive power. For the last 20-plus years, liberals such as Richard Flathman and kindred thinkers such as Anne Norton working at the interface of liberalism and post-structuralism have sought to ameliorate the dangers of liberal atomism by infusing our understanding of liberalism with a greater attention to the power of context and the context of power, gleaned from the insights of Foucault's re-conceptualization of power as productive rather than simply repressive.[7] Attending to the constraints given in those unchosen contexts wherein subjects exercise their liberal freedom, these theorists have unsettled the representation of individual liberty as pure refusal by folding negotiation, acceptance, and amendment into the practices of the liberal subject. Such sophisticated theoretical efforts to complicate individual liberty must, however, compete in the popular imagination with comparatively simple representations of liberal individualism, such as that of *Into the Wild*, which tend to over-emphasize the idealistic desire for the new and for independence at the expense of a real reckoning with the inescapability of power that necessitates negotiation by foreclosing the fantasy of escape.

"Liberalism" is a famously capacious philosophy and discourse; therefore, let me specify the particular liberalism that I have in mind. The liberalism that draws our focus here is one that occupies a central place not just in the political life of the US but also in its cultural imagination. It is embodied in the seemingly autonomous individual's willingness to cast off the old in search of the new. As such, it is rooted in what poet and art critic Peter Schjeldhal has called "the habit of freedom" that, among other things, informs "nearly all the best American art and literature [which] is about departing, setting off, getting rid of entanglements, breaking loyalties, killing the father."[8] Such a liberalism is deeply individualistic, informed by the discourse and practices of individual rights and freedoms as well as recurrent tropes of individualism and independence, from the Western pioneers to the solitary naturalist to the innovative entrepreneur. Through its many cultural and political manifestations, this vision of liberty has become something approaching a taken-for-granted "second nature" for Americans. As Anne Norton argues in her study of liberal theory and American popular culture, *Republic of Signs*, "Liberalism has become the common sense of the American people, a set of principles unconsciously adhered to, a set of conventions so deeply held that they appear (when they appear at all) to be no more than common sense."[9] Such an exercise of liberal freedom prizes the ease of escape over the difficulty of endurance and negotiation.

There are at least two central components to this American liberal common sense, and broadly speaking they concern freedom, subjectivity, and power. The first is an individualistic sense of freedom, a kind of Romantic individualism that conflates individual freedom with freedom *from* the determinations of context and freedom *from* others, rather than a freedom *with* others or a freedom *within* context and power. Owing much to John Stuart Mill, this component is often criticized as atomism, as if individuals were unattached atoms floating free, and thus points toward liberalism's problematic understanding of the subject (more on this below). The second component is a nearly innate suspicion of government in particular and power more generally. This suspicion is infused with a binary understanding of the relationship of freedom and power and often takes the form of a conflation of government with power, such that only the government is perceived as a troubling source of power. On this view, escaping government's reach becomes synonymous with escaping power itself. This aspect of liberalism owes much to John Locke, whom political theorist Sheldon Wolin says holds a "tough-minded view of power [that] is interesting for the way it identifies power with physical coercion [...] The identification of government with coercion became part of the liberal outlook."[10]

By contrast, Foucault's influential insights into the productive mode of power – whereby power does not just "say no" but also "produces things [...] induces pleasure, forms knowledge, produces discourse"[11] – challenge this stark opposition by highlighting the inescapability of power, its distribution throughout society, and the persistence of freedom within power. Indeed, Foucault deconstructs the opposition of freedom and power at the heart of liberalism, claiming that "power relations are possible only insofar as the subjects are free," and further that "if there are relations of power in every social field, this is because there is freedom everywhere."[12] Whereas liberalism holds a stark, zero-sum view of this relationship, seeing freedom where power is absent and power where freedom is absent, Foucault sees power and freedom as inseparable, where the one is the condition for the other. Foucault challenges liberalism's characteristic Lockean suspicion of government by asserting instead that "power relations are rooted deep in the social nexus, not a supplementary structure over and above 'society' whose radical effacement one could dream of [...] A society without power relations can only be an abstraction."[13] And yet, the aspiration to a space free from power is exactly what is offered by the representation of Chris McCandless in the film *Into the Wild*.

The kind of liberalism that *Into the Wild*'s McCandless enacts and represents owes much to the Romantic, individualist liberalism of John Stuart Mill, who was self-consciously inspired by Romantic thinkers such as Wilhem von Humboldt and Romantic poets such as Lord Byron. There are two telling influences from Romanticism in both Mill's liberalism and the film: (1) the opposition of individual to society; and (2) the privileging of impulse and feeling over reason. For instance, the film version of *Into the Wild* opens with a full-screen quotation from Byron's *Childe Harold's Pilgrimage*: "There is a pleasure in the pathless woods; / There is a rapture on the lonely shore; / There is society, where none intrudes, / By the deep sea, and music is its roar: / I love not man the less, but nature more." This quotation, from perhaps the most famous Romantic poet, appears at the very start of the film before any action happens on screen. The deployment of this quotation at the opening of the film positions the audience to interpret the coming story in starkly individualistic and asocial terms ("There is society, where none intrudes"), mobilizing a familiar trope that pairs a deep suspicion of contaminated society with a solitary embrace of pure nature. As we will see, Mill deploys the very same stark opposition between individual and social context. Thus, the film is already positioning its protagonist, Chris McCandless, as representing a liberalism of will, desire, and refusal. Additionally, the privileging of emotion and feeling over reason is another element of Romanticism that attracts Mill and finds expression in the McCandless story, especially the film version. Mill's contention that "desires and impulses are as much a part of a perfect human being as beliefs and restraints"[14] resonates with this feature of Romanticism, as does Mill's rejection of mechanical in favour of arboreal imagery for thinking about human nature (more on this imagery below). Later in the film, McCandless in voice-over recites Leo Tolstoy but echoes Mill when he says, "If we admit that human life can be ruled by reason, the possibility of life is destroyed." In depreciating reason in the service of individual freedom, McCandless' own self-conception resonates with Norton's description of a "Liberalism [that] desires not the boundary but what lies beyond it. In that desire, will triumphs over rationality."[15] *Into the Wild* represents a particular form of liberal individuality as an object of will and desire, one in which individuality is constructed as an escape from troubling social influences, from subjection to the ordinary norms of American suburban life. The liberalism that the film itself offers up for admiration is therefore not so much deliberative and rational, or concerned with rights and procedures, as it is intuitive, Romantic, and impulsive. *Into the Wild* showcases a vision of freedom as self-making, apart from society and away from power. Such a liberalism is as much a cultural force and an indirect influence on politics (depoliticizing though it may be) as any formal political liberalism.

John Stuart Mill, in particular, infuses the theory and practice of liberty with a naturalistic and individualistic ethos. Mill's liberalism values above all "the free development of individuality," for, as he famously wrote, "The only freedom which deserves the name is that of pursuing our own good in our own way, so long as we do not attempt to deprive others of theirs or impede their efforts to obtain it."[16] As compelling and familiar as it may be, this vision of freedom is conspicuous in its lack of attention to culture and context, focusing instead on the purity and integrity of the individual agent. In keeping with the Romantic emphasis on the authenticity of nature, Mill offers a rather telling arboreal analogy: "Human nature is not a machine to be built after a model, and set to do exactly the work prescribed for it, but a tree which requires to grow and develop itself on all sides, according to the tendency of the inward forces which make it a living thing."[17] The analogy is revealing because it emphasizes freedom as the cultivation of the individual's "inward forces," revealing the extent to which Mill's liberalism rests on an atomistic and decontextualized view of the naturalized individual, who need only be freed from external constraints in order to achieve freedom. There is hardly any acknowledgement of the social, cultural, legal, and other supports that enable individual liberty to function smoothly and not become a free-for-all or a war of all against all. In other words, Mill again reinforces some of the fundamental tendencies of liberalism, namely the freedom–power opposition as well as an individual–society opposition.

Mill's conception, to be precise, lacks a more complex reckoning with the power of social, cultural, and political context in shaping the individual, transforming him/her from a mere individual into a situated subject. Such a transformation owes much to Nietzsche and Freud's insights into the way in which cultural context impacts identity, as Norton reminds us:

> Liberals – and romantic existentialists – identified self-expression and self-discovery with liberation. Their enterprise was predicated on the notion of an autonomous self, an independent will that the individual could discover within. Freud's [and Nietzsche's] writings reveal the impossibility of such an enterprise. The self was necessarily constituted as such in a cultural framework; it was dependent upon, and followed from, a political order.[18]

Acknowledging such dependence on cultural and political frameworks pushes us away from Mill's individualism and toward an acknowledgement of subjectivity, such that persons are less "free individuals" than they are subjects, necessarily situated in and influenced by their cultural and political context. Norton goes on to remind us of the resonance of Freud's insight into "Nietzsche's recognition that 'we are all philologists now,' conscious of ourselves as beings in language. The self at the core of the self, the will, was neither autonomous nor singular."[19] By contrast with Nietzsche's and Freud's recognitions of subjectivity, subjection, and the power of context, Mill not only holds firmly to the autonomous self at the foundation of liberalism but also dismisses custom: "The despotism of custom is everywhere the standing hindrance to human advancement."[20] Not only does he banish custom, but he does so by identifying it with a favourite liberal enemy, the despot or tyrannical monarch. We will return to Mill's cavalier dismissal of custom later in our discussion of *Into the Wild*, but for now let us simply note the rigid opposition between the free individual and the powerful context that Mill sets up in his defence of individual liberty, turning freedom into freedom from others and from context.

Into the Wild and the Fantasy of Liberal Independence

Gaining reinforcement from both philosophy and popular culture, atomistic individualism aiming at autonomy is a powerful ideological representation, claiming, at most, the individual's mastery of context, or, at least, the individual's indifference to context. The desire for autonomy is so powerful in fact that not only Nietzsche, Freud, and Foucault but even some liberals themselves have struggled to unsettle and nuance it. Among the latter, consider the unconventional liberal theorist Richard Flathman. While Mill's Romantic, individualist liberalism shares much with Flathman's "willful liberalism," as he himself recognizes,[21] Flathman is aware of both the failures of a starkly de-contextualized, individualist liberalism and the need to better account for the complex relationship between subjects and contexts. Consider Flathman's own acknowledgement of the contextualist critique of liberalism that he struggles to address:

> Liberalism is said by its most insistent critics to be premised on a philosophically untenable atomism and privatism, inattentive to the enmeshing and frequently determining effects of history, tradition, and culture, indifferent if not hostile to community, productive of virtue-destroying and conflict-generating selfishness, and congenitally incapable of sustaining or even accommodating authority and power and hence government and politics.[22]

Flathman thus recognizes the need for complex negotiations of inherited customs, cultures, and circumstances as part of liberalism's desire and struggle for freedom, as when he writes:

> The fundamental and abiding commitment of liberalism is to the most disturbing moral and political idea of all, the idea that each and every human being should be free to think and act as she sees fit. This idea is no more than barely intelligible, and the ideal of implementing it fully is manifestly impossible to achieve.[23]

His recognition of the impossibility of the total autonomy at the heart of liberalism leads Flathman to an improved account of the individual as acting within contexts not of her choosing. "The view," he writes, "that self-enactment is done in isolation or solitude, that one makes oneself and one's life out of material entirely of one's own creation, is a serious misunderstanding […] [T]he free spirit remains deeply, albeit never complacently or even comfortably, situated in a tradition, culture, and society."[24] This recognition of situated-ness is valuable for the way in which it attends to the self's relation to its context, acknowledging that self-making does not happen in a vacuum but is influenced by and situated in culture and society. However, this recognition seems to stop short of fully reckoning with the pervasiveness and productivity of power that Foucault brought to light. In other words, Flathman does not fully move us from the individual to the subject. For that, we have to turn to Foucault.

Foucault, as noted above, may be understood as working to collapse the familiar liberal opposition between power and freedom by apprehending them as always braided together such that power is inescapable (as is freedom). Shifting linguistically and conceptually from the liberal individual to the subject, we should note that Foucault argues for power's productive role in the formation of the subject. That is, who we are, what we do, and what we become are for Foucault never fully individual questions and never fully under our own control because we are always situated within discourses, contexts, and powers that precede and exceed us.[25] This does not, however, mean that freedom is impossible, but instead means that freedom is always already situated, restricted, or subjected. To be clear, like Mill and Flathman, Foucault is concerned with "how the subject constitutes itself in an active fashion through practices of the self."[26] Unlike Mill, however, who sees the individual developing according to his or her "inward forces," Foucault sees the individual as a subject – that is, he or she has always already existed within power. Thus, Foucault insists the practices of self-making are "not something invented by the individual himself. They are models that he finds in his culture, his society, and his social group."[27] In other words, the process of becoming an individual and acting as one is never purely an internal, personal question but rather a social, cultural, and political one. Therefore, Foucault speaks of a double, paradoxical process of subjectivation (*assujetissement*), by which a subject is formed and acts within power, rather than apart from power as liberalism would have it. Judith Butler explains the paradoxical character of Foucault's idea of subjectivation, which, she writes, "denotes both the becoming of the subject and the process of subjection – one inhabits the figure of autonomy only by becoming subjected to a power, a subjection which implies a radical dependency."[28] Strictly speaking, then, autonomy is only a figure that one inhabits or a pose that one adopts, for it is, strictly speaking, impossible as we are always already dependent. In other words, freedom goes hand in hand with dependence upon unchosen cultural, discursive, and political contexts in which subjects find themselves enmeshed.

Finally, then, Flathman's recognition of situated-ness does not carry the same weight as recognizing the always already subjected character of the self. "The recognition of subjection," Norton suggests, "recasts, even replaces, the liberal struggle for liberation. The recognition of the self, no longer an apolitical and ahistorical enterprise, becomes an activity of comprehension."[29] Subjection means power together with freedom, whereas liberal individuality means freedom in spite of or

Into the Wild and the Fantasy of Liberal Independence

apart from power. *Into the Wild*, as we will see, shows both the power and limits of liberalism: the power of liberalism to become materialized in practice, yet the limits of liberalism to comprehend the complex reality of subjectivation – that is, the ways in which subjects are formed and shaped with, within, and in negotiation with unchosen forces, practices, and contexts. This failure leads to the perpetuation of a fantasy of liberal independence – the fantasy of opting out, an inversion of the social contract – rather than a real reckoning with the dependence and power at the heart of freedom itself.

Approaching *Into the Wild* and/as Liberalism

Into the Wild is the peculiarly beguiling story of Chris McCandless, a young man who, upon graduating from university in May of 1990, opted out of society by hitting the road in search of "ultimate freedom" and an "authentic" experience of nature. For over two years, he travelled the country as a completely free agent, moving from place to place, holding odd jobs now and then, and all the while charming many people whose paths he crossed. Yet even as he enchanted strangers along the way, he remained purposefully alienated from his family, having completely disconnected from his previous life and refused to inform them of his whereabouts. McCandless even marked this new life by choosing a new name for himself: Alexander Supertramp. He did not, however, live to tell his story, for he died of poisoning and starvation in August 1992, over 100 days after walking into the Alaskan wilderness to escape civilization's poisoning.

Originating as an article by Jon Krakauer in the January 1993 issue of *Outside* magazine, then becoming a bestselling book by Krakauer upon publication in 1996, and finally a feature-length motion picture written and directed by Sean Penn in 2007, the story of Chris McCandless has proven to be very popular and alluring. Not only has the story sold books, movie tickets, and DVDs, it has also turned the site of his death, the Fairbanks 142 bus marooned on the Stampede Trail in Denali National Park, into a destination for dissatisfied, searching individuals. And yet, as Krakauer indicates, from the moment of the original *Outside* story, responses to McCandless have also always been divided. While there are many people, Krakauer notes, who "admired the boy immensely for his courage and noble ideals," there were many "others [who] fulminated that he was a reckless idiot, a wacko, a narcissist who perished out of arrogance and stupidity."[30] The release of the film in 2007, however, seems to have shifted the balance of power in the contest over the meaning of McCandless' life and death. For while Krakauer's book works hard to strike a balance between the competing interpretations of this individual – courageous or reckless, noble or narcissistic – the film veers decisively toward hagiography in its representation of McCandless' story as a courageous search for freedom. Here, I will concentrate primarily on the film of *Into the Wild* because it presents such a strong representation of Romantic, liberal individualism, almost without reservation.

What are we to make of this story and its popularity? What kind of cultural, political nerve has it struck? The figure of McCandless presents the paradox of an impetuous young man traipsing off from the society he had known in search of total independence and "ultimate freedom"[31] in the wilderness of the American West, only to come to the conclusion "happiness only real when shared,"[32] as McCandless himself wrote in the margins in his copy of *Doctor Zhivago* just before he died. Krakauer reports that many readers of *Outside* magazine wrote in to express their astonishment with McCandless' incompetence and arrogance at having gone into the wilderness so woefully and willfully unprepared, and some readers even interpreted it as suicide. Others, especially viewers of the film, as evidenced from numerous fan groups on the internet devoted to McCandless' story and memory, take much inspiration from his refusal of ordinary American norms, admiring his courage to pursue a course of total freedom and independence.

More particularly, how might political theorists read McCandless' journey, a journey that is culturally and politically significant not only because of the self-conscious inspiration it takes from the likes of Thoreau but also for the inspiration provided to many liberal subjects in turn? The film itself offers two common responses on the part of the liberal subject – either refusal of others or embrace of others – both of which are insufficient to the negotiation required by the complexity of the contexts in which subjects always already find themselves. Thus, the liberal individualism enacted in *Into the Wild* proves radically insufficient to the situated, circumstanced character of social and political life.

Into the Wild is exemplary of the way in which liberalism becomes ambiguously realized in popular culture. The fascinating and ultimately mystifying character of this story derives from the way in which it simultaneously confirms and subverts the ideals of liberalism, as Norton claims is often the case with liberalism and popular culture.[33] There is certainly an expression of freedom and individuality, and a strong desire for independence and self-sufficiency, at the heart of the story of Chris McCandless. More significant, however, are the ways in which his enactment of liberal independence ends up revealing the inescapable reality of dependence, subjection, and power, thereby offering a powerful, if unintentional, critique of liberal ideology. Try as he might, McCandless cannot escape enmeshment in relations and contexts over which he does not have full control.

Into the Wild and the Fantasy of Liberal Independence

Interestingly enough, the book is more honest in hinting at his subjectivity, for it complicates the representation of McCandless as a heroic, Romantic individual by situating him in a cultural tradition and discursive context stretching back in history to literary icons like Thoreau and Jack London and outdoors explorers like Everett Reuss and even Krakauer himself. The film, however, ignores such cultural models and literary precursors, giving the impression that McCandless is the first to pursue such a journey, that he is a true original. The film virtually erases the question of ambiguity and interpretation by offering something approaching hagiography. The differences between the book and the film derive less from differences of genre and medium (journalistic reportage versus dramatic character narrative) and more from the choices made by "authors" Krakauer and Penn, according to the stories that they seek to tell. On the one hand, Krakauer, himself an outdoorsman, de-individualizes McCandless by situating his journey within a long tradition of nature-seeking young men, emphasizing his courage but also his unprepared-ness. On the other hand, Penn, the Hollywood iconoclast, by holding McCandless up as a unique and principled critic of contemporary society, turns him into an unambiguous hero. In fact, the film elevates him in such heroic and solemn fashion that it concludes by positioning and inviting the audience to mourn his loss as the final scene mimics the ascension of his soul with a long crane shot. While the book reveals the limits of the ideal of sovereign autonomy, the film tries to mask these limits.

What is especially striking about *Into the Wild*, the film (going forward, the focus here is on the film), from the perspective of contemporary political theory, is the kind of liberal subjectivity on display. There is a fantasy at work in the film of being free from subjection, as when McCandless burns his money and cuts up his credit cards and driver's license (events substantiated by his own journal entries), freeing him from external constraints and definitions of his identity. Thus, *Into the Wild* participates in the (re)production and circulation of a particularly individualistic representation of liberal subjectivity, and yet it is a representation which erases subjection from subjectivity, leaving only pure individuality and "ultimate freedom." In contrast to either of these readings (Krakauer's or Penn's), I would like to suggest that McCandless' story and its popular reception may be productively read as simultaneously confirming and subverting the ideals of liberal common sense and desire. The subversion of liberalism, however, points not in the direction of a communitarian critique of atomistic individualism but rather toward a post-structural critique of the subject as always already formed by and embedded in productive power. And yet, what I seek to offer is a subversive confirmation of liberalism – or more precisely, a post-structural qualification of liberalism – by tracking the ways in which freedom and subjectivity go hand in hand, how power *conditions* without eliminating choice.

Into the Wild Confirms Yet Subverts Liberal Individualism

> I know all the rules, but the rules do not know me.
> (Eddie Vedder, "Guaranteed," from *Into the Wild* soundtrack)

A journey like the one that Chris McCandless undertakes is colloquially called a journey of self-discovery. From McCandless' perspective, however, it is better understood as a journey of self-making – or self-re-making, to be even more precise. As depicted in the film, his expedition is primarily about putting into action what he has already learned and discovered. For what McCandless sets out to do is cast off the shackles of the old and embrace the thrilling uncertainty of the new in order to remake himself through the freedom of ultimate independence. With striking energy and desire, he takes up the central challenge of liberalism, crafting a uniquely individual life for himself and overthrowing what John Stuart Mill famously called "the despotism of custom."[34] In undertaking this adventure, McCandless appears determined to exercise his individual social liberty to the utmost so as to avoid the customary conformity that Mill memorably condemns when he writes, "He who lets the world, or his own portion of it, choose his plan of life for him has no need of any other faculty than the ape-like one of imitation."[35] The last thing McCandless would want to be accused of, it seems, is slavish imitation of the ordinary, normative lives lived in American society. (Yet in his imitation of literary and historical figures, such as Thoreau, he shows himself to be conforming to a different plan, a different model, and thus a subject like any other, only with different influences). Mill's harsh judgments on custom and society are echoed by McCandless' own unforgiving judgments of his own parents and the "sick society" in which he finds himself and from which he seeks escape, with Alaska as his ultimate destination.

McCandless' judgments of the past and present and his desire for a different future, at least for himself, fuel his courageous willingness to carve out his own path and remake himself. As Krakauer relates:

> Driving west out of Atlanta, he intended to invent an utterly new life for himself, one in which he would be free to wallow in unfiltered experience. To symbolize the complete severance from his previous

life, he even adopted a new name. No longer would he answer to Chris McCandless: he was now Alexander Supertramp, master of his own destiny.[36]

It is this willing severance from the past combined with the deeply felt need to chart a new and different future, symbolized in the taking of a new name, that constitutes the best of liberal individualism, encompassing refusal and risk, optimism and utter confidence. Anne Norton, in her discussion of Flathman's willful liberalism, captures this noble strain of liberal self-making:

> For the individual, the willingness to become what one is requires that one be willing to become other than what one is. The desire to make oneself in accordance with one's will is a refusal of the present self for a future self that exceeds it. This future self, surpassing the first, is beyond its comprehension, almost beyond its grasp.[37]

As portrayed in the film, McCandless/Supertramp commandingly demonstrates his willingness to cast off the old in order to make a new self. For instance, when, before setting off West in his car, Chris not only refuses his parents' graduation gift of a new car but also cuts up his bank card and driver's license, burns his social security card, and writes a check for the balance of his college fund in the amount of $24,000 to Oxfam America.

It is with "Alexander's" behavior in regard to property that we can begin to see a complication in his neat identification with liberalism, suggesting some limits to his understanding of liberty and power. One of the cornerstones of liberalism, stretching back to John Locke, is individual property rights, and property is linked not only to self-expression and self-making but also to the inescapability of power as the necessary complement to freedom. Norton draws out this key ambiguity when she writes, "Property shows itself not only as a means for self-protection, self-expression, and self-discovery but also as a means for subjecting us to the authority of others."[38] In a series of defiant acts – including refusing his parents' gift of a new car, donating his remaining college fund, ditching his car in the Arizona desert, and setting fire in the desert to his remaining cash – McCandless reveals a recognition that property subjects us even as it expresses us. Yearning for total independence and "ultimate freedom," McCandless wants to renounce property and the subjection that is bound up with it in the name of a pure freedom. For instance, after leaving his car in the desert, he catches a ride with a couple of "rubber tramps," Jan and Rainey Burres, travelling in a recreational vehicle, a mobile camper. One night around the campfire, a conversation between Alex and Jan Burres about why he burned all his money gives him the opportunity to proclaim,

"I don't need money – makes people cautious." To which Rainey responds, "Come on, Alex. You gotta be a little cautious. I mean that book of yours is cool and everything, but you can't depend entirely on leaves and berries." Then, McCandless responds in a way that shows the depth of his radical individualist aversion to dependence: "I don't know if you want to depend on much more than that." This exchange is quite revealing, but Alex's attempted refusal of money and property does not undermine his identification with liberalism; rather, it speaks to his identification with a particular strain of liberalism. His refusals of property complicate rather than negate his liberalism because his refusal may be read in a liberal individualist vein as part of his efforts at self-making, trying to free himself from dependence and power. But try as he might he cannot escape the need for property and hence the dependence it brings, for, along his journey, he works a series of jobs to earn money to support himself as long as he still resides among others, not yet in the wild. These jobs bring him into contact with various people – some likable, some not – whom Alex most often views as encumbrances on his freedom. Though the film does not emphasize it, the inescapability of property within the terms of the liberalism in which Alex remains caught reminds us of the extent to which self-making always happens in a context not of our choosing, and that is a message that he needs but which never seems to get through to him. Again, Alex illustrates that without recognizing his subjectivity there can be no larger political comprehension, as he remains bound up in the personal and apolitical search for liberty.

In the film, Chris/Alex's self-making is rendered as self-writing, as it periodizes his journey into chapters, titled on screen as "Chapter 1: My Own Birth," "Chapter 2: Adolescence," "Chapter 3: Manhood," "Chapter 4: Family," and "Final Chapter: Getting of Wisdom." This transformation of self-making into self-writing is characteristic of American liberalism, echoing Norton's claim that Americans are always already constituted in language.[39] Norton, however, goes on to remind us that self-making/self-writing always happens in a context and with language that precedes and exceeds our individual, non-sovereign grasp. "The selves of liberal practice are not the selves of liberal theory," Norton writes, "Convinced, in theory, of our individuality, we find ourselves in common languages and express ourselves (even rebel) in conformity with existing conventions."[40] With this in mind, we may begin to understand how McCandless represents simultaneously the confirmation and the subversion of liberal ideals of freedom and individuality. For in reaching for the cherished fantasy of independence, he ignores the reality of subjection to social relations and conventions, and even to nature itself. Certainly, Chris/Alex appears here as a defiant picture of individual freedom, such that even while the absoluteness of his refusal leaves little space for complexity or negotiation, the film positions its audience to see these moves as courageous acts that wipe the slate clean. Early in the film, as McCandless abandons his car in the desert for the life of a "leather tramp," his sister Carine in voice-over claims to understand what he is doing, saying, "He'd spent four years fulfilling the absurd and tedious duty of graduating from college. And now he was emancipated from that world of abstraction, false security, parents, and material excess – the things that cut Chris off from the truth of his existence."[41] While Carine gives voice to Chris' liberal critique, resonating with Mill's judgment against "the despotism of custom," her statement, like Mill's thought, mobilizes a stark binary between duty and emancipation, between unchosen and chosen, between society and the individual, and pushes the audience to identify with Chris/Alex's absolute, individualistic refusal of entangling social duties and contaminating social concerns.

The lodestar for McCandless' project of self-re-making is Alaska, particularly "the great Alaskan wilderness," as he takes inspiration from the novels of Jack London as well as Thoreau's experience at Walden pond. In the film, responding to the question "What's the fascination with Alaska?" McCandless tells Wayne Westerberg (his friendly farm employer) that "I'm gonna be all the way out there, on my own – you know, no fuckin' watch, no map, no ax, no nothin'. Just be out there in it, out there in it [...] In the wild."[42] Here, McCandless/Supertramp configures the wild as free, free not only from power and the subjections of others but practically from time and space per se. By such a configuration, McCandless' representation of "the wild" bears a sharp resemblance to figure of the "state of nature." The ahistorical condition of a state of nature as a space of pure freedom without government has been a choice trope for liberal thinking about politics and society for centuries, perhaps finding its most salient expression in Thomas Hobbes' *Leviathan*. McCandless seems to want to enact not only the liberal fantasy of the state of nature, as an abstractly pure space of freedom, but also the possibility of a return to it.[43] McCandless thus offers a representation of liberal freedom that is not only radically individualistic but also radically naïve insofar as it is pure and free of any power or subjection at all.

What this representation of individual liberal freedom suggests is that Alex's project of self-re-making has become conflated with extreme, total self-reliance and complete rejection of society altogether. Revealing further evidence of this view, a little later in the same conversation with Westerberg in a South Dakota bar, McCandless says, "Maybe when I get back [from Alaska], I can write a book about my travels, about getting out of this sick society" adding, " 'Cause you know what I don't understand, I don't understand why people, why every fuckin' person is so bad to each other so fuckin' often. It doesn't make sense to me – judgment, control, all that, the whole spectrum." Then, when asked by Westerberg, "What people're we talkin' about?" McCandless responds, "You know. Parents. Hypocrites. Politicians. Pricks." Here again, the film's portrayal of McCandless' reasoning suggests not just the possibility but the reality of a stark division between the individual and society, freedom and subjection, individuality and control. It is a binary that goes unchallenged in the film, when, for instance, all that Westerberg says in response is: "This is a mistake. It's a mistake to get too deep into all that kinda stuff [...] You're a young guy." In various parts of the book, Krakauer offers a slightly more jaundiced view of McCandless' naïve arrogance, but mainly with reference to his outdoors skills and preparation rather than his socio-political philosophy. Nevertheless, one of Krakauer's judgments, gleaned from interviewing Chris' parents, is particularly telling in regard to McCandless' binary thinking: "Nuance, strategy, and anything beyond the rudimentaries of technique were wasted on Chris. The only way he cared to tackle a challenge was head-on, right now, applying the full brunt of his extraordinary energy."[44]

Reinscribing Hyper-Individualism

> On bended knee is no way to be free.
> (Eddie Vedder, "Guaranteed," from *Into the Wild* soundtrack)

In its portrayal of McCandless and his journey, the film version of *Into the Wild* consistently reinforces a troublingly rigid binary, privileging the free individual and condemning the oppressive society. While the film offers a striking representation of Romantic, liberal individuality in the figure of Chris McCandless and his effort to refuse the ordinary and remake himself by his own lights, it does so at the expense of depicting a real reckoning with political circumstances and dramatizing a complex negotiation of social relations. The object of desire for the protagonist as well as the audience is a purely individual freedom apart from others; away from society; and, ultimately, fantastically free from power and dependence. At its heart, *Into the Wild* is a fantasy of escape that in some respects is innocuous, except for the fact that this escape is quite obviously and self-consciously motivated and carried out in the familiar liberal idiom of freedom and individuality, citing Thoreau, Byron, and others. For while the film portrays the admirable desire and courage of a liberal subject to cast off the old and make the new, it does so at a cost – a contextual and a political cost. Again in the context of addressing

Flathman's liberalism, political theorist Ronald Beiner assesses such costs when he writes, "The rhetoric of self-making and the notion that it should be the ideal of liberal politics to leave individuals as much as possible to their own devices reinscribe the idea that individuals can make a life for themselves in abstraction from social relations and larger political realities."[45] Because "language and social convention thoroughly constitute human experience," Beiner contends that hyper-individualism can lead to a constant temptation to wish away the reality of the social constitution of individual experience. It is just such a risk of reinscribing a hyper-individualist fantasy of being free from subjection altogether that *Into the Wild* runs up against.

The very construction of *Into the Wild's* narrative arc – beginning at the end of the long journey with McCandless' great Alaskan adventure, intercutting scenes along his journey prior to his arrival in Alaska, and ending with his desperately lonely death – works to privilege that solitary experience as an achievement more valuable than the social relationships and situations that McCandless discovers and experiences along the way. From the opening Byron verse through to the end credits (over which the song "Guaranteed" plays, including the line "On bended knee is no way to be free"), the film labours to valorise the lone individual as the ultimate expression of freedom while concurrently casting society as controlling and constraining – as, in a word, unfree. For although the film portrays McCandless' relationships along his journey with care (chiefly through sterling performances that bring out the pain caused by McCandless' inevitable fleeing), *Into the Wild's* narrative structure nevertheless puts the audience in the position of identifying with the eventual goal of a solitary, courageous, and noble life in the wild. As an audience, we are encouraged and expected to root for Chris' success. Indeed, throughout the story, the audience is urged, via the identification with McCandless, to see any kind of society – not simply the mainstream American consumerist suburbia that he so loathes, but also the kind-hearted, kindred souls he meets along the way – as an expression of unwanted entanglement, as an unnecessary and unnatural constraint on his freedom and individuality. This is perhaps most dramatically illustrated with McCandless' refusal of Ron Franz's offer of adoption near the end of the film. The warmth, tenderness, and longing expressed by the elderly Franz toward the young McCandless generates some hope that Chris might choose to honour Franz and sustain some kind of relationship. Yet Hal Holbrook's affecting performance as Franz registers the pain left in the wake of McCandless' commitment to a freedom from others rather than a freedom with others.

By depicting McCandless as repeatedly fleeing others in pursuit of liberating self-discovery, the film constructs a representation of "ultimate freedom," as

McCandless himself puts it in his carving in the Fairbanks 142 "Magic Bus," as a solitary, autonomous enterprise requiring social sacrifice for the achievement of such independence. The film encourages an identification of freedom with solitude and of society with stifling power. Therefore, for McCandless freedom is freedom from society and unchosen, prohibitive power rather than freedom within society and along with productive power. In the film's representations, the assertion of individual will to achieve "ultimate freedom" requires refusal, pure and simple – refusal not just of one's prior self, but refusal of others, refusal of society, and even refusal of power itself. McCandless says as much himself. Early in the film, alone in the 142 bus upon his recent arrival in the Alaskan wilderness, he sits at the desk and says to himself, "Strong. You can do anything. You can go anywhere. Power is an illusion." Though he is shown speaking to himself, he is also, of course, effectively addressing the audience, exhorting them to develop the courage to pursue an authentic project of self-making. Such a statement is emblematic of how Chris/Alex, as a representation of liberal self-making, becomes an object lesson in the delusions of hyper-individualism and the inability to recognize subjection. Such a representation depoliticizes the subject and reinscribes the problematic notion of self-making "in abstraction from social relations and larger political realities."

Resisting, Complicating Refusal

> Got my indignation, but I'm pure in all my thoughts.
> (Eddie Vedder, "Guaranteed," from *Into the Wild* soundtrack)

One of the central tactics in McCandless' practice of individual liberty is refusal. He refuses his former self, his parents, his society, maps, food, assistance, and more. His refusals, principled as they may be, serve to further the fantasy of pure independence as well as the individual–society dichotomy that structures the film's narrative. As noted earlier, refusal and the desire for the new, the better, and the different are at the heart of liberalism, especially liberal individuality. McCandless, however, fetishizes refusal in his search for purity. Thus, the film layers onto the "free individual"-versus- "oppressive society" trope another related binary, one that sets out the terms for thinking about resistance – namely, a refusal–amendment or escape–negotiation binary. This additional dichotomy is as problematic as the first in its fantastic starkness, because it reduces resistance to refusal, eschewing and condemning negotiation, amendment, and engagement. Both binaries are rooted in McCandless/Supertramp's aversion to dependence and his yearning for independence and "ultimate freedom." Ironically, his near-absolute refusal of negotiation and dependence constitutes his undoing.

Consider, for example, Chris/Alex's refusal of a map as he ventures into the Alaskan wild. While McCandless, as depicted in the film, wants to portray travelling without a map as liberating (as he tells Westerberg, noted earlier), it repeatedly gets him into problematic entanglements – from paddling the Colorado River all the way into Mexico and getting stranded, unable to reach the sea as he imagined, to his fatal adventure in the Alaskan wilderness.[46] Ultimately, it is precisely his refusal of a map that may have contributed to his death. As both the film and book present it, having just finished reading Tolstoy's *Family Happiness* and marked the passage "the only certain happiness in life is living for others," McCandless decides to leave the Alaskan wilderness and head back to society. The film shows him packing up and departing, with a smile on his face and a proverbial "spring in his step." As he hikes back toward civilization, the song "No Ceiling" plays on the soundtrack – a song that celebrates a wisdom made flesh, the completion of the project of self-making: "No my heart will never, will never be far from here […] / I'll keep this wisdom in my flesh / I leave here believin' more than I had." However, Chris/Alex's joy begins to turn to anguish when he reaches the Teklanika River and cannot find a way across. For while it had been only a trickle in the spring when he crossed it on his way into the wilderness, by the time he reaches it upon his return the summer snowmelt had swollen it to a wide, deep, and raging torrent. The film then shows McCandless falling into the river and then later returning in a rainstorm to the 142 bus. Given the way in which the film encourages the audience's identification with McCandless, this failed exit is a rather dispiriting moment, something like a cruel twist of fate, and it begins to suggest a darker turn in the narrative. However, according to Krakauer, who retraced McCandless' Alaskan trip for his book, there were options available for crossing the swollen river that McCandless did not pursue. "Because he lacked a good map," Krakauer reports, "the cable spanning the river [which Krakauer himself used to cross it] also remained incognito. Studying the Teklanika's violent flow, McCandless thus mistakenly concluded that it was impossible to reach the eastern shore. Thinking that his escape route had been cut off, he returned to the bus – a reasonable course of action, given his topographical ignorance."[47] Weeks later, when he was dying of poisoning and starvation, McCandless also could have benefitted from "a U.S. Geological Survey topographic map, [which] would have alerted him to the existence of a Park Service cabin on the upper Sushana River, six miles due south of the bus, a distance he might have been able to cover even in his severely weakened state."[48]

McCandless' refusal of a map recalls Edmund Burke's caution against arrogantly refusing inheritances and remaining unaware of context. Like Foucault, Burke understands the ways in which a politico-cultural field saturated with power simultaneously enables, orients, and constrains practice. In other words, both Burke and Foucault comprehend the extent to which, as political subjects, we are constrained, whether we like it or not, by the unchosen forces, relations, and circumstances of our position and condition, which cannot simply be willed away, but instead must be negotiated.[49] To illustrate, consider Burke's condemnation of the *philosophes'* rejection of prejudice and inherited knowledge:

> We are afraid to put men to live and trade each on his own private stock of reason, because we suspect that this stock in each man is small, and that the individuals would do better to avail themselves of the general bank and capital of nations and of ages. Many of our men of speculation, instead of exploding general prejudices, employ their sagacity to discover the latent wisdom which prevails in them.[50]

Burke, of course, argues for working within existing, inherited institutions and availing oneself of accumulated wisdom and knowledge because he recognizes, as Beiner does, that "language and social convention thoroughly constitute human experience." McCandless, on the other hand, refuses to recognize such saturation, and suffers from a fatally seductive idea of autonomy when he rejects any dependence upon a map (knowledge inherited from others). Refusing maps is symptomatic of McCandless' urge to be a sovereign "master of his own destiny," as Krakauer has noted, refusing any dependence, any inheritance that might compromise his ideals. And yet even liberal individualists are always already subjects, and thus cannot live by ideals alone. "In a liberalism of institutions as well as ideals, singular individuals will be obliged to accord themselves to laws, customs, regulations, and practices alien (and often hostile) to their ideals," Norton reminds us, "Liberals must accommodate themselves to liberalism."[51] Chris/Alex's ethos of refusal brooks no accommodation or compromise for he remains locked in rigid binary, searching instead for purity, denying any subjectivity or dependence.

Reducing the liberal subject's agency to refusal leaves many practices and approaches out of view and constitutes a dangerously de-politicized representation of liberal individuality. Consider, for instance, Norton's subtle rendering of refusal's place in the predicament of the liberal subject hungering for freedom:

> The will to become other than one is thus entails the refusal – or more properly, the refusal, acceptance, and amendment – of a complex of languages, traditions, customs, practices, ideals, values, beliefs, and

experiences. The richer that array, the more thorough the individual's engagement with and knowledge of the forces that fashioned the inherited self, the more important (and the more impressive) the refusal of that self will be. Self-overcoming is, in this account, a public process, a critical engagement with inherited traditions and extant discourses. Only through a critical engagement with inherited constitution can the singular individual learn, in Nietzsche's words, "how to become what one is".[52]

The critical engagement with inheritance entailed in Norton's formulation suggests a rather different image of individual freedom and individuality than that epitomized by McCandless in the film. His sovereign dismissal belies a necessarily complex negotiation with inheritance, unchosen contexts, and power.

The film's glorification of all-out refusal certainly works to create an inspiring representation of individual courage but as a representation of liberal individualism it greatly oversimplifies, and thereby misses an opportunity to better attend to the subtleties of liberal subjectivity and agency. For liberalism and individual freedom are rather more capacious than *Into the Wild* gives them credit for, as it never fully reckons with subjectivation. By reducing liberal individualism to extreme refusal, the film silences other avenues open to the subject and forecloses the recognition of the subjected self through "an activity of political comprehension."[53] "Liberalism can," Norton tells us, "accommodate calm adherence to ancient custom, the relentless quest for novelty, quietism, and restlessness – and these all within the same subject. Passions and appetites; desires, hopes, and fears; defiance and refusal – all contend on equal terms with the commands of reason."[54] The danger of the film, then, resides in its celebration of depoliticized resistance as refusal, pure and simple, rather than a complex negotiation with the given context. The figure of McCandless/Supertramp simply refuses, and shows no attention to the difficult work of negotiating and amending the inherited "complex of languages, traditions, customs, practices, ideals, values, beliefs, and experiences."

Anne Norton's insights into the power of contextual factors help to complicate the character of resistance for and against liberalism, combining refusal, engagement, and amendment. Simple and pure refusal has to be overcome as a model of resistance available to liberal subjects, for what it does is leave out subjectivity altogether. Resistance, including refusal, always happens in an unchosen context, and *Into the Wild* scrupulously avoids engaging this issue. "There is no culture without resistance," writes Norton, adding:

> Living within a culture entails a complex of relations to its practices and institutions. A subject will admire some iconic cultural figures

and despise others, adopt some practices, reject others, affirm some institutions, and oppose others. The cultural identity of each individual is fashioned through these negotiations of networks of meaning and materiality. These negotiations fashion individual identities from and within an economy of acceptance and rejection, accordance and resistance.[55]

The representation of Chris/Alex's dissident search for freedom in the film gives no sense of this "economy of acceptance and rejection, accordance and resistance," instead reducing resistance to refusal and reducing dissent to rejection. Yet, as long as we live in community with others we are always already subjects, and these kinds of negotiations are necessary and inescapable. Still, *Into the Wild* not only holds out but indeed glorifies the possibility of simply refusing, of opting out, of finding and occupying a space free from power where such negotiations are not necessary. There is, however, no such space.

Conclusion: Subjects Negotiating Power

> [T]o live is to live a life politically, in relation to power, in relation to others, in the act of assuming responsibility for a collective future.
> (Judith Butler, "The Question of Social Transformation")[56]

There may be, finally, a temptation to read *Into the Wild* as a caution against atomistic individualism and an affirmation of community, particularly because of two final, discursive acts depicted in the film. Firstly, near the end of the movie, a weakened, starving, and dying McCandless writes "HAPPINESS ONLY REAL WHEN SHARED" in his paperback copy of *Doctor Zhivago*, suggesting that, in typically Hollywood fashion, he has finally learned the error of his hyper-individualist ways. Secondly, and seconds later, McCandless quotes *Doctor Zhivago* in voice-over – "To call each thing by its right name, by its right name" – as the camera reveals a last handwritten note: "I HAVE HAD A HAPPY LIFE AND THANK THE LORD. GOODBYE AND MAY GOD BLESS ALL." Significantly, the camera slowly reveals the bottom of the note, where it is signed "Christopher Johnson McCandless," suggesting an end of his refusal of inheritance and unchosen context. As Jon Krakauer construes it, "Recognizing the gravity of his predicament, he had abandoned the cocky moniker he'd been using for years, Alexander Supertramp, in favour of the name given to him at birth by his parents."[57] These two discursive acts, together with McCandless' earlier attempt to leave the wilderness and return to society, might plausibly be read as registering a victory for inter-subjectivity and community over atomistic individualism. And yet, I would argue that such a reading must be eschewed because these two acts do not go far enough in registering a full reckoning with subjectivity and the inescapability of power. To be sure, the "choice of inheritance," as Burke would say,[58] a choice reflected in the resumption of his given name, is a start. More work, however, must come in negotiating the unchosen contexts in which subjects find themselves, and although McCandless did this work along his journey it was overshadowed by the vision of solitary "ultimate freedom" that he relentlessly pursued. That is to say, such deathbed redemption does not fully come to terms with the reality of how our situated-ness in institutions, inheritances, customs, and language demands more than simple refusal.

As painful and distressing as the alienation that McCandless must have felt is, the search for a space of pure escape, free from power, proves dangerously illusory. "Identity and alienation are coeval," Norton instructs us, "As the ideas of individuality and community are entailed in one another and necessarily come into being simultaneously, so too do belonging and alienation."[59] The audience can see this braiding together of belonging and alienation at every step along Chris McCandless' journey – not simply in what he perceives to be his stifling, mainstream, suburban upbringing, but also when he works with Wayne Westerberg, when he travels with Jan and Rainey Burres, and when he befriends the grandfatherly Ron Franz. All along, in each set of relationships, there is neither pure belonging nor pure alienation, but rather a complex and changing mix of the two. Indeed, McCandless seems to have at least an intuitive understanding that "community entails alienation," for he is critical of existing capitalist society and wants to resist it. The problem, however, with his resistance is its extremity, as if one could choose to be outside of community. In other words, because community entails alienation he rejects and refuses community altogether. In fact, a large part of the pathos of the film comes from McCandless' narcissistic insistence on his autonomy at every step along the way, as he in fact alienates those closest to him again and again.

Given the inescapable and messy reality of the "economy of acceptance and rejection, accordance and resistance" in which identities are formed, the *Into the Wild* audience as well as McCandless himself are ill served by rigid binaries: free individual versus oppressive society, escapist refusal versus situated attachment. In addition to representing the liberal subject as no subject at all but rather an individual, the figure presented by *Into the Wild* of the radically natural and independent individual suggests not just that the liberal subject can affirm, amend, or reject itself but that social and power relations themselves can be rejected. Such a suggestion is deeply problematic, but nevertheless a recurrent risk with liberal individualism and its discursive representation. By contrast, Michel Foucault teaches us that while subjects are always situated among circumstances and power relations that are not of their choosing, and that cannot simply be willed away, still they are not trapped. Instead they must reckon with power, and their efforts at resistance or change must involve some negotiation the given. As Foucault says,

> So we are not trapped. We are always in this kind of situation. It means that we always have possibilities, there are always possibilities of changing the situation. We cannot jump *outside* the situation, and there is no point where you are free from all power relations. But you can always change it.[60]

The cultural and political legacy associated with the ideals of liberal freedom still haunts, even saturates, the American political and cultural imagination, and yet the unchosen power of context inevitably undercuts the fantasy of independence at the core of liberalism. The challenge, then, not just for liberalism itself but for a culture drenched with it, is to come to terms with the limits of individual freedom by eschewing easy binaries and comprehending the inextricable intertwining of freedom and power, identity and subjectivity. Recognizing the limits and context of liberal individualism directs our attention to the other half of the familiar construction "liberal democracy" – namely, the collective, democratic struggle to shape and amend the conditions that impact our individual and collective lives. "The practices of a liberalism triumphant in the commonplace points to the capacity of democracy to exceed itself."[61] As the protagonist of *Into the Wild*, Chris McCandless not only realized the limits of liberalism, the limits of a hyper-individualized freedom, but also disavowed the democratic and productive context that he could not escape. While as a film *Into the Wild* offers a seductively compelling vision of "freedom from" – freedom from government, from coercion, from society, from others – the difficult task for political theory, political practice, and popular culture is to offer a less liberal and more democratic vision of "freedom with" (freedom with others) and "freedom within" (freedom within power, unchosen conditions), recognizing without wishing away our subjectivity.

2

Avenging Dependence: *Mystic River* and the Political Ontology of Vulnerability

> [I]t is characteristic of political philosophers that they take a somber view of the human situation: they deal in darkness. Human life in their writings appears generally not as a feast or even as a journey, but as a predicament [...] [T]he human predicament is a universal appearing everywhere as a particular.
> (Michael Oakeshott, "Introduction to Leviathan")[1]

For Judith Butler, the particular events of 9/11 suggest a universal human predicament that challenges Hobbes' construction of political society in opposition to insecurity. Butler sees in these events a reminder of the reality of persistent insecurity rooted in a constitutive and persistent vulnerability. Specifically, she refers to this vulnerability as "a collective condition, characterizing us all equally,"[2] a condition of "exposure to violence" and "vulnerability to loss" that we "cannot will away."[3] This exposed vulnerability is, to be sure, a contingent universal in Butler's view, yet nevertheless, as a universal it is a constitutive feature of our social and political ontology that "we cannot easily argue against; or, rather, we can argue against it, but we would be denying something fundamental about the social conditions of our very formation."[4] Given the fact of "our fundamental dependency" and the tendency of acts of vengeance to generate cycles of violence, Butler interprets violent vengeance as both a denial of vulnerability and a threat to, rather than guarantor of, security, and she sounds "an ethical caution against enthusiasms that might make one impervious to the precariousness of life."[5] The precariousness of life, in Butler's felicitous phrase, suggests the ambiguity – both promise and precipice – entailed in the very predicament of vulnerability as the ontological condition of possibility for subjectivity.

In this chapter, we will explore the political limitations and possibilities that this condition of precariousness or vulnerability entails, through a juxtaposition of two particulars illuminating the universal: Butler's thoughts on vulnerability and (non-)violence and Clint Eastwood's cinematic critique of revenge, *Mystic River* (2003). Both Butler and Eastwood examine the ties (chosen and unchosen) that bind us together, and explore the consequences of violent loss. In the eyes of Butler and Eastwood, loss reveals the condition of common vulnerability and challenges us to keep our rage from overwhelming our common humanity. Their works share an emphasis on the fact that we are not autonomous subjects but rather dependent upon, yet vulnerable to, each other. Butler summarizes the political question that loss amidst vulnerability forces upon us:

> That we can be injured, that others can be injured, that we are subject to death at the whim of another, are all reasons for both fear and grief. What is less certain, however, is whether the experiences of vulnerability and loss have to lead straightaway to military violence and retribution [...] If we are interested in arresting cycles of violence to produce less violent outcomes, it is no doubt important to ask what, politically, might be made of grief besides a cry for war.[6]

Butler's theoretical insights into the ambivalence of vulnerability and the dangerous seductions of vengeance parallel the dramatization in *Mystic River* of both the consequences of a violent response to grief and the opportunities for peaceful resolution. Sharing and illustrating the view that socially situated subjects are dependent upon yet different from, and vulnerable to, others, these two sombre views of the human situation suggest a need to rethink both our use of violence and our understanding of community in light of vulnerability and difference.

Vulnerability as the Ontological Condition of Possibility for Subjectivity

In some of her post-9/11 writings, Butler has taken a dark and revealing view of the human situation, wrestling with the political consequences of violence and loss and trying to elucidate our common condition of vulnerability. The touchstone for her political theory of vulnerability is the essay "Violence, Mourning, Politics" in her book *Precarious Life*, which presents a suggestive new agenda for her readers in political theory. Preserving and extending her critique of the sovereign, autonomous subject, Butler begins the work of "reimagining the possibility of community on the basis of vulnerability and loss."[7] This text not only resonates with insights from her earlier work on the sociality and materiality of bodies in *Bodies that Matter* (1993), on subjection and vulnerability in *The Psychic Life of*

Mystic River and the Political Ontology of Vulnerability

Power (1997), and on grief in *Antigone's Claim* (2000), but also presages ideas on ethical responsibility and violence presented in *Giving an Account of Oneself* (2005). Perhaps most interestingly for the discourse of political theory, Butler's interest in reimagining community in light of vulnerability, loss, and difference signals an effort to complement the struggles of identity politics with another struggle for what might be called a non-communitarian idea of community. In that vein, she offers this provocative political question to readers familiar with her work on identity and resistance: "If I am struggling for autonomy, do I not need to be struggling for something else as well, a conception of myself as invariably in community, impressed upon by others, impinging upon them as well, and in ways that are not fully in my control or clearly predictable?"[8] This section explores the sense in which the turn toward vulnerability and community that marks Butler's recent thought simultaneously (a) preserves her interest in power and the ways in which subjects are authored by what precedes and exceeds them; and (b) shifts focus to the social realm of bodies, where the inescapable facts of interdependence and vulnerability might (or might not) be recognized in the service of working toward a less violent political life.

In "Violence, Mourning, Politics," Butler starts from the fact of the 9/11 tragedy and the feelings of loss that it generated, and proceeds to reflect on what she calls "the problem of a primary vulnerability to others, one that one cannot will away without ceasing to be human."[9] The common experience or spectacle of such a traumatic violation of security serves for Butler as a terrible unmasking of the fantasy of autonomy and invulnerability, "challeng[ing] the very notion of ourselves as autonomous and in control."[10] Specifically, it also serves as a reminder of the ways in which we are, in her view, always already non-autonomous and implicated in lives that are not our own. The possibility of "undergoing something outside one's control," she claims, "does not dispute the fact of my autonomy, but it does qualify that claim through recourse to the fundamental sociality of embodied life, the ways in which we are, from the start and by virtue of being a bodily being, already given over, beyond ourselves, implicated in lives that are not our own."[11] The idea of autonomy as qualified by the sociality of embodied life sounds a chord recurrent in Butler's work – namely, her concern with "the way in which we are constituted in relationality: implicated, beholden, derived, sustained by a social world that is beyond us and before us."[12]

The notion of an embodied political vulnerability in her "Violence" essay appears against the backdrop of Butler's earlier examination of the necessary discursive vulnerability of the subject to the ambivalent effects of power in *The Psychic Life of Power*. There, Butler argues that "the vulnerability of the subject to power is unavoidable,"[13] because all subjects are necessarily constituted within norms, power, and social relations that they do not choose. Such power *conditions* – that is, makes possible as well as limits – the agency of subjects. In a recent interview, Butler expressed the point in this way: "We're not in control, but that does not mean we don't exercise a certain kind of conditioned agency. That's what it means to live in a community. That's what it means to live in society."[14] As a consequence of this necessary yet unchosen vulnerability to power, such that the subject "can never produce itself autonomously"[15] but is dependent upon power and norms as well as caregivers, Butler claims that "vulnerability qualifies the subject as an exploitable kind of being."[16] Power, like vulnerability – and, indeed, like community itself – is, for Butler, an ineluctable and constitutive condition, yet one must not forget that it is essentially ambiguous insofar as it necessarily restricts but also enables, simply by being a condition of possibility. Butler's understanding of vulnerability as a socio-ontological condition of possibility of subjectivity means that the subject "is implicated in a loss of autonomy that is mandated by linguistic and social life"[17] – that is, we are never autonomous but always already related to, and dependent upon, others as well as conditioned by power. Though not explicitly thematized as such by Butler (certainly not in *The Psychic Life of Power*, though she comes closer to it in later work), there is in her cumulative corpus the suggestion of a more somber understanding of community than usually appears in political theory. Sombre because her notion of community constituted via shared and inescapable, yet ambiguous, vulnerability entails not only the possibility for attachment, enrichment, and affection but also detachment, loss, and mourning. As such, Butler's community of shared vulnerability, when recognized as such, represents a more realistic, if contingent and uncertain, picture of political community than appears, for instance, in either Hobbes' contractual order of absolute security or communitarianism's traditional order of salutary attachment.

There are two ways in which Butler's more recent account of vulnerability differs slightly from that in *The Psychic Life of Power*, but these are more differences of emphasis than revision. First, in the post-9/11 essay in *Precarious Life*, Butler subtly shifts the emphasis from the influence of the impersonal power of discursive norms to the personal power of bodies by virtue of their sociality. She notes that "each of us is constituted politically in part by virtue of the social vulnerability of our bodies – as a site of desire and physical vulnerability, as a site of a publicity at once assertive and exposed."[18] At its simplest, this bodily vulnerability means for Butler the real possibility of being affected by others in ways that we do not choose – whether it is as infants, as adults, or as states: "We are affected by others. I mean, 9/11 was being affected in a very big way, in a violent way that we radically

Mystic River and the Political Ontology of Vulnerability

did not choose."[19] This unchosen vulnerability derives from the fact of living in society with, and being dependent upon, others – that is, not being fully autonomous, self-determining, or self-sufficient. Most saliently for a post-9/11 politics of security, Butler's view of vulnerability as autonomy qualified by sociality means that my security is not fully in my control, for it depends on not just what I do or control but on what others do or do not do. In other words, she says that "my body," insofar as it is "given over from the start to the world of others" and "formed within the crucible of social life," both "is and is not mine"[20] because it is subject not only to my actions but also to the actions of others. This ambiguity is fundamental to what it means to be a subject.

A second difference of emphasis between her earlier account of vulnerability and the recent return to the subject is that in addition to the unchosenness of social vulnerability that qualifies autonomy, Butler in her post-9/11 work bolsters this claim with the idea that this bodily vulnerability, as a condition not just for the inauguration of the subject but for the continued existence of subjects, is inescapable.[21] It cannot be willed away; it cannot even be argued with.[22] Rather, she conceives vulnerability as an ontological condition of possibility for social, political, and ethical relationships: "If my fate is not originally or finally separable from yours, then the 'we' is traversed by a relationality that we cannot easily argue against; or, rather, we can argue against it, but we would be denying something fundamental about the social conditions of our very formation".[23] This understanding conveys Butler's understanding of the always-social individual who, because of interdependence, is always implicated in the lives of others – indeed, always living in community with others, where community is understood to connote by sharing, not only the good but also the bad: in short, vulnerability.

Finally, though this persistent vulnerability cannot be willed away it can be exploited, and Butler remarks that "violence is, always, an exploitation of that primary tie, that primary way in which we are, as bodies, outside ourselves and for one another."[24] Butler's invocation of vulnerability in a political context prompts the need to question political theory's traditional opposition between anarchy and order, which Sheldon Wolin frames in this way: "In the ontology of political thought, order has been the equivalent of being, anarchy the political synonym for non-being."[25] The ineliminable condition of vulnerability suggests (contra Hobbes) the persistence of the threat of non-being within being at the hands of others – that is, the inescapable threat of death even within political community. By arguing that this vulnerability cannot be willed away and is a constitutive aspect of sociality, Butler suggests that there is no perfect security that might be achieved or purchased at the price of civil liberties or anything else, exploding the familiar post-9/11 political choice. Indeed, she cautions against the impulse to eradicate the vulnerability with which we all live, and must live: "To foreclose that vulnerability, to banish it, to make ourselves secure at the expense of every other human consideration is to eradicate one of the most important resources from which we must take our bearings and find our way."[26] Thus, vulnerability's constitutive ambiguity points not toward the mere toleration of vulnerability but toward an attention to and care for it. In addition to pointing out the ambiguity of vulnerability, this remark suggests that politics should involve coming to terms with this inescapable condition. In seeing the intersubjective or communal dimension of experience as a condition of vulnerability, Butler reveals a sensibility that is sombre, almost tragic, and thus distinct from the more salutary views of deliberative democrats and communitarians.

Constitutive Vulnerability in *Mystic River*

The condition of being vulnerable to others – in the sense of being "implicated in lives that are not our own" in ways that are "irreversible, if not fatal"[27] – finds cinematic representation in the very first scene of *Mystic River*, an opening that conditions the rest of the film's narrative. As the haunting initial scene begins, three boys are playing street hockey in a Boston neighbourhood, yet by the end of the scene, one boy, Dave Boyle, is seen through the back window of a car, leaving with two male abductors. This scene of Dave's abduction together with the ensuing 4-day-long molestation marks an initial traumatic event that challenges the audience to identify and come to terms with the terrible facts of vulnerability and loss. This exploitation of childhood vulnerability remains in *Mystic River* like a barely-healed wound for the rest of the film as the setting jumps 25 years ahead to the same neighbourhood, where the boys still live as grown men, more or less shaped and haunted by the initial trauma.

The initial abduction of Dave as well as the damaged figure of Dave as an adult later in the film together serve to illustrate some key insights from Butler's understanding of subject formation and the limits of subjects' ability to "give an account of themselves." First, the three boys are approached by the abductors while scratching their names in some wet concrete on the pavement. After the other two boys write theirs, Dave begins to write his, but he is interrupted when one of the abductors approaches and asks menacingly "Let me ask you something. You brats think it's okay to destroy municipal property?" The intimidation is compounded by the handcuffs and badge hanging on his belt that he makes it a point to reveal. The incomplete name that Dave writes in the wet cement pavement ("DA") before his abduction together with his struggles as an adult to come to terms with, and tell the story of, what happened to him suggest a parallel with Butler's account of the necessary partiality of any account of ourselves.[28] None of us can fully give an account of ourselves from our very birth, because of the way in which we develop and our fundamental dependency on care by others. This failure is doubly significant in Dave's case, for it speaks to the awful exploitation of that dependency by his tormentors. A second way in which Dave's abduction speaks to Butler's theory of subject formation involves the impersonation of a police officer by the would-be captor. The scene of Dave's abduction by a man impersonating a policeman offers a suggestive echo of Butler's discussion of how the figure of "the turn" inaugurates the subject. For Butler invokes Louis Althusser's "infamous example" of interpellation, wherein subjects are drawn into the realm of law, culture, and ideology by the police hailing them with "Hey you!"[29] When one responds to this hailing, one becomes a subject. But more than that: in the film, when Dave responds to the man's command to "Get in!" the car, he becomes a wounded and even more incomplete subject as the abductors exploit his dependence.

Through the three adult male characters, the film offers representations of three different conditioned responses to later experiences of vulnerability and loss. Whereas Dave (played by Tim Robbins) finds himself impaired and unable to come to terms with vulnerability, Jimmy Markum (Sean Penn) and Sean Devine (Kevin Bacon) represent two different ways of responding to vulnerability and loss – Jimmy choosing vengeance, Sean choosing non-violence. Before turning to a discussion of how Jimmy's and Sean's reactions to later experiences of vulnerability map onto Butler's understanding of the political possibilities that attend vulnerability, let us consider the ways in which the film's opening scene illuminates some other aspects of Butler's concept of vulnerability.

The lingering force of the initial scene brings into view the sense in which vulnerability entails the ever-present possibility for loss that Butler contends is a constitutive feature of social life. More specifically, the scene helps to illustrate the ambivalence that Butler attaches to the concept of vulnerability. While the term vulnerability often carries a negative connotation both in her work and in ordinary language, Butler plays on the ambiguity of the term to also suggest the stance of opening oneself up to connection with others, in the sense of emotional availability. "Loss and vulnerability," she claims, "seem to follow from our being socially constituted bodies, attached to others, at risk of losing those attachments, exposed to others, at risk of violence by virtue of that exposure."[30] Thus, Butler's understanding of vulnerability encompasses an ambivalence consistent with her view of the very social possibility of subjectivity as subjection to power, both attached and exposed to others. On this view, vulnerability is not just a threat but also a chance, and thus vulnerability "means that we are […] vulnerable to violence; but also vulnerable to another range of touch, a range that includes the eradication of our being at the one end, and the physical support for our lives at the other."[31] The initial scene sets the stage for the film's consideration of a shared condition of ambiguous vulnerability, by showing the enriching connections that the boys share through play as well as the damaging connection that they share through vulnerability and loss. The very fact of potential violence from our fellow humans dramatizes the point that there are some things, some forces, that we cannot control and to which we are vulnerable, but also that our lives are made richer and more valuable through our connections with others (when those ties are not exploited). This initial scene establishes a common condition of interdependence among the three boys that persists through the rest of the film in the form of the ties that the grown men later share, as well as through the film's attention to the context of the community in which they live and die, flourish and falter. Thus, *Mystic River* conveys a parallel understanding of the inaugural and persistent condition of vulnerability to others.

Juxtaposing Butler's thoughts of vulnerability with the opening scene of *Mystic River* reveals vulnerability to be a constitutive and inescapable, thus universal, feature of the human condition, yet one that appears everywhere as a particular. Simply put, vulnerability is an essential feature of what it means to live in society with others. As a universal characterization, it brings together under one rubric the three "ontological forces" that Stephen White identifies as constituting Butler's ontology: "interpellating power, materialization, and the desire to desire."[32] As such, vulnerability must be understood as a foundation for her thinking – but is it a foundation that is, in her famous formulation, both "contingent and indispensable"?[33] As presented in "Violence, Mourning, Politics," Butler's answer is that while vulnerability cannot be willed away, the contingency of vulnerability consists in the question of its recognition: "A vulnerability must be perceived and recognized in order to come into play in an ethical encounter, and there is no guarantee that this will happen […] But when a vulnerability *is* recognized, that recognition has the power to change the meaning and structure of the vulnerability itself."[34]

The crux of Butler's normative political theory, as it has come into view since the traumatic events of September 11, 2001, lies in the contingency attending the recognition of vulnerability. Consistent with her view of the operation of power, Butler argues that "if vulnerability is one precondition for humanization, and humanization takes place differently through variable norms of recognition, then it follows that vulnerability is fundamentally dependent upon existing norms of recognition if it is to be attributed to any human subject."[35] Given that we cannot will away this vulnerability, Butler addresses the question of what our political and ethical responses to this condition should be, and argues that "We must attend to it, even abide by it, as we begin to think about what politics might be implied by staying with the thought of corporeal vulnerability itself, a situation in which we can be vanquished or lose others."[36] *Mystic River* offers dramatic personifications of the two main responses that Butler identifies to the kind of loss or injury that attends vulnerability: revenge as a denial, or non-recognition of vulnerability and grief as a recognition of the inescapability of this condition of vulnerability.

Violent and Non-Violent Responses to Losses that Expose Vulnerability

Loss for Butler produces grief, which exposes our relationality and vulnerability, the sense in which we are tied with others. In contrast to a vengeful response to loss that denies vulnerability, Butler insists that we ask "what, politically, might be made of grief besides a cry for war."[37] Butler urges us to forego "terrible satisfactions of war" and revenge, and instead to learn to live with grief and vulnerability and forge a conception of responsibility appropriate to vulnerability.[38] Again, Butler's thought suggests not only a rethinking of responsibility in light of non-autonomy and dependency, but also a re-consideration of our understanding of community and what it means to live amongst others and share with them. These two contrasting characters in Clint Eastwood's *Mystic River* are suggestive for thinking about different responses to loss, responses that not only either deny or recognize vulnerability but also therefore either retard or advance a re-conceptualization of community and responsibility constituted on a shared, yet ambiguous vulnerability.

In contrast to Clint Eastwood's career-long association with unrepentant violence, vigilantism, and vengeance, *Mystic River* is a thorough-going critique of vengeance, exploring the lingering, tragic consequences of each violent act depicted. In other words, there are no gratuitous or enjoyable acts of violence in *Mystic River*, as each one has real consequences and dangerous implications for the characters and the story. Therefore, it is with this film rather than *Unforgiven*[39] that Eastwood signalled a real transformation in his approach to violence, as he shifts from encouraging his audiences to identify with vigilantism to forcing them to confront vulnerability. Whereas in previous Eastwood films vengeance and vigilantes are portrayed positively insofar as the right person, the "evildoer" always gets killed, *Mystic River* frustrates audiences' expectations and troubles their reactions by culminating in a misplaced act of murderous vengeance, as the wrong man is killed in return for something he did not do.

After the opening scene, which exposes the common condition of vulnerability, *Mystic River* jumps ahead more than two decades to the same Boston neighbourhood, as the three men once again become implicated in each other's lives – this time because of another terrible loss, the murder of Jimmy Markum's 19-year-old daughter, which re-exposes and recalls their common vulnerability. This murder sets in motion two parallel investigations that diverge with tragic consequences: one, a police investigation headed by Sean Devine, now a police detective; and another, launched by the ex-con Jimmy and carried out on his behalf by the aptly named Savage brothers. While Sean pursues a series of leads, Jimmy and the Savage brothers hone in on Dave, their suspicions aroused by his badly bruised hands.

In the climactic scene of *Mystic River*, as a consequence of his vigilante investigation, Jimmy exacts a fatal vengeance upon his scarred childhood friend Dave Boyle. He refuses to believe Dave's denials and his explanation that his suspiciously bruised hands are the result of his own vengeful act: killing a child molester, who triggered memories of his own childhood trauma.[40] Displaying only a steely desire for retribution and an utter lack of empathy, Jimmy, full of whiskey, suspicion, and rage, begs Dave, "Admit what you did, and I will give you your life!" before stabbing him to death. Through his words and actions, Jimmy is repeatedly figured in the film through violence and rage. Through his personification of self-righteous vengeance and the search for clear answers and decisive resolutions, even when they diverge from the truth, Jimmy represents the violent delusion of a sovereign, autonomous subject unable to recognize a constitutive vulnerability that cannot be willed away. Thus, Jimmy's pursuit of vengeance reveals the truth of Butler's view that

> Revenge tries to solve the problem of vulnerability. If I strike back, then I am not vulnerable but rather the other person is. I transfer vulnerability from myself to the other. And yet by striking back, I produce a world in which my vulnerability to injury is increased by the likelihood of another strike."[41]

More, indeed, than a failure of violent revenge, Jimmy's vengeance also represents a failure of recognition – a failure to recognize the shared and inescapable condition of vulnerability. Repeatedly in the film, he is identified not only with violence but also with a lack of communication, imagination, and understanding – an identification that is fully realized in the climactic murder of Dave. After Jimmy's refusal to accept his alibi, Dave seems to see the inevitability of his own death at Jimmy's hands and thus admits to killing Katie, even though he is innocent. Interestingly, however, in submitting to Jimmy's wish, Dave offers Jimmy one last opportunity to identify with Dave's suffering and acknowledge the possibility that it might easily have been Jimmy who was abducted and molested that day while playing street hockey decades earlier. Dave tells Jimmy that seeing his daughter that night at a pub reminded him of a dream: "a dream of youth – I don't remember having one." At this grave moment, Jimmy greets Dave's talk of dreams, lost youth, and missed opportunities with utter contempt, saying, "So it was a dream?" In response, Dave says, "You know what I mean, if you'd got in that car instead of me." In an act that displays the full horror of vengeance as a refusal of empathy, Jimmy then says, "But I didn't get in that car, Dave. You did," and fatally stabs Dave. This murder, stemming from Jimmy's refusal to abide with his grief, resonates with Butler's description of revenge: "The quick move to action is a way of foreclosing grief, refusing it, and even as it anaesthetizes one's own pain and sense of loss, it comes, in time, to anaesthetize us to the losses that we inflict upon others."[42] Indeed, the full weight of the vengeance problematic is revealed in the following scene, when Jimmy (and the audience) discovers the next morning that he killed the wrong man, and that his daughter's murderer is actually the son of a man Jimmy had murdered decades earlier. This final revelation deepens not only the film's critique of the futility of the cycle of violence but also its understanding of the ineluctable condition of vulnerability.

Jimmy's refusal to identify with suffering, in favour of vengeance against what turns out to be the wrong man echoes the notion of the futility of savage vengeance and reveals the psychological and political force of Butler's view that, following an experience of loss, it is impossible to "turn around and foreclose or somehow get rid of the fact that we are affected by others in ways we do not choose. We have to figure out what we can do in light of that very condition of vulnerability."[43] The vicious ending of *Mystic River* shows, with depth and feeling, the senselessness of the self-righteous yet misplaced violence of which humans, perpetually prone to error, are capable. The fact that Jimmy kills the wrong person only strengthens the sense in which vulnerability is not a problem to be solved but a condition to be attended to, to be tolerated.

In *Giving an Account of Oneself*, Butler poses the question of a non-vengeful response to loss: "What might it mean to undergo violation, to insist upon not resolving grief and staunching vulnerability too quickly through a turn to violence, and to practice, as an experiment in living otherwise, nonviolence in an emphatically nonreciprocal response?"[44] Her idea of a "process by which we develop a point of identification with suffering itself"[45] finds expression in the character of Sean. In contrast to Jimmy's illustration of the futility of vengeance, Sean depicts the political virtue of identifying with suffering and "abiding with" vulnerability.[46] Throughout the film, Sean as a police officer not only represents law and order as opposed to violent vengeance, but also Sean as a husband represents a capacity for identification with others through an empathic understanding of social relationships. He shows this capacity not only in his investigation of Dave as a suspect in Katie's murder, but also in a subplot from his private life, vis-à-vis his wife, who has left him (for reasons unclear to the audience) but who still calls him yet does not speak. Rather than hang up in frustration and close the lines of communication, Sean stays on the line, even in silence. Indeed, in one of the final scenes, she calls and Sean initiates a reconciliation by saying, "I'm sorry. I need to you know that. I pushed you away." Sean's statement reveals not only an understanding of the pain and suffering that his own actions have caused but also an identification with what his wife has suffered. Sean's sincere apology leads her to finally break her silence and apologize too, adding that "Things have been so messed up. Loving you, hating you." The differences between them are thus resolved through imaginative identification and communication, through an appreciation of the positive potential of vulnerability.

Sean enacts a similar appreciation of the ambivalence of vulnerability in the film's central plot around Katie's murder, wherein he remains much more reluctant than his police partner to cast suspicion on Dave because of his almost first-hand knowledge about what happened to Dave when they were children playing in the street that fateful day. Sean implicitly identifies with Dave and shifts suspicion to others, a move that results in the capture of the true killers of Jimmy's daughter Katie. In another dramatic moment, Sean reveals his capacity for abiding vulnerability the morning after Jimmy's murder of Dave, when he returns to the very street where the three boys played hockey decades ago to find Jimmy and tell him the news of the real perpetrator's capture. This news causes Jimmy's face to sink as he realizes that Dave was in fact innocent. Sean asks Jimmy when he last saw Dave, to which Jimmy responds with a statement that betrays the kind of recognition characteristic of classical tragedy: "That was 25 years ago, going up this street in the back of that car." Jimmy's statement registers his tardy awareness of not only Dave's suffering and impairment but also of the tragic consequences of his own vengeance, and yet it is not the same full recognition that Sean has of the constitutive and persistent condition of vulnerability. After Jimmy responds to Sean's further question about Dave ("What did you do, Jimmy?") by saying, "Thanks for getting my daughter's killers, Sean. If only you'd been a little faster," Sean knows that Jimmy has exacted his revenge, but his response stands in direct contrast to Jimmy's act of vengeance and his limited recognition. For Sean extends the condition of vulnerability from Dave to all three boys by saying to Jimmy, "Sometimes I think all three of us got in that car. And all this is just a dream […] In reality, we're still 11-year-old boys locked in a cellar, imagining what our lives would've been if we'd escaped." Sean understands not only the randomness and contingency of life and the ways in which the past weighs on the present, but also the very given-ness of the condition of vulnerability as the sense in which our sociality, our connections with others "tear us from ourselves, bind us to others, transport us, undo us, implicate us in lives that are not [our] own, irreversibly, if not fatally."[47]

In the closing moments of the film's final scene, Sean, with a single gesture that illustrates the ambivalence of vulnerability as well as the possibility for a new understanding of community, brings together the twinned themes of a critique of vengeance (together with an affirmation of the rule of law) and a capacity for identifying with suffering. A few days after Dave's death, Sean's and Jimmy's eyes meet across the street as they watch a parade pass through their neighbourhood. Once again echoing the tragic contrast between vengeance and vulnerability, Sean appears holding his newly born child and reunited with his wife, while Jimmy appears flanked by the Savage brothers. As they stare at each other – Sean knowing that Jimmy killed Dave, and Jimmy knowing that Sean knows – Sean points his finger in Jimmy's direction and "mock-shoots" him with his finger as if to say, "I'll get you for what you've done." But because of who Sean is, because of the slight smirk on his face, and finally because his family reunion evinces willingness to abide vulnerability, the audience understands that Sean's response will not be executed on the street in cold blood, but rather through dedicated detective work carried on in memory of Dave and through identification with the experience of vulnerability learned at too early an age.

Community and Politics in Light of Vulnerability

Beginning from the insight that "Loss has made a tenuous 'we' of us all" and investigating the condition of vulnerability and how we might respond to such loss, Butler in her post-9/11 work sets for political theory the ambitious task of "reimagining the possibility of political community on the basis of vulnerability and loss."[48] Indeed, the deep and admirable concern to arrest cycles of violence by resisting the temptations of revenge in response to loss and exposed vulnerability finds inspiration not only in a film like *Mystic River* (or Steven Spielberg's *Munich* [2005]) but also in America's open-ended "war on terror" (the ongoing practices, if not the slogan) and the continuing Israel–Palestine conflict. For what these examples reveal are the fatal and inhuman consequences that result from vengeance overwhelming capacities for not only compassion and communication but also any recognition of the inescapability of vulnerability. Responding to loss with an understanding of ineluctable vulnerability and an identification with suffering – rather than denying vulnerability and violently transferring suffering – represents not an excuse or approval of that suffering, but an improved step in coping with loss, as it harbours the seeds of a wisdom that recognizes our fundamental sociality and vulnerability, as well as a different kind of politics. Butler says,

> I think an entirely different politics would emerge if a community could learn to abide with its losses and its vulnerability. It would know better what its ties to other people are. It would know how radically dependent it is on its interrelationship with others [...] I think we would be able to understand something about the general state of fragility and physical vulnerability that people – as humans – live in.[49]

The different kind of politics that Butler envisages, based on abiding with loss and vulnerability, necessitates reimagining political community in light of vulnerability. Butler's proposal to reimagine political community with attention to the fundamental condition of vulnerability is a wonderfully suggestive avenue for further political theorizing, and represents a challenge to some of the most familiar discourses within political theory – including contract theory's binary understanding of anarchy and order, communitarianism's overly optimistic and salutary vision of community, and deliberative democracy's excessively rational understanding of community. Firstly, the contrast between contract theory's narrative opposition of security and insecurity (such as that of Hobbes) and Butler's notion of vulnerability could not be sharper, for Hobbes' contract theory allows us to imagine escaping vulnerability through the institution of a sovereign, whereas Butler contends that an ambiguous vulnerability entailing promise and precipice cannot be willed away and must be continually attended to as the very condition of possibility of power and freedom.[50] Secondly, communitarianism – in its emphasis on the positive, sustaining aspect of community – attends to only one aspect of the necessary vulnerability that Butler identifies, refusing a more somber view of the human condition that understands the ways in which others can impinge on us. Butler tries to rethink community on the basis of vulnerability and loss, as well as difference, which communitarianism traditionally has difficulty accounting for. Thus, in contrast to communitarianism, Butler seeks "another way of imagining community, one in which we are alike only in having this condition [vulnerability] separately and so having in common a condition that cannot be thought without difference."[51] With her theorization of a constitutive, inescapable, and ambiguous condition of shared vulnerability, Butler moves us toward being able to (re)think community, again in a post-identity-politics world.

Thirdly, extending her thought beyond identity politics and toward something like a precarious politics, Butler urges us to cultivate a recognition of a fundamental dependency that is not chosen and cannot be willed away, one which all individuals and groups as well as communities and states must reckon with. This extension of her thinking is nevertheless consistent with the critique of the sovereign, autonomous subject that Butler has pursued throughout her work. In this respect, Butler's recent political theory of vulnerability and precariousness runs counter to the theory and premises of deliberative democracy, such as when she echoes Adriana Cavarero's claim "that it is not because we are reasoning beings that we are connected to one another, but, rather, because we are *exposed* to one another, requiring a recognition that does not substitute the recognizer for the recognized."[52] Indeed, Butler's recent political theory of vulnerability takes inspiration from Cavarero's vision of politics as "a field of plural interaction and hence of contingency," such that politics and political theory not only must start from a principled recognition of "the plurality of human beings insofar as they are unique beings rather than fictitious entities like the individual of modern political doctrine," but also must therefore account most importantly for "a relational dimension of reciprocal dependency, which exposes as false the autonomy and self-sufficiency on which individualism insists."[53] While Butler's political theory of vulnerability recalls Cavarero's politicized theory in its attention to difference, plurality, and constitutive sociality, Butler's recent thought differs slightly from Cavarero, as the former insists on retaining the notion, and affirming the possibility, of a "we" – especially in the sense of "Loss has made a tenuous 'we' of us all."[54] After reiterating her familiar claims about our fundamental dependency/sociality that cannot be willed away, Butler distinguishes her perspective from Cavarero's by asserting the possibility of a kind of community, writing parenthetically "(You can see here that I resort here to the plural *we*, even though Cavarero advises against it, precisely because I am not convinced that we must abandon it.)"[55] Indeed, Butler returns to the primary individual subject's experience of loss (one might say not only violent losses of others, but also the constitutive loss of autonomy theorized in *The Psychic Life of Power*) in order to articulate a political vision, writing, "Despite our differences in location and history, my guess is that it is possible to appeal to a 'we,' for all of us have some notion of what it is to have lost somebody."[56]

Finally, however promising Butler's proposed reimagination of community, it remains politically speaking only a norm and an aspiration – partly because of the difficulty of translating and shifting from the level of the individual subject to the level of collective, political subjects. Butler cautiously suggests that the sociality and vulnerability of the subject applies not just to individuals but also to "state-centered political cultures,"[57] though not necessarily in easy or direct ways. For Butler holds that "when we are speaking about the 'subject' we are not always speaking about an individual: we are speaking about a model for agency and intelligibility, one that is very often based on notions of sovereign power."[58] Butler wants to challenge the notion of sovereign power at the level of the individual subject by reminding us of a constitutive and ambivalent vulnerability, but it also seems that she wants to argue something similar for states in the realm of the society of states. That is a worthy but complicated goal, because the issue of violence is more complex at the level of state interaction as opposed to intra-state action. In the international realm, a key question of political practice to which Butler's normative political theory of vulnerability provides some tenuous guidance, given the variability of circumstances, is exactly how to abide with losses and vulnerability and how to resist the temptations of revenge. Indeed, one could say that Butler's political ethic raises some difficult political questions, such as whether all acts of violence are vengeful, or, if not, which ones are and how do we read violence? Though I would not suggest that every violent act is vengeful or illegitimate, Butler comes close to this position through a near conflation, at times, of violence and vengeance. While she argues that it is not appropriate to the condition of vulnerability to respond to loss with vengeance, Butler leaves some uncertainty as to the parameters of legitimate response to grievances or offenses short of (fatal) loss. In terms of politics, Butler's key terms of loss and vengeance will require interpretation in context. While she may overestimate the power or capacity of abiding with loss and vulnerability as the (contingent) foundation for community, or may draw too sharply the contrast between violent and non-violent responses to loss, Butler nevertheless illuminates the political predicament and offers a particularly significant lesson for our age, an age of terrorism as a sudden address that we do not choose. It is a lesson about our vulnerability, a condition amplified by our recognition of an increasingly global interdependence that we cannot will away but with which we must deal.

3

Grieving Identity Politics: *The Three Burials of Melquiades Estrada* and the Question of Grievability

> [A]n obligation does emerge from the fact that we are, as it were, social beings from the start, dependent upon what is outside ourselves, on others, on institutions, and no sustained and sustainable environments, and so are, in this sense, precarious.
>
> (Judith Butler, *Frames of War*)[1]

Introduction: Revisiting the Western

For the better part of the twentieth century, the Western reigned as one of the most durable and capacious genres in American popular culture, comprising countless novels, films, and television series, from *Riders of the Purple Sage* to *High Noon* to *Gunsmoke*. The Western also epitomized the careers of numerous writers, directors, and actors, from Louis L'Amour to John Ford to John Wayne. While the genre has in recent decades been eclipsed in popularity by others, many scholars and critics argue that the Western played a significant role in moulding the American social and political consciousness, through its popular depictions of conflicts between natives and settlers, and lawmen and outlaws – as well as tensions between rival values such as freedom versus restriction, honour versus institutions, solipsism versus democracy, tradition versus change, and nature versus culture.[2] The political resonance so often carried by Westerns has been noted time and again by critics and scholars alike. Recently, Robert Pippin, in his study *Hollywood Westerns and American Myth* (2010), argues that "the great Hollywood Westerns present in a recognizably mythic form dimensions of an American understanding of great relevance to the question of the nature of the political in the American imaginary."[3] The genre of the Western has been culturally and politically significant for its role in not merely reflecting but in constructing such an imaginary. "The Western, and the larger cultural movements of which the Western is a part," argues literary scholar Jane Tompkins, "have taught people to see the world in a certain way."[4] The former predominance as well as the continuing structural legacy of the Western make it an appealing genre for contemporary films that seek to subvert conventional ways of seeing and help to reorient American perceptions of the social and political world.[5]

In particular, the impressive contemporary Western *The Three Burials of Melquiades Estrada* (*Los Tres Entierros de Melquiades Estrada*) (2006, dir. Tommy Lee Jones) makes a significant political intervention of just this sort, helping to reveal more than just an unrecognized identity. In typical Western fashion, *Three Burials* returns its audience to the familiar visual territory of the dusty West and the customary characters of taciturn cowboys, yet the story is not set in a romanticized and distant "frontier" past but in a present-day Texas border town, where cultural hybridity is the norm. Indeed, the film itself is culturally hybrid, through and through. Written by Mexican screenwriter Guillermo Arriaga and directed by Texan-American Tommy Lee Jones, *Three Burials* is that rare American movie in which the behind-the-screen production is as bicultural as the on-screen content. "This film insists on cultural parity from the get-go," observes film scholar Jim Kitses, such that even the "title credit announces simultaneously *The Three Burials of Melquiades Estrada* and *Los Tres Entierros de Melquiades Estrada*, the former above, the latter below, the symmetry conferring absolutely equal weight."[6] Moreover, the origins of the film's story demonstrate the very real political stakes for this cinematic intervention. Director Jones explains that the film is "based on the true story of West Texas teenager of Mexican descent who was shot dead by US marines on a border anti-drug patrol as he tended his family goats."[7] The film substitutes an undocumented Mexican cowboy, Melquiades Estrada (Juilo César Cedillo), for the teenager and a US Border Patrol officer, Mike Norton (Barry Pepper), for the US Marine, and also introduces a third key character, Pete Perkins (Tommy Lee Jones) as Melquiades' friend and fellow cowboy. Still, what remains unchanged is the structure of the narrative concerning a refusal to tolerate the disposability of lives different from the norm. For, as the film unfolds in Arriaga's characteristic non-linear narrative style (cf. his previous works *Amores Perros*, *21 Grams*, and *Babel*), it becomes clear that the shooting of Melquiades is only an introduction to the long, involved journey of his body through three different interments: the hasty first burial at the scene of the crime by his killer, Officer Norton, in order to cover up the murder; the procedural second burial in an unmarked grave by the local government, callously without notifying Melquiades' family or friends; and the reverential final burial that Melquiades' asked for in his Mexican "home," thanks to Pete's unwavering respect for Melquiades' request.

Three Burials and the Question of Grievability

However, just how Pete goes about carrying out Melquiades' last wishes is what distinguishes this film from countless others.

Among the many ways in which the Western genre has taught Americans to see the world, two are of particular interest for the manner in which they have been appropriated and subverted in *Three Burials of Melquiades Estrada*: the othering of Mexicans and the murderous drive for vengeance. *Three Burials* challenges the norms of the Western genre, turning these two familiar Western tropes upside down from within, confounding expectations, and helping the audiences to see the world, particularly the US–Mexico border, in a less hostile and less violent light. Together, these two genre subversions point toward an affirmation at the heart of this film: an affirmation of the precariousness of life. For the change of perspective that this film accomplishes is less about identity than about political ontology.[8] Despite some critics' claims to the contrary, the real political force of this film lies not in recognizing a formerly unseen or illegitimate identity, i.e. that of the undocumented Mexican migrant. Rather the distinctive intervention that this film accomplishes involves subverting the audience's expectation for murderous vengeance by instead embracing grieving as a response to loss. In connection with affirming the practice of grief, the film also attests to the relationality – or the sense in which we are "given over from the start to the world of others"[9] – that conditions all subjectivity.[10] To be sure, an essential part of what makes *Three Burials* such a compelling film is its very sympathetic portrait of its eponymous Mexican subject, but it is a portrait that not only sets the film apart from most Westerns but also lays the ground for a remarkable political intervention, undermining the familiar expectation of sovereign vengeance and instead affirming precariousness.

Instead of arguing for the film's participation in a politics of recognition, I want to argue that its attention to "grievability"[11] and precariousness reveals something more complex – something along the lines of what Markell refers to as an "alternative diagnosis of relations of social and political subordination, which sees them not as systematic failures by some to recognize others' identities, but as ways of patterning and arranging the world that allow some people and groups to enjoy a semblance of sovereign agency at others' expense."[12] Refusing and confounding the generic expectation of vengeance, the film presents both a sustained critique of sovereignty and a stout affirmation of precariousness.

The conflict at the heart of *The Three Burials of Melquiades Estrada* is a conflict of political ontologies: sovereignty versus precariousness. To put it briefly, sovereignty denies the insight that precariousness affirms – an insight that Markell traces to Hannah Arendt: "Because we do not act in isolation but interact with others, who we become through action is not up to us; instead, it is the outcome of many intersecting and unpredictable sequences of action and response, such that 'nobody is the author or producer of his own life story'."[13] Throughout the film, Pete and Mel (as Pete calls him) are shown to grasp the power of relationality and the truth that 'nobody is the author or producer of his own life story,' while Officer Norton stubbornly clings to pretensions to self-sufficiency and control. Thus, in the conflict of ontological perspectives staged by *Three Burials*, Pete's refusal of vengeance through his insistence on burying his friend in his hometown constitutes a victory for precariousness over the sovereignty represented by the brutally callous, attempted mastery of Officer Norton's murderous cover-up.

While *Three Burials* subverts genre expectations of the Western from within by sublimating the drive for vengeance and representing Mexicans in a sympathetic manner, it is nevertheless still recognisably a Western in two important ways: its respect for the dignity of a proper burial and its wrestling with the fear of losing mastery. Subverting some generic tropes associated with Westerns while affirming others, *Three Burials* illuminates the value of the political ontology of precarious life by daring to grieve not only the loss of the undocumented migrant cowboy, Melquiades Estrada, but also the loss of individual sovereignty. Before turning to a closer examination of the concept of political ontology, as well as Judith Butler's conception of precarious life, let us first examine the limits of a politics of recognition and its relationship to identity.

Subverting Mexican Otherness, Welcoming and the Limits of Recognition

The sympathetic figure at the centre of *Three Burials*, Melquiades Estrada, is exceptional among generic Western representations of Mexicans for the way in which he appears "ordinary," a working (family) man who develops a strong friendship with fellow cowboy Pete (Tommy Lee Jones). (Melquiades speaks of his family back in Mexico, but they never appear on screen except in a photograph he carries and shows to Pete.) The success of the film hinges on the audience being able to see and respect the character of Melquiades, such that once he is shot to death by Officer Norton for doing nothing more than trying to scare a coyote away from his goats, the audience chafes at the way in which the authorities disrespect his body and instead wants to see him honoured in death, his loss marked with respect. Eventually, after two less-than-perfect burials and a long, torturous journey on horseback through the desert, Pete and Norton do honour Mel's last wishes and bury him for the third and final time in his "home."

Three Burials and the Question of Grievability

The fact that the film achieves this empathetic identification with Melquiades throughout speaks to its ability to subvert a set of durable cinematic misrepresentations of Mexicans and Mexico. Film scholar David Lusted observes that "Historically, Mexicans in Westerns are devious 'greasers,' violent revolutionaries, or exotic heroes like Zorro and the Cisco Kid," and that typically in Westerns, Mexico is represented as "a refuge for Americans on the run."[14] Yet this film defies such norms by figuring Mexicans throughout as universally non-threatening and "ordinary," and Mexico as "home." (At one point along the journey to Melquiades' final resting place, Pete himself even expresses a desire to stay and settle in Mexico.) "The Mexicans are treated sympathetically but are not patronized," notes critic Philip French, himself a keen student of Westerns, such that "the film implies that the Southwest belongs as much to them as to the white newcomers. This is extremely refreshing and positive."[15]

The Three Burials of Melquiades Estrada is, of course, not the first Western to feature Mexico centrally in its plot. In fact, it shows some influence from a revisionist trend vis-à-vis Mexico in Hollywood Westerns rooted in the 1970s. Literary scholar Lee Clark Mitchell observes, in the context of a discussion of how Sergio Leone and Sam Peckinpah reinvigorated the Western in the 1960s and 1970s, that

> both [Leone and Peckinpah] turned away from fixed generic assumptions, most prominently in turning the Western itself to a Mexican context, placing Anglo-American characters in a culturally alien setting rather than loose in wilderness space. The shift south of the border contributed to the overall process by which the genre was further defamiliarized, diverting attention yet again from plot to questions of character.[16]

To be sure, *Three Burials* owes much to this defamiliarizing revisionist legacy in Western genre film, and yet what distinguishes it still from many such films of the 1970s is its consistently sympathetic and non-threatening, indeed welcoming, portrayal of Mexicans and Mexico. For instance, critics reviewing *Three Burials* often compare it to Peckinpah's *Bring Me The Head of Alfredo Garcia* (1974), in which the white American protagonist navigates through "a culturally alien" Mexico with the eponymous head, dodging and confronting dangerous rivals. (Both films derive moments of black comedy from the constant toting of dead bodies.) However, the only violent Mexican character in *Three Burials* is Mariana (Vanessa Bauche), a woman who, after healing Officer Norton's snakebite with herbal remedies, pours a hot pot of coffee on his lap. Yet unlike many traditional representations of violent Mexicans in Westerns, Mariana is not violent a priori and for no reason, simply because she is culturally different and presumed hostile. Rather, the film provides specific and powerful motivation for her actions, as earlier she is seen to be the victim of terrible police brutality at the hands of none other than Officer Norton. To be sure she was trying to cross the border illegally, but Norton unnecessarily beats her with excessive force and receives a reprimand from his commanding officer. In the larger context of the film, the point of these two exchanges is not to establish the suspicious and violent otherness of Mexicans, but rather that of Norton, who as a border patrol agent is the very definition of sovereign violence. In fact, Norton's sovereign violence finds its ultimate expression in not only his killing of Melquiades but also in his effort to cover up his misdeed.

Set in the US–Mexico border area and involving action in both Texas and Coahuila, *Three Burials* supplies many examples of welcoming on both sides of the border in order to suggest a general ease with cultural difference characteristic of such a culturally hybrid area. On the Mexican side of the border throughout the latter half of the film, Pete and Officer Norton encounter many people willing to help them on their journey with everything from directions and coffee to snake-bite remedies. Similarly, on the Texas side of the border, Melquiades, though undocumented and ever vulnerable, is nevertheless able to build a life for himself, a project that takes root when he becomes friendly with Pete. There is theoretical significance to such welcoming, as Markell suggests: "To welcome someone says more about the welcomer than the welcomed: it represents a slackening of the urge to convert an uncertain activity into a predictable process by setting and enforcing strict boundaries to participation."[17] Most every character in the film demonstrates a welcoming ethos, suggesting an appreciation of the uncertainty and relationality inherent in their social condition.

The one striking exception in the film to this welcoming ethos is Officer Mike Norton, who, having just arrived in south Texas from his hometown of Cincinnati, is shown to be consistently different, isolated, self-serving, and violent. The exceptional Officer Norton is both literally and figuratively identified with sovereignty. Literally, because he works for the federal government policing the border, and figuratively, because as the character who kills Melquiades, brutally beats border-crossers, and quietly rapes his wife (all with impunity), he is the very embodiment of what Markell calls "sovereign agency." Markell argues for "a broader idea of sovereign agency, which can be attributed as easily to persons as to institutions. In this broader sense, sovereignty refers to the condition of being an independent, self-determining agent, characterized by what Hannah Arendt calls 'uncompromising self-sufficiency and mastership.'"[18] Markell's deployment of sovereignty carries a sharply critical edge, because he argues that the ontological social conditions in which we find ourselves cannot bear out such uncompromising "self-sufficiency and mastership." Indeed, "the basic aspiration behind" sovereignty, he claims, is "the aspiration to be able to act independently, without experiencing life among others as a source of vulnerability, or as a site of possible alienation and self-loss."[19]

Two key scenes in the film epitomize the fundamental difference between Pete, on the one hand, as someone who rejects sovereignty and welcomes vulnerability, and Norton, on the other, who rejects welcoming and embraces the aspiration to sovereign invulnerability. First, in a scene glimpsed by the audience in flashback early in the film, Pete, immediately after exiting the morgue where he has identified Melquiades' body, remembers first meeting Melquiades. In the remembered scene, Melquiades rides up on horseback to the barn where Pete and fellow ranch-hands are taking a midday break and asks in Spanish for water for his horse. In a shot that finds echoes in many a Western, Melquiades is seen on horseback from within the barn, the door framing him in near silhouette. With a slight suggestion of suspicion that matches the generic expectations associated with Westerns regarding Mexicans, Pete asks in Spanish "Where'd you come from?" When Melquiades responds "Coahuila," Pete continues the interrogation in Spanish asking "What are you doing in Texas?" And when Melquiades responds "Looking for work," Pete again responds quickly with a question, again in Spanish: "What kind of work?" Melquiades then pauses, and in a close-up the camera tracks his eyes as he surveys the other ranch-hands sitting around the barn. Finally, Melquiades diffuses tension and suspicion among Pete and his fellow ranch-hands by cracking a knowing half-smile, nodding his head and saying in Spanish, "I'm just a cowboy." The film's representation of Melquiades here is doubly subversive of generic Western conventions for representing Mexicans, for not only does he appear non-threatening and "ordinary" as a family man, but he also occupies the iconic and distinctively American position of the cowboy, a figure usually reserved in Westerns for heroic white American males and structurally opposite darker-skinned others. Perhaps this helps the audience feel Mel's loss even more. For immediately after Melquiades saying "I'm just a cowboy," the film brutally cuts to a brief shot of the "first burial" as Officer Norton drags Mel's body into a shallow desert grave.

What is striking about the scene of Pete and Mel's first meeting that makes it worth examining closely is the way in which it tracks the subversion of Mexican otherness, suggesting a distinction between welcoming and recognizing, where welcoming is, we might say, agnostic about identity. This early sequence illustrates not only Pete's fond remembrance of first meeting the now-dead Melquiades, but also the way in which Melquiades overcomes the generic, othered suspicions of both Pete and audiences alike in order to become welcomed as an empathetic figure. After welcoming such a figure, Pete and the audience feel his loss deeply and feel that a wrong needs to be righted: Melquiades needs to be buried and grieved properly. Welcoming is precisely what Pete does on first meeting Melquiades, for after Melquiades identifies as a cowboy, he and Pete go on to work together on the ranch and form a true friendship – all seen in bittersweet flashbacks in the film. Again, Markell captures the essence of the welcoming that Pete gives Melquiades, without reference to national identity:

> Arendt commented that 'if it is good to be recognized, it is better to be welcomed, precisely because this is something we can neither earn nor deserve.' Welcoming, here, refers to the risky inclusion of another in a shared activity, without reference to her identity, or state of character, or degree of merit.[20]

The fact that Pete welcomes and includes Melquiades without regard to identity (except as a "cowboy") also speaks to the force of the film's intervention beyond the identity politics of recognition. The film addresses more than identity. It addresses relationality, grievability, and precarious life.

The importance of welcoming reminds us how significant the hybrid nature of the border town is for the story of *Three Burials*. For Pete and others welcome Melquiades, while Norton is consistently unwelcoming to Mexicans, border-crossers, and non-Americans, even while he as a white American male has been welcomed into the small Texas town. While Pete welcomes Melquiades, and in turn Mexicans later welcome Pete along his journey to properly bury Mel, Officer Norton does not welcome Mexicans but insists on seeing them as suspicious at least and enemies at worst. Norton's point of view is evidenced not only in his beating of the border-crossers but also his killing of Melquiades (more on this momentarily). Thus, early on in the film, the audience can glean quite a lot from Pete's welcoming ethos and Norton's hostile mode of being. Indeed, from the beginning, Pete is identified with a certain "slackening" of the urge to control associated with mastery and sovereignty, while Norton is tightly bound up with the drive for self-sufficiency and control.

Now let us turn to a key scene in the film that illustrates not only Officer Norton's unwelcoming attitude but also an important aspect of political ontology. Later we will examine the political ontology of precariousness, but first we turn to what Markell calls the "impropriety of action," or the lack of control and inability to master the conditions in which we act. Markell suggests that this lack of control over the conditions and consequences of our actions is "a constitutive feature of

Three Burials and the Question of Grievability

human action" – that is, it cannot be eliminated, regardless of our pretensions to self-sufficiency or sovereignty. Indeed, "the very conditions that make us potent agents [our materiality and our plurality]," Markell goes on to say, "also make us potent beyond our own control, exposing us to consequences and implications that we cannot predict and that are not up to us."[21] In some ways, one might see *Three Burials* as one long meditation on the truth of this insight, given the circumstances of the deed that sets the film's action in motion. Consider, for instance, the circumstances of Melquiades' murder by Officer Norton and what they reveal about our inability to fully control the implications of our actions. The shooting of Melquiades initiates in Norton's misreading or misunderstanding of the cowboy's own rifle shots, which were intended to scare a coyote away from his grazing goats. In the midst of an impromptu masturbation session during his quiet patrol (a further suggestion of disturbing self-sufficiency), Officer Norton hears those shots and (mis)reads them as being directed at him. (Remember that in the non-linear chronology of the film, Officer Norton has already been shown to the audience to be prone to hostility when he used excessive force against an attempted border-crosser – who in turn even later will be revealed to be Mariana, the woman who will save his life). At this point, Norton immediately reaches for his own rifle and thus returns fire, killing Melquiades. He then rushes over to Melquiades and, seeing both the coyote wounded by Melquiades as well as his scattered goats, seems to regret having been instinctively suspicious and hostile, saying in English, "Hey man [...] You OK?" This remark and the worried look on Norton's face are the first hints given in the film that Officer Norton is capable of empathy. For up to this point, he has quietly raped his wife in the kitchen of their home and brutally beaten a female border-crosser. Finally, then, he has gunned down an innocent man, who was merely tending his goats.

This "accidental" shooting, a most unwelcoming act which initiates the main action of the film and its three burials, but is only glimpsed in flashback in the middle of the film, serves as a vivid illustration of the "impropriety of action." It illustrates, firstly with respect to Melquiades' warning shots and later with respect to Norton and the government's cover-ups (first and second "burials" respectively), the fact that we cannot fully control the consequences of our actions in social space given the fact of plurality. (The second burial in an anonymous grave is carried out by local Texas government officials; anonymous, because the sheriff callously refuses to attempt to notify Melquiades' family, assuming that he has none.) Characteristic of the ontological conflict at the heart of the film, the "improper" killing of Melquiades serves as a reminder of the dangers of pretensions to self-sufficiency and points toward the need to attend better to the materiality and plurality of the social relations in which we inevitably find ourselves. For Melquiades only intended to scare the coyote away, and yet his shots were interpreted in a hostile light by Officer Norton. The film goes on to illustrate the impropriety of action not only in the case of Melquiades' shooting, but also by not allowing the intended cover-up of his murder as well as his anonymous first and second burials to stand. Pete's quest to honour Melquiades by kidnapping Norton and forcing him to dig up the body and accompany Pete on horseback to Mel's homeland represents many things, but chief among them is the double acknowledgement of the impropriety of the action and the dependent truth that 'nobody is the author or producer of his own life story.' Pete knows that Melquiades needs him to complete his life story, and Pete is determined not to let him down.

Such moments of welcoming and suspicion are quite telling and theoretically significant beyond the cultural hybridity of the setting and the film's production. They speak to the film's larger socio-political argument, one that pushes beyond identity and toward political ontology. The prevalence of welcoming, with Norton being a stark exception, argues against the film's central argument being the recognition of different identities. Instead, because different identities are generally welcomed without concern, we can see that the film is pushing its audience to look beyond identity to the conditions in which identity is formed. And yet, some critics have insisted on reading the film as an argument about identity rather than political ontology.

In light of *Three Burials*' generic subversions of Mexican otherness and the recent political discussions of immigration and border security in the US, it has been tempting to read the film as doing work on the racialized political anxieties surrounding illegal immigration and the US–Mexico border. Fredric Jameson has noted that popular culture texts, such as Westerns, can be seen as doing "transformational work on social and political anxieties and fantasies which must then have some affective presence in the mass cultural text in order to subsequently be 'managed' or repressed."[22] Such a reading suggests the film's participation in the politics of recognition, seeking recognition of difference and redress of injustices related to misrepresentation and misrecognition of identity. In an essay in *Sight & Sound*, film critic and scholar Jim Kitses makes just such an argument, claiming that the film is "an evocative border tale that's also a forceful social analysis of America and Mexico's shared tragedy of the illegal immigrant."[23] Kitses' interpretation of the film, even as it illustrates the value of such recognition, inadvertently exposes the limits of a politics of recognizing identities. For his argument is built around many of the assumptions and ideas that are the very object of Markell's critique of the politics of recognition. "[T]he politics of recognition," argues the latter, "is characterized by certain important misrecognitions of its own – not misrecognitions of identity, but failures to acknowledge one's own basic ontological conditions – and [...] these arise from the fact that the pursuit of recognition expresses an aspiration to *sovereignty*" (emphasis original).[24] Critics like Kitses, who insist on reading *Three Burials* as an intervention in the politics of recognition, are unwittingly reenacting these ontological misrecognitions.

Throughout his essay, Kitses insistently eschews analysing aspects of the film that point to political ontology (relationships, vulnerability, and agency), turning instead to questions of identity. For instance, Kitses claims that many reviewers of *Three Burials* have unfortunately overlooked "the film's title immigrant" and "have simply praised the film as a testament to friendship and loyalty, ignoring Melquiades' ethnicity and the recuperation of the 'wetback.'"[25] While Kitses is right to note the unusually sympathetic, for the Western genre, representation of Mexicans in the figure of Melquiades, his insistence on shifting attention away from the relationships among the characters and toward ethnic identity is but one indication of his effort to read the film as contributing to a politics of identity recognition. In fact, Kitses goes on to reinforce his main claim by contending that "central to the [film's] project is the fact that Pete's friendship is with someone who is trapped by national identity in a destitute and dependent state."[26] In claiming that the film is about the recognition of Melquiades' national identity, Kitses confirms one of the misrecognitions identified by Markell as being at the heart of such a politics: the insistence on seeing identity (national and ethnic identity, in this case) as a fait accompli. There is a serious problem with Kitses seeing identity as so fixed that one could be trapped by it, and Markell states the problem in this way: "Invoking 'identity' as a *fait accompli* precisely in the course of the ongoing and risky interactions through which we become who we are (or, more precisely, who we will turn out to have been), [the politics of recognition] at once acknowledges and refuses to acknowledge our basic condition of intersubjective vulnerability."[27] In other words, invoking identity as Kitses claims the film does goes directly against the ethos of respecting and welcoming the uncertainty inherent in social relations noted earlier. Moreover, Kitses' framing of the issue overlooks the fact that vulnerability and dependence are not something to which only illegal immigrants or people of difference are subject. Rather, these are fundamental conditions of the intersubjective social world of plurality that we all inhabit, though vulnerability and precariousness may be unevenly experienced across groups.

Still, when Kitses persists in arguing finally that "At the end the broken American's abject apology crowns the film's action of recognition, documenting the undocumented worker,"[28] he misunderstands the point of the film's intervention. Once Norton has dug the final grave and he and Pete have fixed up the remains of Mel's home, Pete forces Norton to beg for Melquiades' forgiveness before letting him go and even giving him a horse. But the film does more than document the undocumented, or recognize the unrecognized. Rather, it foregrounds Pete's effort to make Norton acknowledge the basic "ontological conditions or circumstances" of life and the "finitude" of an individual – in other words, dependence, interdependence, precariousness. To fully understand the problems with Kitses' argument, however, we must turn again to Markell's critique of the politics of recognition – specifically, to an alternate politics rooted in a different ontology. Ironically, Markell argues that

> something like this alternative [ontological] view of action, identity, sovereignty, and recognition is already implicit, but half-buried and disavowed, in the politics of recognition itself. That politics, after all, is in part a response to the experience of vulnerability, to the fact that our identities are shaped in part through the unpredictable responses of other people.[29]

However, unlike the politics of recognition's fixed view of identity, Markell sketches what he calls the politics of acknowledgement, which involves "accepting that the existence of others – as yet unspecified, indeterminate others – makes unpredictability and lack of mastery into unavoidable conditions of human agency [...] since part of the point of acknowledgement is to expose ourselves to surprise appearances and unexpected developments."[30] Claiming that *Three Burials* is about recognizing the unrecognized, as Kitses does, overlooks the significance of the long final "journey" that constitutes the majority of the film. The purpose of that journey is not simply to get Norton to recognize Melquiades. The final burial journey is about grievability (more on this below) and about "dismantling or attenuating"[31] the privilege of a white American border patrol agent who, by killing with impunity, has aspired to an impossible sovereignty. As a refusal of murderous vengeance, the final journey represents an "acknowledgement" of the ties that bind us to each other and the relations to which we are always already given over. Pete acknowledges this throughout, and also in refusing to kill Norton forces him to acknowledge it as well. From the moment that Melquiades meets Pete until Mel's final burial, the film concerns the acknowledgement of precariousness and vulnerability as constitutive features of life. *Three Burials* tries to unearth what is half-buried in the politics of recognition – namely the necessary and inescapable condition of dependency and attachment that is vulnerability and precariousness.

Subverting Revenge and Affirming Precariousness

Another trope familiar to many Westerns that is subverted by *Three Burials* is the central drive for vengeance. Although vengeance is now rather ubiquitous in movies and popular culture, it is worth remembering the central role of the Western in "teaching" Americans about the necessity and legitimacy of violent revenge. In fact, the drive for vengeance is so structured into the makeup of the genre that it "reproduces itself in a thousand Western novels and movies," insists Jane Tompkins. In most Westerns, "Vengeance, by the time it arrives, feels biologically necessary."[32] By contrast, the main engine of *Three Burials*' plot is not vengeance, but something rather more interesting and complicated. While Pete's quest for justice for his murdered friend "Mel" does provide the narrative energy of *Three Burials*, it becomes clear about a third of the way into the film that justice will not come in the usual vengeful form of "an eye for an eye." For once Pete learns that Norton shot Melquiades, he does not seek to kill him in turn, but instead kidnaps him, forces him to dig up Melquiades' body, and journey on horseback to Mexico to return Mel to his home. Before they set off for Mexico, however, Pete forces Norton to walk a mile in Melquiades' shoes, literally, taking him to Melquiades' house and making him sit in his chair, drink from his cup, and finally put on his clothes. Such a forced identification of perpetrator with the other suggests that Pete is not driven in the customary, generic manner by a desire for murderous vengeance, but rather that he acts as an agent of empathy, mourning, and a different understanding of social relations than is customary in most movies, let alone Westerns.

As much as *The Three Burials of Melquiades Estrada* is in essential ways a meditation on the "impropriety of action" in the circumstances of Melquiades' shooting, the three interments of the title also constitute an extended reflection on another theme related to political ontology: grievability. Indeed, perhaps more than any other film in recent memory *Three Burials* engages the question of grievability, or "who is grievable?" That is, whose lives matter enough to be mourned when lost. This question is not as simple as it may appear, for it harbours deep undercurrents related not just to identity and culture but also to ontology and politics. For the "mattering" of lives is not simply a function of individual choice or abstract right, but rather a function of shared social norms. Judith Butler has done much to raise grievability as a political and philosophical question in recent books, most notably *Precarious Life* (2004) and *Frames of War* (2009), arguing that "Only under conditions in which the loss would matter does the value of the life appear. Thus, grievability is a presupposition for the life that matters."[33] In charting the journey of

Melquiades' body through three different burials, each with its own socio-political valences, the film emphatically challenges the dominant understanding that as an undocumented migrant in the US he is ungrievable – that his loss is invisible and insignificant, that his life is insignificant. Throughout the film, as the action moves forward through the three different burials, the audience also sees flashbacks of the friendship between Melquiades and Pete, the friendship that Pete seeks to honour in spite of the government's willingness to overlook injustice done to a "nobody." Butler asks the question to which Norton, the government, and Pete in turn may be said to provide very different answers: "After all, if someone is lost, and that person is not someone, then what and where is the loss, and how does mourning take place?"[34] In fact, the first two burials confirm that Melquiades is ungrievable in exactly the sense that Butler suggests: "An ungrievable life is one that cannot be mourned because it has never [been] lived, that is, it has never counted as a life at all."[35] In the moment that he shot Melquiades, Officer Norton, it seems, cannot imagine that his victim enjoys a life in Texas with a house and a small flock of goats. By contrast, Pete's taking charge and kidnapping Norton to make a proper burial happen is about two things: one, he brings about an acknowledgement of vulnerability and action's impropriety; two, he makes Melquiades count for Norton (and, by extension, for the American public/government), he makes him grievable.

As if it were starting from Butler's claim that "specific lives cannot be apprehended as injured or lost if they are not first apprehended as living,"[36] *Three Burials* sets out to tell Melquiades' story in order to help the audience to apprehend his life and make it count, no matter the reigning norms or politics of recognition. Making elegant use of a non-linear narrative structure, the film affirms the value of Melquiades' life, even as it has already been lost. In its first scene, two hunters discover Melquiades' body, already resting uneasily in its hasty first grave in the desert hills of south Texas. It is only later revealed, in an all-too-brief flashback, that this first burial was performed by Officer Norton near the scene of the crime (we only see him dragging the body into the shallow grave). The fact that Norton, as an officer in the United States Border Patrol, thought he could cover up his shooting of an undocumented Mexican says much about the privilege of sovereign power with which he is literally and symbolically identified. In fact, it speaks again to the existence of "ways of patterning and arranging the world that allow some people and groups to enjoy a semblance of sovereign agency at others' expense."[37]

The troubling fact that this film does not shy away from is that such "ways of patterning and arranging the world" are not merely a function of individual rogue officers, or "bad apples." Indeed, the film barely lingers on the isolated, individual effort of the first burial, and instead devotes considerable screen time to the more politically significant second interment. According to the film, what is worse than an individual not apprehending a life as living, as counting, is a whole community or society and its government not apprehending a large set of lives as living, as counting, as mattering. Yet that is exactly what the film shows through the way in which Officer Norton is aided and abetted in this crime by the local Texas government, which buries Melquiades for a second time in a grave marked only with a small cross and a hand-written notation: "Melquiades. Mexico". (Additionally, it should be noted that the film offers no indication that Norton faces any disciplinary action from the Border Patrol agency, much less criminal charges from the local government.) The local government, particularly Sheriff Belmont (Dwight Yoakam), does this in spite of Pete's explicit request that he be given the body once the autopsy is finished, effectively identifying as Mel's family in the absence of any other.

In another striking scene of sovereign privilege, Sheriff Belmont, upon hearing the autopsy report in the morgue from the medical examiner, immediately and cavalierly gives approval to inter him, saying, "OK, bury him." When the medical examiner halfheartedly objects, saying, "Need to notify his relatives," Belmont looks him straight in the eye and says coldly, "He ain't got any." And he does that in spite of Pete's request to receive the body as Mel's proxy family. Belmont's dismissal represents a doubly damning condemnation of a sovereign power that not only cannot imagine Melquiades' life as a life, but also cannot respect the ties and relations that make up his life. In fact, Belmont's action effectively illustrates Butler's criticism about ungrievable lives: "Those we kill are not quite human, and not quite alive, which means that we do not feel the same horror and outrage over the loss of their lives as we do over the loss of those lives that bear national or religious similarity to our own."[38]

The first two burials of Melquiades Estrada, performed under the aegis of the sovereign power of the government, deny that his loss matters. But more than that, they reinforce a troubling individualistic ontology of autonomy by denying that "my existence is not mine alone, but is to be found outside myself, in this set of relations that precede and exceed the boundaries of who I am."[39] According to this alternate ontology, which acknowledges the inescapability of precariousness, "life itself has to be rethought as this complex, passionate, antagonistic, and necessary set of relations to others."[40] Pete's effort to see Melquiades buried according to his final wishes is about more than making his life count, though it certainly is that. It is about acknowledging the necessary relations to others that enable and sustain our lives. Even when, near the end of the film, Melquiades' family turns out to have been a fiction (nobody in the town knows of Melquiades, and no one knows of the place where he wishes to be buried, Jimenez), Pete continues to try and honour his burial wishes and perhaps even Mel's desire for and appreciation of family even if he hadn't actually made one of his own. Unlike Belmont, Pete's actions effectively respect this alternate frame of reference, as if he were saying along with Butler: "If I survive, it is only because my life is nothing without the life that exceeds me, that refers to some indexical you, without whom I cannot be."[41]

After the first two burials, the film's continued engagement with the grievability of Melquiades derives from Pete's devotion to him and the latter's refusal of murderous vengeance. (At the end of the film, as Pete prepares to leave and tells Norton he can go, Officer Norton says "I always thought that you'd end up killin' me.") Instead of allowing himself to be consumed by loss and seeking to deny our constitutive vulnerability, Pete seeks to honour a promise he made to Melquiades. He does so in spite of the government's insistence that Melquiades' life does not count and his loss cannot be grieved. In another poignant scene, again glimpsed in flashback, the audience sees Pete and Melquiades sharing a moment on the ranch beside a small pond. Melquiades says, in Spanish: "Promise me one thing, Pete. If I die over here, carry me back to my family and bury me in my hometown. I don't want to be buried on this side among all the fucking billboards." Given this vision of tombstone billboards, it seems that Melquiades knows he will not be grieved properly if he dies on the American side of the border, that he will not be placed in the context of the social relations that matter to him. His fear of not being respected even after his death surely derives from the feeling of invisibility that he has as an undocumented person.

It is telling that Mel's expression of this last wish is seen by the audience only after Pete has kidnapped Norton and forced him to dig up Mel's body. For since Melquiades is always already dead in this film, one might say that the film tells the story of Melquiades' body – but not merely his dead body, also his social body. The film refracts the story of Melquiades' body through the prism of his social relations, especially his relationship with fellow cowboy Pete. After the second burial and throughout the latter half of the film, as he transports Mel's body across the desert, Pete attends very carefully and lovingly to it attempting to preserve it until the final burial. Many of these moments – such as when Pete pours whiskey on the body and lights it on fire to get rid of ants, or when he combs Mel's hair with a horse brush only to have much of it come out – come off as effective moments of black comedy. Still, the tender care of one friend for another carries another meaning in light of Butler's social ontology of the body. If "the body implies mortality, vulnerability, agency," as Butler has claimed, then Pete's care for Mel is an extended reminder of our shared vulnerability and dependency as well as Pete's respect for that. The fact that Melquiades' body is such a central part of this film speaks to the fact that "Constituted as a social phenomenon in the public sphere, my body is and is not mine."[42] Such a social reading of the body undercuts all pretensions to self-sufficiency, emphasizing instead relationality and dependency. In insisting that Melquiades be grieved and his loss acknowledged, the film, through the character of Pete, teaches us that "to be a body is to be exposed to social crafting and form, and that is what makes the ontology of the body a social ontology."[43]

By engaging the question of "who is grievable?" through these three burials, taking a resolutely social view of Melquiades, and revealing how he is constituted in and through his social relationships, the film encourages its audience to confront the limits of individual sovereignty and begin to envision a different political ontology, one based on "the insight that our very survival depends not on the policing of a boundary – the strategy of a certain sovereign in relation to its territory – but on recognizing how we are bound up with others."[44] Moreover, the film makes it clear that it is not just the marginal or the ungrievable (people like Melquiades) who are always already bound up with others, for not only is Pete undone by the loss of his friend Melquiades but Officer Norton is also made to experience the meaning of being "given over from the start to a world of others."[45] Constituting a sophisticated political intervention, for instance, in the context of the US debate over immigration and the border, *Three Burials* seeks to make Melquiades' life (and by extension, those of millions of others like him) matter, and yet the substance of the matter is more ontology than identity. In other words, the key to grasping the significance of the film's political and philosophical intervention requires that we neither reduce the question of who is grievable to a question of identity nor restrict the film's politics to a politics of recognition. The question of grievability is broader and deeper than the question of identity and recognition, and the film's political intervention is not solely in the service of a politics of recognition, identity, or difference. Rather, as Butler notes, "The apprehension of grievability precedes and makes possible the apprehension of precarious life."[46] Precarious life or precariousness names the political ontology at the heart of both Butler's and the film's intervention.

Conclusion: Losing Mastery, Affirming Precariousness

While *Three Burials* subverts the Western from within by sublimating the drive for vengeance and representing Mexicans in a sympathetic manner, it is nevertheless still recognizably a Western, and not simply because of the horses trotting across the beautiful landscape. Above all, *Three Burials* is a Western in the slightly unconventional sense established by Tompkins when she notes: "The Western doesn't have anything to do with the West as such. It isn't about the encounter between civilization and the frontier. It is about men's fear of losing their mastery, and hence their identity, both of which the Western tirelessly reinvents."[47] Indeed, *Three Burials* does more than engage the fear of such loss; it explores the experience of the loss of mastery and identity via its three main characters, who must confront what Judith Butler calls the precariousness of life – or, "the fact that one's life is always in some sense in the hands of the other."[48] The film helps us to see the meaning of precariousness as the inverse of sovereignty. Each of the film's three main characters – Melquiades, Pete, and Norton – carries some of the burden of this fear of losing mastery and identity, and thus each in his own way faces the limits of individual sovereignty.

As we conclude, consider a key plot development that sets the film in motion. Already an undocumented migrant without a legal identity, Melquiades feels the limits of self-sufficiency insofar as he experiences the precariousness of his political and legal vulnerability almost constantly while living in the US. Yet he also still manages to form a strong friendship connection with Pete. Nevertheless, he experiences, in the most profound way, the loss of control in the circumstances of his death. In one of the key scenes in the film, brilliantly revealed only in flashback, we see that Melquiades' death comes as a result of him merely shooting at a coyote that he saw threatening his goats, as Officer Norton, already shown in the film to be prone to hostility, then misinterprets Melquiades' shots as threats against him and "returns fire," killing Melquiades instantly. For a period of time thereafter, Melquiades' loss of mastery is matched by Norton's mastery insofar as he avoids sanctions or prosecution of any kind for the murder that he has committed. Pete, of course, feels the loss of his self-sufficient mastery to the extent to which he is undone by the loss of his friend, whose memory and dignity he feels he must honour. But Norton's sovereign escape lasts only until Pete learns that Norton killed Melquiades and undertakes to "make it right," by foregoing easy vengeance and instead forcing Norton to confront his own lack of mastery. The accidental shooting that brings these three characters together illustrates all the key themes of political ontology explored here: the impropriety of action; the aspiration to sovereign self-sufficiency; and, above all, precariousness. The relationships between these three characters in this remarkable film illustrate the resonance of Butler's claim that "the subject that I am is bound to the subject I am not [...] we each have the power to destroy and to be destroyed [...] we are bound to one another in this power and this precariousness. In this sense, we are all precarious lives."[49]

Three Burials and the Question of Grievability

The Three Burials of Melquiades Estrada is a superlative Western in the way in which it dramatizes the loss of mastery (and an identity bound-up with mastery) because, along with Norton, the audience is forced to confront the vulnerability and precariousness entailed in the loss of mastery, which accompanies the fact that we are always already given over to others. *Three Burials'* redirection of the desire for justice in the murder of Melquiades away from vengeance and toward grieving is doubly instructive in this respect, for the film encourages the audience to mourn not only the loss of Melquiades Estrada but also the loss of individual mastery, control, or sovereignty over our surroundings. What the film, then, seeks to bury is not only Melquiades but also a particular idea of sovereign individualism. And in grieving the loss of sovereignty, the film affirms a rival political ontology: "Precarious life implies life as a conditioned process, and not as the internal feature of a monadic individual or any other anthropocentric conceit […] all life is precarious, which is to say that life always emerges and is sustained within conditions of life."[50] In grieving Melquiades, this film asks us to acknowledge and attend to the relations and conditions that sustain life.

4

A Predicament of Precarity: *Wendy and Lucy* and the Impossibility of Neoliberal Self-Care

> At root precarity is a condition of dependency – as a legal term, precarious describes the situation wherein your tenancy on your land is in someone else's hands.
>
> (Lauren Berlant, *Cruel Optimism*)[1]

Introduction: Precarity on Film

Films both reflect and construct social reality, especially in the way in which they participate in the reproduction or interruption of not only the discourses but also the affects, images and sensory perceptions through which we grasp political life. Often, contemporary films represent the exercise of freedom in a decontextualised and depoliticised way, ignoring the dependent and precarious character of social and economic life while at the same time eschewing the attendant anxieties. *Into the Wild* (Penn, 2007) is one example of this approach. Other films, however, do attend to the unchosen relations and circumstances that cannot be willed away but must instead be negotiated, putting the work of such negotiation at the centre of their on-screen drama. What is more, some of these films also address the fretful insecurity that is increasingly inescapable in today's neoliberal political economy, and which is characterised by the notion of precarity. Films of this sort illuminate precarious lives, shedding light on the ways in which individual subjects are always already non-sovereign – dependent upon, as well as sensing and acting in, conditions and contexts not of their own choosing. As part of our investigation into the dependence and subjectivity that necessarily accompany freedom despite liberal common sense's claims to the contrary, we now turn our attention to a consideration of the contemporary economic pressures shaping freedom and subjectivity, examining in particular the contemporary film *Wendy and Lucy* (Reichardt, 2008). Director Kelly Reichardt's focused and contemplative piece offers a compelling

Wendy and Lucy and the Impossibility of Neoliberal Self-Care

portrayal of a woman negotiating a set of unchosen circumstances and affects, indeed foregrounding the unchosen in a way that many movies do not.

The two films *Wendy and Lucy* and *Into the Wild* are effectively mirror images in terms of their representations of freedom and the unchosen, even as they share many similarities of plot and imagery. Both are variations on the "road movie," a genre that has always played a role in the construction of a certain imaginary of freedom in the United States. "Forging a travel narrative out of a particular conjunction of plot and setting that sets the liberation of the road against the repression of hegemonic norms, road movies project American Western mythology onto the landscape traversed and bound by the nation's highways."[2] Both *Into the Wild* and *Wendy and Lucy* tell stories of protagonists travelling West and North to Alaska, representing in a sense the final American frontier of freedom and self-determination. These characters, Chris McCandless and Wendy Carroll seek freedom – or, at least, an opportunity to make ends meet – each in the spirit of the American tradition of self-reliance.

Whereas *Into the Wild* is a more traditional road movie in contrasting the freedom of the road with stifling, ordinary society, *Wendy and Lucy* turns the genre upside down, interrupting Wendy's planned journey with car trouble and other unchosen events in order to offer the audience a clear-eyed vision of the harshness exerted by the expectation of autonomy in a world of dependence. By contrast Chris McCandless holds a seductive but illusory vision of freedom as freedom from the unchosen, freedom from dependence. Though compelling in a way, Chris' vision is impossible given the necessity of unchosen powers and influences on subjectivity, though the film underemphasizes these forces and instead foregrounds Chris' courageous deviance. However, when compared with the realistic hardships and setbacks that Wendy must face on the road, the class and male privilege in McCandless' choices comes into view. In contrast, Wendy is presented on screen not as a hero/heroine or "free agent" but rather as someone who adapts and survives, someone who is connected to and dependent on others (including non-human others, especially her dog Lucy) in ways that are sometimes challenging to sustain. Wendy tries her best to preserve the relationships that she depends on, even as everything threatens to slip away. In other words, *Wendy and Lucy* is captivating for the manner in which it addresses and makes visible some of the ways in which precarity is lived in today's America.

In addition to offering incisive critiques of the American mythology of independence and "free agency" through its depiction of multiple and complex dependencies, *Wendy and Lucy* also helps to illuminate the contemporary condition of precarity that characterizes more and more of the experience of working people in today's capitalism. In particular, this film can be helpfully situated within what Lauren Berlant has called the "Cinema of Precarity." While the discourse of precarity charts some of the consequences of neoliberalism's advance and the State's retreat, Berlant does excellent work detailing the way in which some cultural texts, including films, bring into view both the ordinariness of economic crisis and the affective demands and challenges induced by precarity. Or, to be more precise, Berlant's intervention supplements the discourse of precarity with precarity's affect, for as she notes "the present is perceived, first, affectively."[3] The cinema of precarity, she argues, "melds melodrama and politics into a more reticent aesthetic to track the attrition of what had been sustaining national, social, economic and political bonds and the abandonment of a variety of populations to being cast as waste."[4] Berlant's insight illuminates the important intersection of structural economic conditions and stories of particular lives lived amidst prevailing norms about "what it means to have a life." She highlights the affective challenge of trying to survive economic precarity and live. In writing, for instance, that "Even those whom you would think of as defeated are living beings figuring out how to stay attached to life from within it, and to protect what optimism they have for that, at least,"[5] Berlant wants to help us better appreciate those cinematic narratives that offer insight into the affective structure of our precarious times. Though she focuses on a handful of contemporary European films and analyses no American movies, *Wendy and Lucy* shares many of the characteristics that she outlines.[6]

Wendy and Lucy focuses on a marginalized younger white woman who struggles against being cast off and seeks help navigating the challenging situations with which the unchosen presents her. The fact that Wendy is precarious and dependent is revealed directly in her need for help, while the larger "precarious public sphere" is exposed indirectly through Wendy's difficulty finding that help. There is no shame in needing support, but this story, and others like it, of trying to find help while facing the daunting prospect of being completely on one's own reveals the inescapability of dependency. It is this dependency that the individualistic ideology of liberalism (and neoliberalism) consistently disavows. Dependency is not merely something to be suffered, however, for there is of course always the possibility and potential for enrichment and happiness from our dependency on, and relations to, others (just as there is from the constitutive ambiguity of our vulnerability). Thus, dependency is ambiguous, and as such can be considered a feature of our political ontology.[7]

This film, coupled with Berlant's analysis, gives strong insight, affective as well as conceptual, into the political ontology of precarious dependency. The attrition of sustaining bonds together with the casting off of these populations points to two

Wendy and Lucy and the Impossibility of Neoliberal Self-Care

of the central features of precarity: economic insecurity and an impossible expectation of independence and self-sufficiency. The first becomes manifest in the film through an economic as well as a temporal index. While Wendy struggles to sustain herself and the one she cares most about, her dog Lucy, she seems to occupy a perpetual present, barely able to even dream about the future much less plan for it. The second central characteristic of precarity, the expectation of independence, figures in the film through not just the indifference that Wendy encounters when seeking assistance but also her own reluctance to ask for help. For she seems to have absorbed the (neo)liberal expectation to the point where she wears it with pride. Before turning to a reading of *Wendy and Lucy* that reveals the merciless logic of individual self-sufficiency that inspires today's neoliberal capitalism, let us begin to appreciate the harsh experience of trying to stay afloat in today's economy with a consideration of one of the more intriguing theoretical political concepts of recent years: precarity.

Precarity's Dependency and Neoliberalism's Self-Care

Precarity is a capacious term that has in recent years come to do a lot of work, theoretically and politically, to illuminate the changing conditions of contemporary life under capitalism. Part of the argument connected to precarity suggests that the experience of uncertainty derived from contingent labour is no longer, if it ever was, confined to the workplace. Instead, the practices of contingency come to permeate the atmosphere, as it were, "becom[ing] a byword for life in late and later capitalism."[8] Uncertainty and insecurity are everywhere. The effects of atmosphere and structural conditions, together with those on leisure and labour, can be hard to capture and harder still to use as the basis for political organization, and yet the discourse and politics of precarity has more than made an attempt to do just that. Surveying the various uses of precarity among analysts and activists, Lauren Berlant in her recent book *Cruel Optimism* registers the compound nature of the term:

> This emergent taxonomy raises questions about to what degree precarity is an economic and political condition suffered by a population or by the subjects of capitalism generally; or a way of life; or an affective atmosphere; or an existential truth about contingencies of living, namely, that there are no guarantees that the life one intends can or will be built."[9]

Indeed, it is all these things, depending on who is using the term and in what context.

In this account, I want to try and preserve some of the connotative multiplicity associated with the term precarity, for two reasons. Firstly, as a node of thought and action, precarity represents a rather distinct and productive site for grasping the contemporary links between structure and agency, conditions and subjects, affect and action. Secondly, the audiovisual medium of cinema proves to be a valuable means through which to explore and explain the many valences of precarity, especially given its relation to the senses and to affect. Moreover, not only is precarity a capacious concept, it also names a relatively ambivalent condition – one that is sometimes praised, sometimes condemned by both workers and employers, and that is in some ways beneficial but in other ways detrimental to workers. Primarily, however, it is used to talk about a historically particular experience of unsecure labour under capitalism.

A term rooted in political analysis and organization, "precarity" originated in Europe in the 1980s in response to deepening conditions of economic insecurity associated with the advance of neoliberalism coupled with the retreat of the welfare state. Indeed, the primary connotation of precarity concerns the uncertainty and anxiety related to unsecure employment. The term speaks to the way that late capitalism is experienced today, and points toward links between economy and psychology, structure and experience. For instance, on the economic and structural side, Andrew Ross explains in his book *Nice Work if You Can Get It* that precarity

> is most often used as shorthand for the condition of economic insecurity associated with post-Fordist employment and neoliberal governance, which not only gives employers leeway to hire and fire workers at will, but also glorifies part-time contingent work as "free agency," liberated from the stifling constraints of contractual regulations. Low-wage immigrant service workers and high-tech consultants alike might share these conditions, and this commonality has inspired activists who see the opportunity for cross-class solidarity.[10]

Notice that Ross' characterization is not simply economic and structural, for his description also points to the way in which capital legitimizes, rhetorically and culturally, the structural changes that it undertakes, even as it exploits them. Or, as Rob Horning puts it,

> Though the word *precarity* is only necessary because of the political urgency of describing this widespread insecurity, the experience of precarity is not inherently or completely negative. The "positive" components of precarity – the sense that it provides for the freedom

of flexibility, rewards certain kinds of creativity and opportunism, promotes a kind of absolute individualism that can be taken for dignity, and accommodates or even requires a degree of social and geographic mobility – are part of what has allowed for neoliberalism's implementation.[11]

These linguistic and political ambiguities, which are associated with the condition of precarity, point to the ideological contradiction at the heart of neoliberal capitalism itself: neoliberalism demands self-sufficiency or self-care while disavowing the realities of social dependency, even as it increases workers' reliance on help from others by shrinking the State. Precarity, then, is a lens through which we can apprehend the social wreckage done by neoliberalism to workers in the name of "freedom." Wendy Brown has written insightfully about the political rationality associated with neoliberalism, and in particular about the kind of subjectivity that neoliberalism solicits through its devious use of the idea of individual freedom. Thus, she writes that "neoliberalism normatively constructs and interpellates individuals as entrepreneurial actors in every sphere of life. It figures individuals as rational, calculating creatures whose moral autonomy is measured by their capacity for 'self-care'–the ability to provide for their own needs and service their own ambitions."[12] Precarity, then, registers in part the anxiety of trying to meet the demand for an impossibly complete self-care in today's economic environment.

Of course, the liberalism of neoliberalism is primarily economic in the usual gloss – and yet there is a clear resonance with political liberalism's idea of the free individual, but less as a bearer of rights and more as a framer of life plans. (This idea often implies pretentions to control or mastery, such as in John Stuart Mill's comment that "He who lets the world, or his own portion of it, choose his plan of life for him has no need of any other faculty than the ape-like one of imitation.")[13] There are, as Brown notes, political implications to the demands for self-care issued by neoliberalism, particularly when it comes to the inevitability of hardship and failure. "Correspondingly," she asserts, "a 'mismanaged life,' the neoliberal appellation for failure to navigate impediments to prosperity, becomes a new mode of depoliticizing social and economic powers and at the same time reduces political citizenship to an unprecedented degree of passivity and political complacency."[14] In other words, you might say that it is only big business whose losses are socialized, while everyone else is on his or her own. Precarity, then, might be said to register something more than the kind of dependence that has always characterized labour's relation to capital. It refers a more multiple dependence – on a withered state, on family and other social relations – at the same time that it names a frustration with the impossibility of self-care.

Economic insecurity for workers thus grows as capital becomes more flexible, and this has affected a wider and wider range of people, not just a few marginal groups. Two of the original academic investigators of precarity argue that

> Precarity, then, does not have its model worker. Neither artist nor migrant, nor hacker nor housewife [...] Rather, precarity strays across any number of labour practices, rendering their relations precisely precarious – which is to say, given to no essential connection but perpetually open to temporary and contingent relations. In this sense, precarity is something more than a position in the labour market, since it traverses a spectrum of labour markets and positions within them.[15]

Certainly this is true economically and sociologically, but it is also true aesthetically as well as cinematically.[16] As we will see, part of what characterizes the disparate films of the "cinema of precarity" is not so much the subjects as the subjectivity, not so much the identities of protagonists as the experience of similar structural positioning and similar affective states (and stakes) in the contemporary world. This precarious position is situated and figured both temporally and spatially. That is, from this position subjects suffer relentless economic insecurity in relation to the future and experience their own ineluctable and natural social dependence as a failure of self-sufficiency.

Wendy's Predicament

Wendy and Lucy is an unconventional offering, both stylistically and narratively, as you would expect of a film that speaks to contemporary conditions of precarity. It is a remarkably good example of the cinema of precarity set in an American context. It tells the story of a young woman (Wendy) and her dog (Lucy) navigating a series of challenges as strangers in a small city in Oregon. Over the course of the film, these challenges, namely Wendy's car breaking down and Lucy going missing, turn into real losses that only further confirm Wendy's lonely precariousness. But at first, the film starts with Wendy just passing through with Lucy, trying to make her way to Alaska to find work on the "slimeline" in one of the salmon canneries. As an audience, we enter her story *in medias res* as she has stopped along this journey for the night, somewhere in Oregon. We soon gather that Wendy is living on a very tight budget, tracking her expenses with a pen and a small notebook, counting every penny before she and Lucy bed down in the car for the night. When she is awakened the next morning by a security guard's knock on her window, her journey comes to an abrupt halt. Not because she has broken the law, but because her car will not start when he asks her to leave the parking lot. The rest of the film tracks how Wendy copes with the challenges of losing her car and her dog over the next 48 hours in this small, unfamiliar city. It is a road movie, interrupted: freedom interrupted by the unchosen.

Wendy's general situation of unemployment and itinerancy, together with her specific challenges of car failure and losing her dog, can be helpfully characterized as a predicament. The film's director, Kelly Reichardt, herself, together with reviewers of the film, have repeatedly described the collection of challenges that crop up for Wendy as a "predicament."[17] In particular, predicament is used in ways that emphasize two of the key aspects of precarity – social relations of dependence, and temporal uncertainty – without actually invoking the discourse of precarity. On the one hand, Reichardt's use of the word "predicament" emphasizes social relations and dependence braided together with loneliness, as when she says, "There's a certain kind of help that society will give and a certain help it won't give. So we imagined Wendy as a renter; no insurance, just making ends meet, and a fire occurs due to no fault of her own and she loses her place to live. We don't know her backstory in the film but we imagined Wendy was in that kind of predicament."[18] Much of the drama of the film, such as it is, involves how Wendy will negotiate this predicament socially and economically, and whether she will receive help. On the other hand, reviewer Rick Groen, for instance, writes that "That's the real purpose of *Wendy and Lucy*: to make us see this young woman, to attend to her present predicament – three days and nights stranded in a small Oregon town – and to wonder about her perilous future. And maybe to find a reason to hope, on her behalf but on ours too, because, of course, we're all just passing through."[19] Groen's use of "predicament" brings to the fore the temporal dimension of precarity, the way in which the present threatens to eclipse the future.

Still, the word predicament is perhaps more apt than these critics, and perhaps even Reichardt, realize. As a name for a difficult situation, predicament resonates not only phonically but semantically with the idea of precarity, which is, after all, a situation and an ongoing economic difficulty. What is more, because of the film's particular stylistic choices, predicament names a narrative construct that is not overly dramatic but that unfolds slowly and somewhat flatly, or matter-of-factly. By contrast, there are other, more severe words that could be used instead of predicament to give a more dramatic connotation – such as ordeal, plight, calamity, or emergency. Many of these terms, however, impart connotations of extraordinariness and finality, and yet what is precisely valuable about the idea of a predicament – both for *Wendy and Lucy* in particular, and for the purposes of illuminating precarity more generally – is its suggestion of understatement and ordinariness.

Paradoxically, then, "predicament" might be said to name an "ordinary crisis." In fact, Lauren Berlant suggests that the affects associated with precarity do make crises ordinary and familiar, folding precarity into the normal and transforming it. "Crisis," she points out, "is not exceptional to history or consciousness but a process embedded in the ordinary that unfolds in stories about navigating what's overwhelming."[20] Navigating is a telling word here, for it has the helpful connotation of acting in a context not fully in one's control, which is apt for precarity's dependency and contingency. (It expresses a similar idea as the word negotiation.) But enduring or surviving precarity tends to reduce navigating to merely treading water rather than actually getting ahead.

Through the general effect, as well as affect, created by Reichardt's stylistic choices, Wendy's slowly unfolding predicament comes to reflect the precarious aesthetic that Berlant identifies in some of the films of French director Laurent Cantet. Speaking of Cantet's films in particular and the cinema of precarity more generally, Berlant describes "an aesthetic shaped by the fraying of norms, that is, of genres of reliable being. Fraying implies something slow, delicate, processual, something happening on its own time. Aesthetically, we observe this political-affective condition mainly in messy situations, episodes, incidents, and gestures, and not often in the gesture of the dramatic event."[21] Or, we might add, predicaments. Berlant's invocation of "fraying norms" brings together the two elements of the predicament – social relations and time – that are key aspects of precarity. Thus, we can add the figure of the predicament to this list of messy and less-than-dramatic events. For Reichardt's method of training our attention on Wendy's predicament is very much consistent with the slow, processual wearing out that Berlant discerns in precarity. For instance, Reichardt often uses long takes and employs no music at all in the film, contributing to the experience of the duration of Wendy's predicament. Even the more dramatic moments in this film are represented in a modest and deliberate way, suggesting a distinctive blend of form and content.

Slowness, or Stuck at an Impasse

Reichardt's film represents Wendy's predicament as much through its visual style as through its scripted content. The film is brief, but adept in its focus and compelling in its artistry. For while its running time is a mere 80 minutes, Reichardt's style of direction and editing (she edited the film, too) blends the classical influence of Italian neorealism's attention to working-class characters' circumstances and concerns with a measure of the observation and contemplation more recently associated with "slow cinema."[22] Adopting a more deliberate pace, Reichardt allows the

Wendy and Lucy and the Impossibility of Neoliberal Self-Care

camera to linger, and thereby enjoins the audience to endure Wendy's predicament along with her in this small town where she is marooned without a functioning car. For example, the camera repeatedly tracks Wendy as she walks, and walks, and walks all over this town. She walks to and from the grocery store, to and from the dog pound. She walks around taping up missing posters for Lucy as well as leaving articles of her own clothing tied to signposts for Lucy to find, and finally she walks to and from the woods on the edge of town seeking a place to bed down for the night, since her ordinary sleeping place is locked up at the repair shop.[23] Whereas many other films would use editing to severely telescope the time it takes Wendy to walk these distances, Reichardt's camera forces the audience to accompany Wendy on these walks and induces us to feel the duration and weight of her predicament.[24]

The film's focus on walking is not purely stylistic, of course. Wendy's walking is driven narratively by the loss of her car, a remarkably American symbol of personal autonomy (an auto-mobile for the autonomous individual, you might say)[25] and key to any road movie – except, of course, a road movie that comes to an abrupt, unchosen halt. To depict precarity's ordinary crisis, Reichardt narratively engineers the loss of Wendy's automobile (the antithesis of slowness), making walking a necessity and changing the way in which Wendy experiences space. Wendy's overall predicament has important social dimensions, and yet, more immediately, her predicament is spatial and temporal simply because she is stuck both in this small Oregon city and in the present, with her plans for the future thrown into doubt. So, when her cross-continental trip to Alaska is called into question by these ordinary crises, Wendy arrives at an impasse. She is literally stuck and cannot get moving, and instead the film focuses on the slow fraying of her stability and relationships.

Wendy's impasse turns out to be emblematic of precarity, emblematic not only for her individually, but also for the social and economic context in, and through which, she experiences precarity. The whole town in which she is marooned is figured in the film as being itself at an impasse – having witnessed the departure of a key industry, which has left many people out of work. In one of the few moments in the film that speaks directly to the larger, precarious economic circumstances, the security guard[26] in conversation with Wendy characterizes the town's economic losses and their impact on lives. The conversation occurs after Wendy has just used the security guard's cell phone to call the city dog pound to see whether Lucy has been found (a rare instance when she calls instead of walking). After handing the phone back to the security guard, Lucy says, "Not a lot of jobs around here, huh?" and he responds, "I'll say. I don't know what the people do all day. Used to be a mill, but it's been closed a long time now. Don't know what they do."

He delivers this last sentence with a sense of bewilderment, as if it is such a shame and a puzzle that so many people are unmoored. It is a casual but striking characterization of the effects of capitalist dynamism, or "creative destruction" as Joseph Schumpeter famously put it. Immediately following his remark, Wendy voices her own identification with the uncertain and unrooted character of precarity, saying, "Can't get a job without an address anyway […] or a phone." Her statement serves as a reminder for the audience that in her circumstances of itinerancy and precarity, she in fact lacks all these conventional markers of stability. The security guard then immediately responds with what is certainly the line of the movie: "You can't get an address without an address, you can't get a job without a job. It's all fixed." This line is conspicuous and remarkable, particularly in a film that has less dialogue than most. It is remarkable regardless, and yet when viewed through the lens of precarity, it speaks volumes to the temporality and social conditionality that precarity exposes. For what his comment captures is the almost self-perpetuating character of precarity, such that loss of job or loss of house can cascade and cause other losses that leave one unable to really find one's socioeconomic footing at all. The crowning blow is suggested in his final statement, for when he says, "It's all fixed" he is conjuring a sense of fatalism that comes from one's fate being in the hands of another – namely, capital. We are all always dependent in larger and smaller ways that we may be more or less aware of depending on stability and privilege, but those coping with precarity are constantly, anxiously aware of their dependence.

In addition to this rather explicit thematization of generalized precarity, the film further conveys a sense of precarity through Wendy's particular, personal impasse. The manner in which she is stuck in this impasse keeps her moving in the same space again and again. The impasse is a figure Berlant finds to be characteristic of precarity cinema for just the way in which it uses the personal to track the structural. "The impasse is a *cul-de-sac*," Berlant notes, "In a cul-de-sac one keeps moving, but one moves paradoxically, in the *same space*."[27] What better way to illustrate such an impasse than walking in a small city? Wendy walks and walks and walks in this film, giving us a sense of the duration of her impasse. She is seemingly locked in the same town, walking back and forth, hoping to find her dog, get her car fixed, and get back on the road. In other words, she wants to resume her journey, and by the end of the film, she does – in a kind of way.

Again, however, the payoff from this film comes not in a dramatic and complete resolution of this impasse in any conventional sense. Rather, the film makes a point of attending to the way in which Wendy navigates challenge after challenge over the course of 48 hours in this small town. In this respect, its approach

Wendy and Lucy and the Impossibility of Neoliberal Self-Care

is consistent with the emerging genre conventions that Berlant sees in the figure of the impasse. Firstly, consider that Berlant wants to think "about the ordinary as an impasse shaped by crisis in which people find themselves developing skills for adjusting to newly proliferating pressures to scramble for modes of living on."[28] Wendy's cinematic story fits this description, for even without knowing exactly why she is living out of her car and trying to get to Alaska, as an audience we can see that she adjusts to whatever comes her way as she tries to stay afloat while dreaming of getting ahead. The contending spatial metaphors used to contrast the American dream of getting ahead with precarity's reality of treading water to stay afloat mark a significant shift in the frame of reference for what optimism means.[29] That is just the kind of change that Berlant is interested in tracing through the notion of "cruel optimism," which she says is "what happens to fantasies of the good life when the ordinary becomes a landfill for overwhelming and impending crises of life-building and expectation whose sheer volume so threatens what it has meant to 'have a life' that adjustment seems like an accomplishment."[30] The film puts the audience in the position of rooting for Wendy to simply re-equilibrate herself and get back on track toward the mere possibility of having a life.

Secondly, it is important to situate Berlant's diagnosis of the impasse as part of her larger effort to see the ways in which precarity makes crisis ordinary. As she says, "In the impasse induced by crisis, being treads water; mainly, it does not drown. Even those whom you would think of as defeated are living beings figuring out how to stay attached to life from within it, and to protect what optimism they have for that, at least."[31] While in some ways Wendy is marginalized and defeated, she also has a degree of pride and dignity, and as an audience we see her trying to figure things out and get along, even as the setbacks crop up again and again. In keeping with the cinema of precarity's reticent aesthetic, Wendy's continual adjustments are not portrayed with any melodramatic flourishes, but simply and straightforwardly as what she has to do in order to keep moving (in place). That she appears capable and confident in addressing these challenges makes it all the more frustrating to see her struggling economically. In light of precarity, these continual adjustments are themselves an achievement, Berlant reminds us.

Returning once again, finally, to the scene referenced earlier, we consider the conclusion of the conversation between Wendy and the security guard, for it is also quite revealing. In response to the security guard's distillation of precarity – "You can't get an address without an address, you can't get a job without a job. It's all fixed" – Wendy declares, "That's why I'm going to Alaska. I hear they need people." Her attachment to the idea of life in Alaska is the very seed of her own cruel optimism. In a way, her most significant adjustment is her recalibration of her dreams in light of precarity. It is a statement that betrays the cultural persistence, even under conditions of precarity, of a peculiarly American idea of freedom. For not only does Wendy intend to travel by automobile (a symbol of self-sufficiency, even though its operation relies on a whole host of social and technical infrastructures), but she intends to reach Alaska – perhaps the last instantiation of the great frontier, to which Americans have fled to again and again to start over, remake themselves, and make their fortunes. However, much of this idealism appears drained from Wendy's invocation of Alaska. She does not expect to become rich; she just hopes to be able to land a job for a time without having those conditional roots, phone and address, typically associated with formal employment.[32] The vagueness of Wendy's plan for the future suggests precarity's toll on our very temporality – the way in which it makes the future uncertain and the present intractable.

Precarity's Perpetual Present and Receding Future

Wendy experiences this precarious impasse not just spatially but also temporally, affecting her plans for the future and prolonging her present predicament. In fact, the temporal dimension of precarity is one of its most prominent features. Much precarity talk concerns the anxious relation to the future produced by employment insecurity. What's more, this temporal uncertainty reverberates well beyond mere work such that it becomes difficult to form a credible plan for the future, to "build a life." In a discussion of precarity and performance, Nicholas Ridout and Rebecca Schneider explain, "Precarity is life lived in relation to a future that cannot be propped securely upon the past. Precarity undoes a linear streamline of temporal progression and challenges 'progress' and 'development' narratives on all levels. Precarity has become a byword for life in late and later capitalism."[33] Clearly, the larger precarious predicament in which Wendy finds herself (i.e. whatever has propelled her to live out of her car) makes her economically vulnerable. Given this precarious vulnerability, the film focuses on how car trouble and losing her dog undoes her progression toward her goal of Alaska for a time. To be precise, the extent to which she is delayed in reaching that goal is the exact timespan that this film covers. In the very last scene of the film, Wendy resumes her journey toward Alaska by hopping a freight train (a very precarious mode of transportation in itself). So, by virtue of the film's focus on Wendy's predicament with the car and Lucy, her future is always uncertain for the audience.

In addition to throwing the future into doubt by pushing it out of reach, precarity also transforms one's experience of the present. When one has little security about one's income and consequently the life that one is trying to build, the present comes to feel unending. In a commentary on "precarious dystopias" in today's cinema, Mark Fisher describes "the ambient dread of precarity in a world stripped of (job and social) security, in which the poor are trapped in a perpetual present tense, unable to plan or dream, all their mental and physical resources devoted to the exhausting hardscrabble for bare survival."[34] Fisher captures the aura of anxiety that characterizes today's experience of capitalism for many workers under conditions of precarity. Lest Fisher's language of "perpetual present" convey an inaccurate impression of stability,[35] we should note Berlant's formulation that the cinema of precarity gives audiences an affective sense of "the instability of the ongoing present as the ground for living."[36] The atmosphere of *Wendy and Lucy* echoes Fisher's "ambient dread" to the extent that the audience is led to wonder what else will go wrong for Wendy and how will she continue to adjust. The film is also suffused with a sense of the "instability of the ongoing present" insofar as the audience must endure the ongoing anxious present with her as she tries to regain her footing.

In keeping with precarity cinema's aesthetic, Reichardt allows her audience to feel the seeming permanence of the present through the unhurried nature of the film's pacing, instead of deploying the rupture of the dramatic gesture. This slower style reflects the way in which the future recedes and the present becomes all-consuming for Wendy once her car breaks down. Wendy wants to get to Alaska where she hopes to be able to count on a certain term of employment to replenish her bank balance. But when her car breaks down, that goal quickly recedes and all of her energy becomes devoted to addressing the immediate crisis, in a strange town, with no friends, and little money. This stylistic stretching-out of the present is key to the way in which the film conveys the sense of precarity's affective anxiety that pervades Wendy's lonely present. It is felt throughout the film, whether in waiting for the repair garage to open, waiting for the dog pound to call her back with news of Lucy, or waiting to be released from jail after being picked up on a heavy-handed shoplifting charge.

"Just Callin'," or, Fraying Social Bonds

Shifting registers, consider the uncertainty with which the film addresses the social dimension of Wendy's past as well as her future. It leaves the audience deliberately uninformed about her past, with only the suggestion that she cannot count on her family for help. Kelly Reichardt in interviews suggested that Wendy was the victim of some kind of catastrophe, such as fire or hurricane, that left her living out of her car.[37] And so she is unmoored and alone in the unending present when she loses her car.

While the film never explains exactly why she has undertaken such a long journey for work, what is clear is that Wendy is on her own not only because she is a stranger in this unfamiliar town a long way from home but also because her family offers her no support, neither monetary nor emotional. What is even worse, Lucy (Wendy's best friend, maybe her only friend) goes missing after Wendy spends most of the day in jail on a shoplifting charge (she takes two cans of dog food).[38] An early, telling, and difficult, scene in the film shows Wendy calling (home) to speak to her sister and brother-in-law, just after having learned that she'll spend the night without her car and her dog. We sense that she might ask for help paying for the car repairs, but she does not. Nor does she even solicit any emotional support from her sister or brother-in-law, Dan. Instead, her exchange is terse and awkward, illustrating her isolation as well as a perhaps a degree of pride:

Dan: "So what's up?"
Wendy: "Nothin,' I'm just callin', just ..." [trails off]
Dan: "Nothin'?"
Wendy: "Car broke. [pause] I dunno. It's kinda bad here actually. [pause] Lucy's lost."
Sister picks up phone and breaks in: "Who's that?"
Dan: "It's your sister. She broke down in Oregon."
Wendy: "Hi Deb."
Sister: "Oregon! What does she want us to do about it?"
Wendy: "Nothing. Nothing. I'm, I'm just callin' ..."
Dan: "She's just callin.'"
Sister: "We can't do anything. We're strapped. I don't know what she wants."
Wendy: "I don't want anything, I'm just calling."

As an audience we can sense that Wendy has come to an emotionally vulnerable state that nearly matches her economic vulnerability. She reaches out, in a way, by calling her sister and brother-in-law, but that is all she does: just call.

Wendy's emotional duress is indicated in the slippage in Dan's description of her predicament, when he says to Deb, "She broke down in Oregon." In his telling, Wendy and the car are conflated, such that a car breakdown becomes Wendy's own breakdown, even though Wendy shows little sign of breaking down emotionally. Dan's slippage coincides with Deb's own rebuff of a request that is not even made. For all along, Wendy has seemed reluctant (too proud? too self-reliant?) to come right out and ask for help, but we get the sense she wouldn't refuse it if Dan offered. Once her sister butts into the conversation, however, we intuit Wendy's spine stiffening and her pride swelling, such that her reluctance comes to be infused, even replaced, with the prideful sense that it would be somehow wrong, a failure on her part, to ask for help – as if accepting help would be confirmation of weakness. And she can't allow herself to be seen as this kind of failure, perhaps especially to her sister. Wendy seems to be struggling with the ideological contradictions of the neoliberal expectation of self-care, which become even more difficult under conditions of precarity. She wants to be able to fully take care of herself, and her accounts notebook together with her composure suggest that she is careful and capable. But as unexpected challenges arise through no fault of her own, she finds it increasingly difficult to do it all on her own. This tension persists throughout the film as Wendy faces more challenges and slowly, reluctantly reaches out for help in small ways. The small changes in her relations with others in Oregon over the course of the film suggest that Wendy is becoming more comfortable with the limits of her self-reliance.

In addition to its unsettling temporality, precarity has another important characteristic, and that is dependence. Precarity names not only the social and existential fact of dependence but also registers the anxiety and insecurity associated with it. Such dependence stands in stark contrast to the "brave new world" of neoliberal freedom populated by fully self-possessed individuals (or so the ideology tells us). Berlant thus notes that "At root precarity is a condition of dependency – as a legal term, precarious describes the situation wherein your tenancy on your land is in someone else's hands."[39] Of course this has always been true to an extent as long as people have lived in communities with a social division of labour, not to mention as long as people have participated in family life. In other words, people have always already been dependent, but the contours and valuation of that dependency vary from culture to culture. So what is distinct about contemporary life that has caused the advent of this new concept, this neologism "precarity"? And further – dependent on what? Certainly on capital, as much of the discourse of precarity indicates – but also on others, on conditions, and on norms. Neoliberalism's market ethics trumpets the virtues of free choice and self-sufficiency while denying or diverting us from our dependency on others as well as on larger social and economic conditions.[40] However, "the ambient dread of precarity" increasingly does not allow us to forget our dependency. More than that, it can help to make dependency visible and present (and potentially challengeable and changeable) in new ways. The cinema of precarity generally, and *Wendy and Lucy* in particular, participates in such a project, giving visual and narrative form to this set of conditions and experiences.

In a remarkable pair of comments that bring together the affect of precarity with the social effects of neoliberal rationality's growing normalization, Reichardt and Berlant express very similar ideas but in different languages. Where Reichardt asks whether responsibility is purely personal, Berlant identifies three key elements of precarity and its cinema. Discussing her ideas behind scripting Wendy's predicament, Reichardt speaks to what Berlant calls the fraying of social bonds. "*Wendy and Lucy* asks the question of what we owe each other, and what's our responsibility to each other?" says Reichardt, "Wendy is a stranger: We don't know where she came from, and people have to decide in the moment where they meet her what their obligation to her is. Or maybe there is no obligation. Is it every man for himself now?"[41] Similarly, but in a more theoretical register, Berlant argues that the cinema of precarity "emphasizes the present as a transitional zone where normative forms of reciprocity are wearing out" such that "the films record the loneliness of collective singularity, the impacts of affective fraying, and the tiny optimism of recuperative gestures in the middle of it all, for those who can manage them."[42] These three features – collective loneliness, affective fraying, and tiny recuperative gestures – bring out the affects and consequences of neoliberalism's injunction for self-care. Individuals in the era of neoliberal precarity are supposed to be responsible and self-reliant, and traditional forms of obligation show signs of withering.

Let us return for a moment to the phone conversation between Wendy, her sister, and her brother-in-law: this illustrates the presence of these first two features of precarity cinema (collective loneliness and affective fraying) as well as the absence of small recuperative gestures that suggest a hint of optimism. That is, the phone conversation shows evidence of the impacts of affective fraying and the loneliness of collective singularity, while also allowing us to feel the absence of even the smallest recuperative gestures that might sustain optimism (Wendy's and the audience's), however tenuously. The structure of the conversation, with Wendy's sister interrupting and rebuffing an unstated request for help, shows that with precarity everyone is on his or her own, even with regard to family. The visual presentation of the scene also echoes this loneliness of collective singularity, as the camera shows Wendy talking on a pay phone, seemingly zoomed in from a distance and through glass that reflects car lights as they pass by. (Since the car itself can be seen as a figure of autonomy/loneliness, the shared isolation is doubled here.) The impact of affective fraying is felt through Wendy's reluctance to ask for help as well as her sister's pre-emptive rejection and her brother-in-law's conflation, "She broke down in Oregon." There is a sense of defeated realism from all three sides of this strikingly indirect conversation, and that mood is characteristic of precarity.

In this conversation scene as well as many others, *Wendy and Lucy* puts the audience in the position of enduring Wendy's negotiations of the frayed norms

Wendy and Lucy and the Impossibility of Neoliberal Self-Care

wrought by the neoliberal demand for self-care. For while she has difficulty finding reliable assistance (much less intimacy) in her predicament, the film presents her foundering not in a (melo-)dramatic fashion but rather in an understated and rather naturalistic way.[43] Whereas the phone conversation evidences the absence of recuperative gestures, even from family, another relationship illustrates their presence but also their smallness under conditions of precarity. The setting for these small recuperative gestures is the one human relationship of significance in the film – that between Wendy and the security guard. The same security guard who in the drugstore parking lot near the start of the film wakes Wendy to tell her she can't park there, goes on to show her many small kindnesses over the course of the film. He comes to provide something of an avuncular presence for Wendy, as he is senior, gentle, and wise. He gives her help pushing her car off the lot when it won't start; he gives her directions to the grocery store, and later the dog pound; and he insists that she use his phone to call the dog pound even when she demurs, having only asked for a quarter in exchange for nickels and dimes. The posture of authority that the uniformed but privately-employed security guard adopts as he almost reluctantly enforces the rule that she can't park overnight and sleep contrasts sharply with the pretentions to police authority that a young grocery-store clerk assumes in his effort to make an example of Wendy when he catches her shoplifting. Indeed, the security guard goes on to give Wendy help, whereas the clerk causes her to lose Lucy on top of already having lost her car.[44] And when Wendy later sees the clerk behind the store as she's looking for Lucy, his first response is "What are you doing here?" before getting into his parent's car.

These small kindnesses shown by the security guard to Wendy are the backdrop for the last and most fraught exchange between them, showing just how tiny the optimism of recuperative gestures can be in light of precarity. The exchange occurs on Wendy's last morning in town, after having spent hours in front of the drugstore waiting for the security guard. When he finally arrives, he walks up, sees her and says, "You look a bit stricken." Wendy responds, "Well, I've been here since 8. Where have you been?" in a pointed way that she has not quite shown before in the film. She has endured a strange incident in the woods the night before,[45] and both he and we see Wendy's frayed affect and sense that she is starting to have trouble holding it all together. He tells her that it is his day off, and that she got a call after she left the drugstore last night. He hands her the phone and she calls the pound to learn that Lucy has been taken in by a foster family. Her mood lightens and her face brightens as she lets out a sigh of relief. She then tells him the good news, and this exchange follows:

Security Guard:	"So that's it, you're gonna be pulling out?"
Wendy:	"Yeah, that's the plan."
Security Guard:	"Well, I hope it all works out. I know it will. Uh, I want you to take this. Don't argue. Just don't argue. Don't let Holly see. If you ever come by here again, you just stop by here and say hi."
Wendy:	"Thank you. I will."

As he walks away, Wendy looks down at her hand and unrolls the bills that he has given her to reveal a five-dollar bill and a one dollar: a total of $6. This registers as a small and surprising disappointment, as we might have expected a larger gift. Notice, however, the contrast between the qualification that Wendy offers, "Yeah. That's the plan" and his reassurance "I hope it all works out. I know it will." We sense that she has learned the hard lesson that precarity makes all plans utterly contingent, we also sense that this is more than just pro forma sentiment, given the other generous assistance and understanding that he has given Wendy. (Note that this is the only time we see him in "civvies" rather than his security guard "uniform." Perhaps in staging it this way, Reichardt wants to make sure that his help can't in any way be interpreted as corporate or official help.) And so, the gift is a remarkable example of Berlant's notion of the "tiny optimism of recuperative gestures" because it represents an act of generosity rooted in a real relationship with shades of intimacy, but we also sense that it is constrained by his own precarious circumstances (note how he's concerned for her not to let Holly see)[46]. The gift followed by the revelation of the $6 in Wendy's hand lands with an affective mixture of hope, sadness and realism, registering as a sort of cruel optimism.

Self-Care's Impossibility

Finally, we come to the end point in this film of the experience of precarity, and what we are left with is a pure individual, shorn of meaningful relationships and still trying to find stable footing. After parting from the security guard and his small kindeses, Reichardt gives us a brief shot of Wendy enjoying a pastry and coffee while charting her route on a map and tallying her remaining assets in her notebook. (She is once again humming the same tune that she has hummed earlier in the film at small interludes of peace and stability.)[47] Then she walks across to the car-repair shop, and immediately learns the bad news that her car is broken almost beyond repair. It is going to cost more to fix it not only than the car is worth but also than Wendy has. Having no other choice, she decides to abandon the car, but to add insult to injury, she has to pay $30 for the towing and disposal of it. This loss, following on the cruel optimism of the $6 help, sets up Wendy and the audience for the film's final coup de grâce.

Next Wendy arrives by cab near the address where Lucy has been taken in. After walking the last few blocks with all her belongings in hand (her car is gone for good now), Wendy watches a man leave the house and drive away, and then she approaches the fenced-in area where she sees Lucy. She says, "Hey Lu," and then, "I'm sorry. Come here." As she kneels down outside the fence, she says to Lucy "I know, I know. Come on, Lu, don't be mad." After playing catch with Lucy and a stick, Wendy says "It's so nice here, Lu. That man seems nice," as her face starts to curl up with emotion. Again she kneels down, and says "I lost the car," as a few tears roll down her face. And then she pauses looks intently at Lucy and says, "You be good. I'll come back. I'll make some money and come back." As Lucy whimpers, Wendy gathers up her things and starts to walk away, and soon hop a freight train. This most emotionally laden scene of the film is the culmination of Wendy's predicament, and it exhibits the very personal and affective cost of precarity's cruel optimism. With the loss of her car, Wendy cannot afford to keep Lucy with her, and decides, perhaps cruelly, to leave her there while she resumes her optimistic journey to Alaska in an even more precarious mode of transportation. Still, Wendy maintains hope that she will return once she has made "some money." It is a modest ambition, and it should not be too much to ask to be able to make a living in a way that allows the preservation of such a relationship. But that is precisely the kind of insecurity that precarity sows as it undermines any assurance we might think we have about being able to build the kind of life we desire.

In interviews about the film, director Kelly Reichardt refers again and again to American myths of individual initiative. She notes that she was struck by the idea often publicly expressed after the devastating 2005 Hurricane Katrina that "if people hadn't left themselves so vulnerable, if they didn't live so precariously, they wouldn't have found themselves in that situation."[48] Such a political judgment stems directly from the proliferation of a neoliberal political rationality that, as noted earlier, political theorist Wendy Brown insists casts such predicaments as "mismanaged lives," thereby personalizing failure and depoliticizing precisely those social and economic powers that make people increasingly precarious and vulnerable. The way in which Reichardt tells it, she and screenwriter Jon Raymond were inspired by the idea of challenging and trying to undermine this "bootstraps" myth. She says

> I called Jon Raymond after hearing an interview where someone used the proverbial 'pull yourself up by your bootstraps' image, and we were musing over what happens if, like Wendy, you have no

safety net, you have a nothing education, you don't have family support, and certainly there's no trust fund. How do you pull yourself up by your bootstraps?[49]

Reichardt, then, is clearly self-conscious about the way in which she hopes *Wendy and Lucy* can speak to the impossible demands for personal responsibility that ignore the necessity of various supports and interrupt the familiar judgment associated with this proverbial image. But of course the wonderful thing about a feature film, even an independent film, is that it doesn't speak in these terms, but in more familiar terms and images.

To be sure, Wendy's situation was already precarious and lonely before she ever arrived at this predicament in Oregon, travelling across the country to find work and sleeping in her car along the way. In fact, her past, present, and future are all precarious, and so the predicament in Oregon that is the focus of the film is especially revealing. Wendy's journey is interrupted not just by losing her car, but also by her dog going missing. Therefore, at the same time as the loss of her car puts her literally on her feet and pushes her into the community, the loss of Lucy threatens the apparently only stable and meaningful relationship in Wendy's life. On the one hand, in the American imaginary Wendy becomes less free without her car, while on the other her life threatens to become less fulfilled. The contradictory implications of these two losses – one increasing Wendy's dependence, the other inducing independence, but both unwanted and both arguably contributing to her unfreedom – point to the effects of neoliberal precarity and are key to the way in which the film illuminates Wendy's life as a precarious neoliberal subject. Wendy Brown observes that "Neoliberal subjects are controlled *through* their freedom [...] because of neoliberalism's *moralization* of the consequences of this freedom" (emphasis original).[50] This film refuses to moralize Wendy's challenges as failures of her own rationality, her own fault, but instead offers them for observation as the effects – both structural and affective – of unchosen precarity.

5

Familial Subjectivity and *Winter's Bone*

Introduction

Throughout this book, we have tracked the circulation, reproduction, and interruption of familiar renderings of freedom and vengeance in cinema. The idea has been to bring a critical perspective to the all-too-commonly reductive cinematic visions of freedom and vengeance that underestimate and even deny subjectivity and the relations of dependence through which we are constituted. Seeking to avoid what Edmund Burke derided as "a simple view of the subject, as it stands stripped of every relation, in all the nakedness and solitude of metaphysical abstraction,"[1] I work here against the liberal and neoliberal tendency to valorize and atomize the individual, and instead emphasize the ways in which subjects who seek freedom and vengeance must always negotiate contexts and relations not of their choosing and not fully under their control. I want to bring the political ideas of freedom and vengeance together, and think through their connections and implications for a politics of subjectivity. Family is a valuable lens through which to view these issues, for family is often a locus for freedom and vengeance as individuals struggle to free themselves either from or for family and as they most often seek vengeance in response to familial loss.

In all of the films examined in this book, family has been an important feature, whether explicitly or implicitly, shaping the identity and conditioning the action of protagonists. Consider, on the one hand, that cinematic vengeance is most often figured as a response to the intimate and devastating loss of a family member – a violation that not only cuts deep emotionally, but which also brings to light our vulnerability to, and dependence upon, others. Jimmy Markum in *Mystic River*, for instance, seeks brutal revenge for the murder of his daughter. As Jimmy confronts the loss of his daughter, he defends his dependence on his family even as he rages against vulnerability. Another example is Pete Perkins of *The Three Burials of Melquiades Estrada*, for even though he has no formal or biological relations of family to Melquiades, Pete has no other family to speak of and treats Melquiades as family, rejecting vengeance and struggles to honour his friend's wishes to be buried back home near his family.

Freedom has also been frequently figured in connection to family. A familiar trope of cinematic freedom involves an escape, whether achieved or merely desired, from the restrictions and determinations of family. Chris McCandless of *Into the Wild* suffered betrayal and a sense of loss from his father and then struggled to achieve freedom from the determinations of family and a stark independence. Conversely, estrangement from family can be deployed narratively to offer a picture of lonely and vulnerable individuals, where dependence is neither erased nor fulfilled. Wendy of *Wendy and Lucy* is without family, save her dog Lucy, and her struggles to stay afloat offer a glimpse of precarious freedom as a kind of cruel autonomy.

Winter's Bone (Granik, 2010) is a critically-acclaimed independent feature directed by Debra Granik and based on a novel by Daniel Woodrell, and it offers a star-making performance by Jennifer Lawrence as Ree Dolly, a young woman of 17 from southern Missouri who finds herself in a quandary with familial and economic implications. It is a film about family – about what family promises and how it fails, about family duty and betrayal, about love and loss in the family. While that could in some ways be said of any number of films, what is especially intriguing and effective is the way in which *Winter's Bone* surveys an array of families (and ideas of family) through the perspective of a single subject: the extraordinary protagonist Ree (Lawrence) who negotiates very well a series of family challenges and responsibilities. Ree appears in every single scene in the film, so she is some ways more than a protagonist; the film's perspective is closely identified with hers in terms of perception and mood. As she grows increasingly frustrated by the lack of help, the audience grows more tense, and the film builds suspense along Ree's journey as to whether she will not merely find her father but even survive the quest. While the difficulties with which she must wrestle are extreme, they are also increasingly common in today's unequal economy, in which many populations find it hard to even stay afloat, much less get ahead.

The film's central focus is Ree's quest to preserve her own immediate family in the face of its many failures, both actual and impending. Her father is literally absent, and her mother is psychologically absent, leaving Ree in charge of her younger brother and sister. Set in the rural Ozark mountain region of Missouri today, the film chronicles Ree's struggle to find her father and safeguard their family and homestead. It is clear from the start of the film that the Dolly family is very poor. An early scene, for instance, shows Ree taking her horse to her neighbour Sonya's barn and asking her if she will care for the horse as she simply does not have the means. As an audience, we soon come to learn that her father is involved in the illicit production of methamphetamines, and is thus a direct participant in a socioeconomic epidemic that has hit the rural United States particularly hard in recent years. When the sheriff shows up at her door, Ree learns that her father, out of jail on bail, has gone missing just as his day in court approaches. This piece of information sets the main action of the film in motion: Ree must find him and ensure that he appears in court or they will lose their house and their valuable acres of timber, the only assets that this poor family has. Throughout her ensuing quest, Ree encounters a few families in different forms, but eventually the film concludes with her not only successfully preserving her family and their homestead but also choosing affirmatively to stay with her family in spite of its failings.

In light of Ree's search for, and choice of, family, two important questions guide this analysis. Firstly, what does family mean for her in light of the conditions of economic hardship with which she is confronted and which suffuse the whole movie? Secondly, what does this cinematic meditation on family tell us about the politics of family and subjectivity? Consider the larger context in which Ree negotiates these challenges and in which her family is situated. This film has a distinctive setting and aesthetic that contribute what it has to say about family. The setting is not only geographically and culturally distinct from the rest of the country, but also economically distinct from the too-often glossy worlds depicted in many movies. Immersing us in this area with complete on-location cinematography and a *mis-en-scène* that the director describes as "layered with objects,"[2] the film gives the audience a glimpse of a vibrant sense of the local area: the economically depressed, rural area of the Ozarks in southern Missouri, where economic opportunities are scarce, and drugs are abundant.

The film's aesthetic reflects the poverty and precarity of the Dolly family and the region, and helps to set the mood for the stark, tense narrative. Though the film is not presented in black and white for the greatest part (apart from one impressionistic, monochrome dream sequence, one might be forgiven for having the impression that it was). From the wintry setting and the bare trees to the multiple sequences filmed at night, much of the movie is drained of colour. In addition to reinforcing the general tenor of economic deprivation, its predominantly grey aesthetic works in the service of the increasingly tense and chilly tone – chilly not only in the titular "winter's" sense but also in the sense of unwelcoming. For Ree's repeated pleas for help are almost universally rebuffed, until her uncle, Teardrop, changes his mind in the third "act" of the film. Throughout her quest, whether she is walking or driving from encounter to encounter, Ree travels the rural highways and byways through the nakedly grey trees and under overcast skies. Even when the film goes indoors, scenes are set in spaces lit with severely white fluorescent lighting, such as the high school that she does not attend; the army-recruiter interview; the cattle lot through which she chases Thump Milton, the meth kingpin; and, perhaps most importantly, the barn where Thump's female thugs beat Ree. The frigid and forbidding lighting in these spaces accentuates the sense of disconnection that Ree feels from these institutions and relationships.

The consistent exception to the film's frosty aesthetic is found in scenes of home, where warm and welcoming light of a more golden hue underlines a sense of belonging. In these settings, including Ree's own home and the home where she visits an old girlfriend of her father, the look of things is sharply different, bathed in golden light as if there were a crackling log fire on the hearth. The warmth and togetherness (sometimes more aspiration than reality) in these spaces visibly contrasts with the cold lonesomeness of the many other spaces where Ree searches for her father with little help.

My approach to *Winter's Bone* (Granik, 2010) finds conceptual resources in two recent engagements with family by political theorists, resources helpful in highlighting the intersection of freedom and vengeance as well as the relationship between family and subjectivity. Let us turn to them in order to spotlight two aspects of family that are significant for a politics of subjectivity that runs counter to liberal individualism: the unchosen quality of family and the negotiation that it necessitates within the family. These aspects have been underlined by recent work in political theory attending to the complex dynamics of family, as well as its changing meaning.

Family and the Unchosen

Families are among the most significant and guarded of unchosen relations for many people, and thus family offers a focused scene through which to examine freedom and vengeance together. Family represents the site and the substance of our first and most formative experiences of given or unchosen relations and circumstances, which shape us and condition our subjectivity. The family, whatever its size or "shape," is a scene of investment and anxiety, a formative set of relations alternately defended and spurned, embraced and resented. If, as I argue elsewhere in this project, many mainstream movies often present a misleading picture of individual subjectivity by highlighting an excessively autonomous vision of freedom and vengeance, then we can begin to craft a better representation of the situated subject by attending to relations of dependence, specifically to those that constitute the family. For while family is a place and space where we are perhaps most dependent and vulnerable, it is also a place and discursive site in which dependence is acknowledged and even extolled, in contrast to the dominant liberal vision that prizes independence – sometimes to the extreme of aspiring to sovereignty.

Though the forms of family in contemporary life are multiplying, and recognition of them is growing, Samuel Chambers reminds us that whatever its form, family is necessarily marked by an unchosen quality; otherwise, it loses its distinguishing quality. In his book *The Queer Politics of Television*,[3] Chambers examines the way in which television series such as *Buffy the Vampire Slayer* and *Big Love* have intervened in the cultural politics of family to shift and broaden the meaning of family, moving its locus away from relations of blood and marriage.[4] Those two poles have traditionally served to define family – that is, someone is family either by blood or marriage. To de-centre this traditional notion and recognize a broader range of actually existing families, one must take account of the freedom and choice that people exercise in crafting their lives together. From the perspective of subjectivity, I would like to underline a key point that Chambers makes: that family, no matter its form, must have a combination of chosen and unchosen elements. "Family will always serve to undermine and rework the narrow dichotomy of chosen/determined," he writes. "Family always proves to be partially chosen and partially unchosen, but this does not constitute a limitation or weakness of family. Indeed, the *unchosen* quality of family *makes family*. Being 'beyond choice' is an essential and constitutive element of family."[5] Clearly, family is unchosen in the most common sense that we do not have a choice of the family into which we are born. But even as young or grown adults when we craft our own families, a significant part of what we seek is a sense of belonging that comes from "fit." While belonging is felt subjectively, it must also be reciprocated in order to be full, and the reciprocation is out of our control – thus, unchosen.

Among its unchosen qualities, the family contains a set of dependent relationships that are not simply limitations but also capabilities. In the context of a politics undergirded by liberal common sense, dependence often has a bad name – especially in a neoliberal politics infused with libertarianism. Structurally, the relations of dependence that help constitute subjectivity are similar to the rules of grammar or a system of roads. Yes, they channel and constrain behavior, but they also enable action and creativity. Dependence, then, and family more specifically, is something of a paradox – a limit that enables, a burden that guides. We are in the first instance dependent on our family in the sense of being determined by their will to, and resources for, care from birth. As we grow, the shape and extent of our dependency changes but we remain reliant on their support. Even as "independent adults," we rely on a series of relationships involving friends, colleagues and/or newer families. When we loosen the perceptual grip of (neo)liberal autonomy, we can see that even though something may be unchosen, it is not necessarily threatening. Rather than remaining unacknowledged or feared in pursuit of fantasies of freedom and vengeance, an appreciation of dependence can be acknowledged and woven into the public imagination regarding freedom.

The fact that family is by definition "beyond choice" makes it an especially instructive lens through which to view the politics of subjectivity. Although freedom is often figured in contemporary political discourse in opposition to dependence (those who are most free are those who are least dependent/most independent), appreciating the necessary and unchosen character of subjectivity holds out the possibility of helping to shift the image of freedom away from freedom *from* dependence and toward freedom *with* or *within* dependence. The very crux of the difference between a misleadingly seductive image of autonomous individualism and a richer understanding of individual subjectivity is that the latter accounts for the unchosen influences on subjects – both immediately, as with family, and more obliquely, as with culture, politics, and history. A crucial issue, then, involves recognizing the chosen and unchosen structures and conditions that we depend on whether we know it or not. And family is an instructive space for examining how subjects negotiate their dependence on the unchosen.

Family Negotiation

As the contemporary politics of family shows, families appear in a growing variety of shapes and sizes. Still no matter their type, families are neither pure nor ideal, but instead the real setting for some of our most striking experiences of both intimacy and anguish. In his recent book *All in the Family*, Kennan Ferguson has written insightfully about the political significance of the daily challenges that attend family, and what we can learn about macropolitics from the micropolitics of families. Ferguson shows how the ineliminable fact of radical difference (or "incommensurability," in his terms) does not diminish possibilities for family and/or community, but rather how in families difference coexists along with coherence. In short, families remind us that unity is not necessarily unanimity.

The case that Ferguson makes for taking families seriously from the perspective of political theory rests, then, on an insight into the way in which relationships and cultural experience at the micro-level inform macro-level politics. "Families," he writes, "are the location where most of our political and ethical negotiations take place, where we learn to make sense of our simultaneous connections to, and distances from, other human beings."[6] In Western political thought, the familiar trope of family-as-microcosm-of-the-polity often connotes unified community, but it is precisely Ferguson's point to challenge this trope. Ferguson's insight is to track the coexistence or concurrence of conflict and concord that is characteristic of ordinary family life, not that of an idealized family. The idea is to learn from the give-and-take of attachment and disappointment, the back-and-forth of belonging and alienation that is familiar and intensely felt in all working, non-ideal families. You might almost say that the political insight into family here derives from confronting assumptions about community with the truism that every family is dysfunctional in some way or other, to a greater or lesser extent.

The ordinary, functioning dysfunctional family then is not an ideal model of harmony but rather the locus of quarrel and consensus – and in order for families to persist and survive, their members have to figure out how to cohere and get along. For Ferguson, this means living with difference even when so much is shared and when we are most vulnerable. More than merely "living with" difference, Ferguson makes significant use of an ordinary term for how families do this: negotiation. He presents a recurring characterization of family as a space of political and ethical negotiation. This term is central for Ferguson, as when he writes, "Negotiation is how we live our lives as both communal creatures and individual actors, feeling and creating our way through roles, expectations, obligations, and potentialities."[7] I want to hone in on negotiation as a concept, for the word here not only signals a breakdown of the sharp opposition between choice and determination, but also a shift from the perspective of autonomous individuals to that of subjects. Negotiation thus connotes dealing with something beyond our full grasp, reckoning with something given to us, such as when we negotiate a patch of ice on the sidewalk in winter or negotiate a so-called "minefield" in the office. Echoing Chambers on families as mixtures of chosen and unchosen elements, Ferguson brings subjectivity into view as he reminds us that people "become who they are alongside and within a network of people both given to them and chosen by them."[8] In other words, we are always subjects – formed by more than our choices. You might say that whereas independence connotes creation or sovereign choice, dependence necessitates negotiation, which in turn suggests the necessity of grappling with pre-given circumstances or unchosen structures. In families, members must negotiate "roles, expectations, obligations, and potentialities" that they find themselves situated in because of family relationships, history, and perceptions.

Ferguson's approach to family is very instructive politically, and I would like to view it from a complementary angle, shifting focus from what family means for community to what family means for subjectivity. Ferguson explores family in order to address the communitarian anxiety that difference threatens community, but we can also examine family in order to speak to the inverse liberal concern that dependence threatens autonomy, and subjectivity threatens individuality. Ferguson surveys this territory himself when he writes, "Families are where we feel the critical oppositions of politics – for example between collective identity and liberal individuation – most intensely. They are where we learn how to negotiate identities and differences. They are where we spend much if not most of our political energies."[9] Whereas Ferguson examines family in order to demonstrate that difference or incommensurability does not undermine the possibility, even the reality, of community, I want to take a corresponding look at family from the perspective of individual members in order to see how family qualifies autonomy without eliminating it. Thus, just as Ferguson's appraisal of family brings into focus the ways in which we live together in spite of difference, I want to suggest that family helps us to also see the way in which we still act and choose freely even amidst the unchosen, negotiating a course between rejection of and submission to family, between embrace and forbearance of autonomy.

As family members negotiate the relationships and affects of family, they find out that individual freedom is never completely free or frictionless but always exists within a determining context. Freedom or choice always depends on unchosen conditions and contexts. Families are, then, the locus for our first and ongoing experiences of subjectivity (paraphrasing Ferguson), of being dependent upon others and subject to persons and circumstances over which we do not have full control. My point here is in a sense an alternative view of the same phenomena. To complement Ferguson's point that family is "the site of community most intensely practiced by most people,"[10] I would suggest that family is where most individuals most intensely feel and grapple with their subjectivity – that is, with the fact of their incompleteness and their dependence on others. If we cannot command as sovereigns then we must negotiate as subjects, and family is the space in which we not only learn this but continue to practice it daily.

Both within and beyond the family, freedom and vengeance are connected in deep and powerful ways, which attest to the social condition of vulnerability and dependency that simultaneously limits and enables subjects' action. Elsewhere in this book, I show through a reading of *Mystic River* (Eastwood, 2003), informed by Judith Butler's work on grief and vulnerability, that vengeance constitutes a denial of our fundamental vulnerability while its refusal, through an embrace of grieving, respects that vulnerability. Elsewhere, examining *Into the Wild* (Penn, 2006) and *Wendy and Lucy* (Reichardt, 2008), I have also worked to make perceptible the costs associated with the ravenous pursuit of an autonomous vision of freedom that denies, whether by choice or necessity, the ways in which we are necessarily dependent upon others. It is in that vein that I turn here to *Winter's Bone*, a film that brings the themes of freedom and vengeance together and that stages a double refusal of their simpler expressions. The refusal of both a compulsive, self-defeating vengeance and a seductive, yet ever-elusive, vision of autonomy together constitute a rare and welcome cinematic affirmation of the fundamental condition of dependency in and through which we are all constituted. That condition shows that we are essentially related to others, with all that that entails – attachment and injury, bonds and losses, pleasure and pain. Therefore, the double refusal of freedom and vengeance by the protagonist of *Winter's Bone* expresses a declaration of dependence, offering a different picture of subjectivity than that of the familiar, independent hero/heroine.

Winter's Bone: Family Auditions

Along the course of Ree's quest to preserve the family's house and timber, the film stages an uncommon series of encounters and reflections on the attractions, as well as the limits, of family – both hers and others. Instead of her experience with family failure repelling her from the idea and practice of family altogether, it seems instead to have intensified her desire to be part of a functional family. Over the course of the film, Ree meets (and, you might even say, auditions or flirts) with different families, as she searches for help from someone who will be a partner. Though she is strong and determined, we can sense an undercurrent of desire in Ree. She craves a sense of belonging, and hopes to find someone who will reciprocate her affective investment in a familial scene of belonging. Though the ostensible purpose for her quest is the preservation of her family and their homestead, Ree's journey functions, on an affective level, as a series of circumspect interviews with prospective families: her immediate family, her extended family, what you might call her clan (the Dollys), and the US Army.[11]

Of course, there is, first and foremost, Ree's immediate family, in which her absent mother and father leave her wanting while her brother and sister are more than just responsibilities, they are subjects of her affection. Even in the earliest scenes of the film, the audience can perceive that Ree is a tough and exceptional young woman, and this sense only grows as she navigates the challenges that she encounters throughout the film. Ree, though only 17 years old, cares for her two younger siblings in the absence of her parents. Her mother seems to suffer from some kind of mental illness or may be (highly) medicated (possibly self-medicated), but her condition is left ambiguous in the film so that she could either be in a permanent state of shock or has simply "checked out." At a later point in the film, a friend asks Ree whether her mother is aware of what is going on with her missing father and the threat of losing the house. Ree's response says a lot about her, and how she differs from her mother in handling the unchosen: "This is the exact shit she went crazy trying to get away from. It'd be too mean to tell her." At the same time as Ree indirectly gives voice here to her own frustration with the burden that she must bear, she also paradoxically inhabits a motherly role in protecting her vulnerable mother. Ree's response once again affirms that she bears the responsibility of the unchosen (her mother's illness/abdication) with grace. Indeed, throughout the film the young Ree is the very picture of uprightness and duty as she shoulders the dual unchosen charge of not only primary care giver to her mother, brother, and sister but also de facto bounty hunter of her father. Underlining the familial role reversal and the impact of the unchosen, there is a scene in the middle of the film when Ree, in a rare moment of vulnerability, pleads with her mother to "Please, help me this one time." Even though Ree is nearly overwhelmed because of all the obstacles she has encountered and the little progress she has made in finding her father, her mother nevertheless does not (or cannot) respond to her request. She merely sits there impassively, locked away in her own trauma and emotionally disabled by the unchosen burdens of family and her husband's choices.

The double parental absence that constitutes a large part of the unchosen family inheritance that Ree must handle is reflected in the growing responsibilities with which she must reckon. She is faced with a tough choice in a situation that she did not choose: she can either shirk the responsibility and pursue her own desires and ambitions or she can accept her inheritance and take up the responsibility. Given the absence of her parents, the possibility of her dodging these duties seems a very real option. What is striking in the movie, however, is not just that she takes up the responsibilities but that she handles them as well as she does, without bitterness or resentment. For Ree appears remarkably capable of handling the unchosen responsibilities of caring for and protecting her family. From child care to negotiating with her drug-dealing extended family, Ree continually must cope with and respond to demanding circumstances not of her choosing. She is always, as it were, ably playing the bad hand that she has been dealt. Other than in the case of her horse, Ree does not to ask for help when it comes to daily matters of household and child care. When her little brother suggests that they ask the neighbours for some of their fresh venison, she even scolds him with a principle: "Never ask for what ought to be offered." When the neighbour does offer later that night, Ree graciously accepts. Ree knows that family isn't perfect or ideal. Her own experience with her absent, criminal father and her damaged mother have taught her the disappointment that can attend family relationships. Still, Ree perseveres, taking up the slack from her father and mother, and caring for her two younger siblings. More than that, she perseveres in her yearning for a better, more functional family – one that will care for her as much as she cares for it.

Moving out concentrically from Ree's nuclear family, next there is Ree's extended family – chiefly her uncle, Teardrop (John Hawkes). It is worth noting that even before she asks her mother for help and receives no response (as noted above), Ree first calls on her father's brother, Teardrop, for help finding her father, as the two brothers are still close. Ree only turns to her mother in the middle of the film, once she has experienced multiple frustrations and rejections. Teardrop's first appearance in the film, when Ree comes to ask for help, is a memorable and menacing one. First of all, the film visually conveys his own criminal history by allowing the audience to see his prison tattoos (including a small "x" at the corner of his left eye) as well as the handgun that he loads and cocks while sitting across from her at the kitchen table. Setting up the pattern to follow, Teardrop is the first to refuse Ree any help, saying sternly, "Don't go runnin' after Jessup. Show or don't show, that choice is up to the one that's goin' to jail, not you." In addition to demonstrating what Ree is up against, Teardrop's words of warning suggest a presumption of independent choice that is seemingly alien to Ree and the set of circumstances that she has inherited. While Teardrop implies that her father is completely free to make choices independent of his family (even as they may ostensibly be *for* his family), Ree certainly does not see it that way – nor does she enjoy the same male privilege as her father or uncle. Ree is already dealing with the resulting blowback from her father's "free choices." Teardrop's statement is revealing of the way in which individual choice (particularly white, male choice) is conventionally a narrative focal point, leaving the unchosen consequences for others, who remain out of focus. *Winter's Bone* is exceptional in this regard, placing Ree's negotiation with the unchosen at the centre of its narrative.

Teardrop goes on to counsel Ree to take heed of the silences that she will confront from the Dolly clan if she persists in her effort to find her father. Still, she somehow manages to preserve a strong sense of family. Just as she honours her family dependencies and responsibilities when they arise, she seems to expect others to reciprocate when she is in need. Again and again, however, she runs up against a wall of silence from her family's clan surrounding their criminal enterprise which trumps any claims of family connection or loyalty. Teardrop's explanation ("Show or don't show, that choice is up to the one that's goin' to jail, not you") at an early stage of the film's narrative is, however, given less as a matter of the power of drug traffickers and more as a matter of (implicitly patriarchial) prerogative and autonomy. By contrast, Ree's engagement with the dependencies in which she finds herself enmeshed amounts to a rejection of such autonomy. That she resists the lure of independence throughout the film is not, however, simply a matter of her positioning in the gender order of a traditionally patriarchal society.

To be sure, Ree is situated within her culture's gender norms such that she might well be expected to effectively assume the role of head of the household. But to say, as one reviewer does, that "The place of Ree Dolly in this society is set: She's a woman, so she's meant to take whatever comes, and she's still a kid, so she doesn't matter [...] So Ree chops the wood and feeds the kids and holds the family together because that's what you do,"[12] not only misreads Ree but underestimates the achievement of Granik's film. Her strength and resoluteness (inseparable from Jennifer Lawrence's stellar performance) should push us toward an appreciation of the fact that Ree is not simply conforming or deferring to the prevailing gender norms. After all, there are different ways in which to inhabit the norm.[13] In fact Ree shows herself time and again to be someone who is willing to run the risk and challenge norms (gender norms, norms of silence) in the service of protecting her family and their homestead. If we look at her efforts to care for her mother, brother, and sister through the lens of the determination that she shows in her quest to find her father, we can see that Ree acts in a caring fashion not merely out of a sense of duty or fidelity to norms but out of deep feelings of love and something more than duty, something like dignity – and not just individual dignity, but family dignity. And so, Ree remains steadfast with her family even though she has many reasons – and seemingly every right, by the individualistic norms of American culture – to leave and strike out on her own.

The final family that Ree flirts with is the army, which functions in a sense as a family through rhetoric ("band of brothers," etc.) as well as being a set of unchosen relations meant to inspire attachment, belonging, duty, and sacrifice. An early scene in the film establishes Ree as a high-school dropout when she drops her siblings off at school but does not attend school herself. Still, she lingers at the high school peeking in on different classes: she looks in, with an expression of amusement, on a home economics course involving baby care, and she also gazes longingly upon an ROTC (Reserve Officers' Training Corps) drill in the gymnasium. Even as these scenes present Ree as a dropout, they also establish her once again as an outsider, unattached and longing for something more. In fact, later in the film

Familial Subjectivity and *Winter's Bone*

she does consider the idea of leaving and joining the army, and even attends an army recruiting interview. Again, she experiences rejection and disappointment from a potential family when the army recruiter informs her that at 17 she is too young to enlist without parent/guardian approval. The irony, of course, is that even though "the U.S. government still considers [her] a minor" as the recruiter tells her, Ree is more responsible and more of an adult than anyone else in her family. She is also disappointed to learn from the recruiter that she would not be able to bring her younger siblings along to basic training with her, for she seems to hope that she can graft elements of two families together to produce a functional family for herself and her siblings.

As an audience to Ree's negotiations with and within these different families, we come to see that she is a confident and capable woman, even as she seems to be failing in her quest to find her father, Jessup. Even with the threat of violence continually hovering along with the overcast skies, Ree still perseveres, negotiating obstacle after obstacle. It is against this backdrop of violence that Ree's repeated requests for help stand out as themselves principled, declarations of dependence, acknowledgements of a constitutive vulnerability and a refusal of violent vengeance. Despite her best efforts, however, her search turns out to be a lonely one. For much of the film she is on her own, trying to crack the code of silence among those of her very extended family, her clan, involved in the drug trade who may know something of her father's whereabouts but do not dare tell for fear of betraying the clan's drug trade. Continually, Ree reaches out to these people *as family*, only to be met with utter cautions; stonewalling rejection; or, worse, violence. At an early point in her search, for example, Ree pleads with an older woman for help, saying, "Some of our blood at least is the same. Ain't that supposed to mean something? Ain't that what is always said?" Ree learns the hard way – through repeated silence and eventually violence – that the economic necessity attending the clan's drug trafficking supersedes any claims of family relation. In other words, though family as loyalty is a survival strategy for both Ree and her clan, family means something different for them than for Ree. She asks family for help, seeking to draw on blood relations, a shared heritage, and a shared dependency, and in turn, she is met with indifference (as with her mother, noted earlier), disdain, or violence.

The film climaxes when the tension concerning the Dolly clan's stonewalling of Ree's calls for help comes to a head in a confrontation between Ree and kingpin Thump Milton. Though Ree tracks him to a cattle auction and tries to chase him down in the adjacent stockyards, Thump later retaliates by having his female thugs beat Ree – setting up a meeting between her and Thump on his terms, not hers. Aesthetically, the scene in the barn is explicitly framed by the fluorescent lighting that is consistently associated in the film with an affective coldness and social disconnection. The establishing shot of the barn into which Ree has been dragged is immediately followed by a close-up of the barn's fluorescent lights, part of a montage that represents for the audience Ree's perception as she comes to after having been beaten. This shot is succeeded by others – a horse's bridle, chains – in a sequence that concludes with blurry images, in which members of the Dolly clan slowly come into focus. After we see Ree regain consciousness, we see her raise her head and glance around the room, and the camera identifies with her gaze such that we and she look upon all the characters who had earlier rebuffed her requests for help finding her father. They had tried to tell her not to press forward, but she did not listen, and finally it has come to a head.

After this shared gaze has surveyed the figures who have spurned Ree, the camera cuts to a familiar young woman who says to Ree in a soft, caring tone, "What are we ever gonna do with you, baby girl?" In turn, Ree says "Kill me. I guess," capturing the sense of frustration and hopelessness that her seemingly futile quest has produced. When the young woman then responds, "That idea's been said already. Got any others?" Ree does not dwell on the hopeless but instead immediately seizes the opportunity to say, "Help me. Ain't nobody said that idea yet have they?" The young woman then says, "Tried to help you some before. This is what come of it," referring to the warnings and attempts at redirection given to Ree. But then Thump Milton walks in, and it slowly becomes clear that what has come of her single-minded efforts is in fact an audience with "the Big Man."

Ree's confrontation with Thump Milton is the key "showdown" moment of the film, and it is very revealing of the kinds of negotiations and declarations that Ree is willing to make. Once Thump enters the scene, Ree again makes her claim on "the Big Man" in a fearless way, suggesting that she has nothing left to lose. And yet the face-off is staged and directed in such a way as to suggest Ree's inferior and weak position. For instance, as Ree is slumped on the floor (again having just come to from her beating), Thump walks over to her, kneels down, and grabs her by the chin, pulls her face up and then to each side in a way in which you can very well imagine he inspects a calf or cow in that very barn. He is, however, taking stock of the extent of her beating. Thereafter, he stands and she remains on the floor, further encoding the power differential between the two figures. Then Thump looks down at Ree and gives her an ultimatum: "You got somethin' to say, child, you best say it now." Her reply is fearlessly to the point and declares once again her dependence on her homestead and her family's dependence on her: "I got two kids that can't feed themselves yet. My mom's sick, and she's always gonna be sick. Pretty soon the laws are coming and taking our house, throwing us out to live in the field like dogs." Jennifer Lawrence's performance as Ree is key here, for while such a list of dependencies could sound pitiful or whiny, Ree declares these relationships. She declares them with a hint of defiance, as if she is also saying, you all would've had me and my family just wilt under this pressure and take the punishment. In fact, she refuses punishment, as she continues, "If Dad has done wrong, Dad has paid, and whoever killed him, I don't need to know all that." (Note her suggested refusal of vengeance here, something we will examine more fully later.) Finally, she concludes her uninterrupted announcement with a crowning declaration. She says sternly, not plaintively, "I can't forever carry the weight of kids, and my mom [...] not without that house." In this tense face-off, though the staging suggests her weakness as Thump towers over her, Ree commands the stage, showing remarkable courage and making an intrepid declaration of her dependence. Again, she refuses the fatalism of "kill me, I guess," and instead presses the point "help me." At this moment, the film does not show the successful conclusion of this declaration. It is only later, when three women come to help Ree to recover her father's hands as proof of his death, that we retrospectively realize that her declaration was effective. Such proof of death will allow Ree to keep "that house."

In the moment, however, Ree's statement is left hanging without response, because this climactic scene concludes with the arrival of Teardrop to claim her from the Dolly clan. Though this could be read as further suggestion of Ree's weakness, it is instead an oblique confirmation of Ree's declarations of dependence and her quest for help, as Teardrop has changed his mind.

The film's structure of a single subject engaging a series of families presents an opportunity to think politically about subjectivity and family, for it allows consideration of a single subject's various negotiations with family and dependence as she searches for belonging. The film is so centred on Ree's experience that there is no scene in which she does not appear. In spite of the rejections she experiences, which seem to conspire to return her to her immediate family of love and loss, Ree nevertheless does decide to stay with her own family, damaged though it is, in a way that suggests strength, courage, and negotiation with hardly a note of desperation. One of her very last lines in the film confirms Ree's return to her family. Responding to her younger brother's fears that she will leave them for the army, Ree says, "I'd be lost without the weight of you two on my back. I ain't goin' anywhere." This is Ree's declaration of dependence. How can this be explained? We have something of an answer in Lauren Berlant's discussion of the affective results of economic crisis on desire for family and belonging. Even so, Ree's declaration is instructive for the politics of subjectivity, too.

Ree's "Choice of Inheritance," Her Declaration of Dependence

At the end of Ree's quest for belonging, *Winter's Bone* stages one of the more striking declarations of dependence in recent American cinema. Ree's most compelling and illustrative declaration of dependence, her choice of inheritance, finds expression in a quiet scene at the end of her film-long mission to safeguard her family and homestead. Her quest concludes successfully, but in grisly fashion as members of the criminal extended family take her blindfolded to her father's remains. There she must use a chainsaw to remove both of his hands in order to prove to the bail bondsman that her father is dead. After then reclaiming the bond and securing the homestead, in the film's very last frames Ree settles in on the front porch with her younger siblings to finally take a breath. Just then, her little brother Sonny tentatively and fearfully asks whether she is going to join the army and leave them. As mentioned, Ree answers in a way that encapsulates her character and her choices: "I'd be lost without the weight of you two on my back. I ain't goin' anywhere." In the context of the film, what is so striking and pitch-perfect about this response is the way in which it captures Ree's bittersweet "choice of inheritance" and reflects her negotiated reckoning with the unchosen. Ree authentically chooses to stay, to take up the burden of family and even affirm it. She chooses her inheritance, both literally with the homestead and timber acres and symbolically with her declaration of dependence: "I'd be lost without the weight of you two on my back." Ree has every reason to resent the situation that her parents have put her in, the responsibilities that they have abandoned, and to reject this inheritance. Instead, she has taken the burden, made it her own, and occupied the role of caretaker with real diligence and affection. Viewed in the context of the whole film, Ree's choices not only speak to her sense of honour but also give a rich picture of the situated, negotiated agency characteristic of subjectivity as opposed to a chimera of purely free agency.

This film can be read in part as a study in choices, as can many conventional feature films. Still, *Winter's Bone* depicts Ree's negotiations as a subject with the demands of, pressures on, and attraction to family. The crucial and distinctive accomplishment of this film is to make credible what we might call Ree's "choice of inheritance," recalling both Edmund Burke[14] and David Bromwich.[15] Bromwich adopts the phrase from Burke's *Reflections on the Revolution in France*, but gives it his own fresh interpretation. On the face of it, the phrase appears oxymoronic – for inheritance is customarily bestowed, not chosen. But Bromwich expands the resonance of the phrase, saying that it "implies that something more than a memory binds the past with the present."[16] I read "choice of inheritance" as something of a gloss on the fact that we are always already *in medias res*, simultaneously preceded and exceeded by social, historical, cultural, and political circumstances and powers.[17] Another way to appreciate the situated character of subjectivity that informs Burke's thought is to recognize, as political theorist Stephen White does, that "Burke shares with many contemporary thinkers a deeply hostile attitude toward the figure of the self-determining, rational subject who conceives of himself as the master of all he surveys."[18] Burke's hostility to this figure of autonomy is of a piece with his appreciation of the political resonances that attend family.

To begin to make sense of this paradoxical phrase, consider that Burke is famous for his defence of government as an inheritance. As Burke's primary theoretical metaphor for politics, inheritance connotes an immanent historicist perspective that is consistent with his appropriation and transformation of the metaphor of social contract. "Society is indeed a contract," Burke wrote in his *Reflections*. However, he continues, "As the ends of such a partnership cannot be obtained in many generations, it is a partnership not only between those who are living, but between those who are living, those who are dead, and those who are to be born."[19] Again, this famous phrase is often highlighted in order to demonstrate a notion of Burke's fidelity to tradition. Yet it is not a simple reflexive deference to tradition. Rather, it marks a keen historical and social sense of place and experience. Thus, Burke's transformation of the social-contract metaphor also expresses the underlying immanent and historicist perspective from which he views politics, through its adoption of the social-contract narrative while at the same time injecting "the people" into that narrative *in medias res* while refusing to locate a specific, even abstract, origin for that contract. If this transformed notion of contract points to historical and empirical continuity, then the allied metaphor of inheritance suggests a practical institution to ensure the transmission upon which continuity is based. Burke's transformed social contract locates the choice in the present for each generation as a question of their "choice of inheritance" rather than locating choice in a far-removed moment of abstract origin.

Yet while for most readers of Burke, this defense furnishes evidence of his traditionalism and conservatism, there are many powerful and insightful aspects to Burke's leading political metaphor of inheritance that point to something much less common to the tradition of social-contract theory and liberalism – a political perspective that takes culture seriously. What Uday Mehta says of Burke's understanding of territory or location, that it is "both a metaphor and an important physical fact,"[20] is also true of inheritance in Burke. For the fact that humans are born into a particular socio-political culture means, for Burke, that they are born *in medias res* – that is, in the middle of a whole matrix of institutions, practices, and histories. Since people most often inherit a set of institutions and practices rather than creating them from scratch, the fact of inheritance gives rise to a more apt metaphor for political thought than the more familiar social contract. Still, as they are often inherited with origin(s) unknown, social practices and political institutions betray their immanence through an ineradicable element of contingency and dependence. Such contingencies and dependences make a claim on us, and Burke believes that such inheritances must be accepted, embraced, and fortified through choice – hence, his felicitous phrase: "a choice of inheritance."

Looking more closely at this remarkable expression "choice of inheritance," the context of the phrase speaks to Burke's historicist approach to thinking about politics:

> In this choice of inheritance we have given to our frame of polity the image of a relation in blood, binding up the constitution of our country with our dearest domestic ties, adopting our fundamental laws into the bosom of our family affections, keeping inseparable and cherishing with the warmth of all their combined and mutually reflected charities our state, our hearths, our sepulchres, and our altars.[21]

Many contemporary readers may be tempted to interpret this as a kind of essentialist argument, referring as it does to the family as "a relation in blood." However, that kind of reading would overlook the force of the other terms in this context, especially their relation to nature and affection. Moreover, an essentialist interpretation is undercut from the start by the injection of choice, for essentialisms obviously cannot be chosen. While ordinarily inheritances cannot either, Burke has done much work to make this seemingly paradoxical phrase appear most intelligible. Thus, Burke here announces that inheritance is in the end an immanent choice, never a transcendent right or obligation. Not only the transmission but also the upholding and maintaining of the political inheritance is never a foregone conclusion – never taken for granted, like the rising and setting of the sun. Rather it is a matter of convention and choice to uphold and preserve it. Though it is certainly conservative, Burke's view is a thoroughly immanent, cultural one, and it is an immanent conservatism attuned to cultural determinations. For it is to be upheld not because it is right in a moral or a juridical sense, but because it fits with the texture of the life that includes the affections of hearth and state. Political theorist Stephen White characterizes Burke's "choice of inheritance" in this way: "Political health in the modern world cannot be rooted in unthinking traditionalism, but rather only in affirmative 'choice' to attach ourselves to our collective inheritance. The inevitable *fact* that we are 'encumbered' selves is thus only a starting point."[22] White's encumbrance, you might say, is another way of naming the unchosen. Note, however, that affirming encumbrance does not mean simply submitting to custom as it is, but also reforming it when necessary. For Burke is at pains to distinguish necessary reform from both complacent inertia and speculative revolution. The central idea is that one cannot be free of encumbrances, free of cultural determinations. One is always in the middle of things, negotiating the unchosen and the chosen.

Returning to Ree's particular "choice of inheritance," the trope here expresses an acknowledgement of an inheritance, an affirmation of a given set of circumstances and relations within which we find ourselves. The phrase's resonance with family, the primal scene of the unchosen, is, of course, key. Because the chosen and the unchosen are always imbricated with each other, we are, as subjects, always choosing in contexts not of our own choosing. Some may find themselves resenting the unchosen or raging against it, while others may avow or merely tolerate the unchosen. We can affirm or challenge the unchosen (or elements thereof), declare it or hide from it, but we are not free to simply reject or refuse it – for even a refusal is, in a sense, a response to it. Thus, the unchosen is there in its various elements and manifestations, and must be negotiated. In this way, a choice of inheritance is a declaration of dependence.

Notwithstanding the integrity and generosity of it, Ree's choice to remain with her family can also be read as an affective and politically revealing response to economic crisis. By underlining the context of economic struggle, *Winter's Bone*, like *Wendy and Lucy*, can be situated with what Lauren Berlant calls the cinema of precarity. The Dolly clan of *Winter's Bone* is clearly a "tattered family," registering the very personal costs of macroeconomic hardships.[23] In that light, Ree's seemingly stubborn or perhaps even archaic belief in family seems to attest to family as "the lone institution of reciprocity remaining here for fantasy to attach itself to."[24] Thus, throughout the film, Ree's quest is for a family setting that will function, that will reciprocate her affective investment.

If we read Ree's desire to stay with her family through the lens of precarity's affective impacts, we can see that her unwavering defence of her family speaks to her desire for a future grounded in family, but one different from what she has known with her own parents. She wants to preserve and make right the family (one might be tempted to say restore the family, but it is not clear that the family was ever, on balance, functional – even acknowledging that every family is dysfunctional to some degree). In this view, *Winter's Bone* stands as a striking example of how "the exhaustion and corruption of families in the brittle economy produces, nonetheless, a desire in these children for the 'normal' life, 'the good life.'"[25] Ree's own experience throughout the film with the trumping of family by silence and economic need points to the wider structural, normative context in which hers and other families struggle in today's era of economic crisis – even, or perhaps especially, in the rural context of the Ozarks. Thus, Ree's choice to affirm her dependence by staying with her family and foregoing any aspiration to autonomy also reads as a desire for the normal – a normal condition of dependence and care. While there are many complications, she still sustains the attachment.

Thinking through the impact of precarity on daily family life, recall that Ree as a daughter must "mother" her mother and siblings. Ree taking up these roles serves as evidence of the way in which relationships become scrambled and confused in precarity's tattered family, exemplifying "the immediate crisis out of which children are trying to fight their way."[26] However, in *Winter's Bone* specifically, the economic crisis is not even the most immediate crisis. Finding the father and preserving, for the moment, the homestead is the immediate crisis. Still, even while she holds on to her dreams of a family future, Ree is actually stuck in "what we might call survival time, the time of struggling, drowning, holding on to the ledge, treading water, *not-stopping.*"[27] The fact that Ree is stuck in survival time is nowhere better expressed than in the film's ending, which merely returns her to the *status quo ante* of financial struggle. She manages to preserve her family's homestead, but nothing about their economic circumstances has essentially changed for the better. It has even changed for the worse with the loss of Ree's father.

Further exploring the context of economic uncertainty named by the discourse of precarity, Berlant pinpoints the fact that precarity is generating "new affective practices, in which children scavenge toward a sense of authentic social belonging by breaking from their parents' way of attaining the good life."[28] Even as Ree scavenges for help and seeks to do right by her family, Lawrence's performance as Ree along with the way the story is scripted never allow the audience to doubt that Ree rejects her father's criminal ways. Moreover, that activity of doing-right-by-her-family constitutes part of her attempt at securing some sense of belonging, but ironically it brings her into conflict with the extensive criminality of her extended family. One relationship at the heart of the film, however, does eventually bear out Ree's claims of dependence, her desire for reciprocal affect and action, but not before her repeated experiences of rejection cause her to expect rejection. Ree's quest is eventually redeemed in a sense when Teardrop has a change of heart, rescuing her from the family drug traffickers just when they seem to have beaten her to within an inch of her life. When Teardrop finally shows up to help Ree in her most desperate moment, the dramatic effect is one of surprise – not only because of Teardrop's earlier refusal but because of all the earlier refusals of help that Ree and we have endured.

Vengeance Refused, Vengeance Embraced

Though the film in a sense ends happily – or, at least, not tragically – its ending does still register a bittersweet note, offering a significant affective dimension to the conclusion. Though ostensibly happy, the ending merely concludes Ree's quest for Jessup, leaving her and her family without their father and returning them to the ordinary and familiar dire economic straits they were already in at the start. In particular, the film's closing achieves its poignant affect through an important aspect that we have not yet fully considered: the role of vengeance.

Even as Teardrop and Ree work together, he underlines by contrast what is distinctive about Ree's search for belonging, her choice of inheritance, and her refusal of vengeance. Remember that early in the movie, when Teardrop was hoping to scare Ree off her quest, he said, "Show or don't show, that choice is up to the one that's goin' to jail." Returning to the subject of Jessup's choice later in the film once they are allied, Teardrop offers Ree an explanation for her father's "snitchin," his choice to turn state's evidence against the drug operation, saying, "Well, he loved y'all. That's where he went weak." Teardrop conveys this observation in a sympathetic tone, suggesting that he can understand and does not condemn the choice. Still, the statement speaks to the way in which dependence is conventionally figured as an unwelcome constraint, particularly by men. Ree, in contrast, never expresses any disappointment about her relations of dependency but rather seeks to preserve, and even hopes to improve, the sense of belonging that she feels with her family.

In context, then, Ree's statement "I'd be lost without the weight of you two on my back" represents the conclusion to not only the film's dramatic depiction of Ree's quest to find her father and preserve the family homestead but also her refusal to embrace an all-too-familiar idea of freedom as independence from others. Ree not only refuses an easy and reductive notion of freedom, she also refuses vengeance – unlike her uncle Teardrop. At almost the halfway point of the film's running time, there appears a growing sense for both Ree and the audience that her father may well be dead. Still, Ree soldiers on trying to find her father and save their timberlands. Not only does she refuse autonomy by seeking help and staying loyal to her family, she refuses to seek vengeance for her father's death. For, throughout the film, Ree has not sought to punish those who killed her father but only to gain their help in preserving her family's house and timberland, which her father put up as condition for his bail bond. Ree never complains about the burden the she is carrying, and never gives any sense of resentment.

A key intervention that this film makes into the politics of subjectivity is its attempt to redeem dependence from the perception of it as weakness. One way in which this plays out is in the treatment of vengeance in the film. Consider the contrast between Teardrop's association with independence and Ree's appreciation of dependence, in connection with her refusal of vengeance and his embrace of it. While Teardrop's desire to "get even" for his brother is a further sign of his identification with a dangerous independence, Ree, who we have seen all along to be sensitive to dependence and to preserving relationships, wants to "get past" her father. The difference between a posture of strength connoting independence and a posture of attachment connoting subjectivity comes to the fore in a late scene in which the sheriff pulls over Teardrop and Ree while driving at night. Initially, it appears that Teardop will not even stop at the sight of the flashing lights pulling up behind his truck, but then Ree says, "Teardrop, you should stop. Just see what he wants." So he pulls over his truck and a remarkable confrontation ensues.

Upon approaching the car from behind with flashlight in hand, the sheriff asks Teardrop by name to step out of the truck, adding, "I need to talk to ya." The sheriff's tone is serious but not hostile or threatening. In turn, Teardrop delivers his reply – "I don't think so" – at a much lower volume than the sheriff's request, almost under his breath. Teardrop's posture is a typically masculinist posture of defiant independence, even to the point that he is not even addressing the one who's speaking to him. Apparently not having heard Teardrop's response, the sheriff says in the same tone, clarifying but insisting, "It ain't about you, you're not in trouble. It's about your brother." Again Teardrop responds quietly, almost to himself, "Nope." Then also quietly he says "Tonight I ain't doin' a fuckin' thing you say," and as he says this, the camera cuts from a two-shot, framed with the truck's windows featuring him prominently in the foreground and Ree shadowed in the background, to a close-up of Teardrop gripping his rifle between his legs. Finally, he does make himself audible to the sheriff and manifests his vengeful mindset as he asks, "Why'd you tell? Why?! You went and got his ass killed. You happy now?" Teardrop's clear though implicit aim is to avenge his brother's death. Here, he threatens to hold the sheriff responsible rather than the Dolly clan that actually killed him.

This confrontation between Teardrop and the sheriff is one of the more tense moments in the film, and part of the reason is because it features the menacing figure of Teardrop. It is the closest that the film comes to a scene that does not feature

Ree, though she is present in it and made visible in important ways. Ree's reactions to Teardrop are as significant as the encounter between the criminal and the law. For instance, the film cuts to her for a reaction shot after Teardrop's threatening bit of sarcasm, "You happy now?" Up to this point, the scene has been framed and cut as a confrontation between the sheriff and Teardrop, but from this point forward Ree's reactions become a third "pillar" of the scene. For the look on Ree's face at her uncle performing a credible threat of violence is one of disbelief, as if to say "What?! Are you really saying/doing this?!" Ree's astonishment is legible to the audience precisely because she has never even contemplated vengeance. She has been so identified with the quest to preserve her family that the notion of avenging her father has been practically unthinkable to her.

Ree then shifts her eyes to the sheriff, her face revealing her eagerness to know how this is going to play out. After catching her glance, the sheriff pulls his gun, taps the truck with it, and says, "I know you, I know your family. Get out of the car now." This invocation of family by the sheriff is striking, for it does not mark a typically macho, prideful, or even defensive answer to Teardrop's sarcastic question, of a sort that we might expect from a movie cop brandishing his gun and occupying the traditional subjective position of masculine independence. Rather, the sheriff's "I know you. I know your family" serves as a rebuff of Teardrop's claims of autonomy as he prepares for vengeance. It is a sign of the sheriff's attention to relationships and his appreicration of dependence, and since editing shows us that the sheriff caught Ree's glance just before he says this, his acknowldgement of dependence can be read as an extension of hers. Again, Ree and the sheriff exchange glances, suggesting that his refusal to take the bait of the "guns-drawn showdown" stems from consideration of Ree and Teardrop's family. (Later, after accepting Ree's delivery of her father's hands as proof of his death, the sheriff confirms this reading, as he catches Ree on her way out the door to say, "Hey, I didnt shoot the other night 'cause you were there in the truck. He never backed me down.") Teardrop, however, refuses to engage the invocation of family and instead responds by doubling down on his threat of vengeance, saying, "Is this going to be our time?" The sheriff then slowly backs away from the truck, and when Teardrop turns the ignition and starts the truck, the face-off is over.

Teardrop's invocation of the figure of "our time," though, is, finally, a gesture of sharing and suggests interdependence – but, of course, only in death. For "our time" signfies the mutually assured death to come from a shoot-out fuelled by Teardrop's own pride and vengeance. The way in which the film cuts between the confrontation and Ree's viewing of it serves to register the significant distance between Ree and Teardrop on the issue of not merely vengeance but dependence and precarity as well. We can read both stances in the context of the desperate social and economic conditions that these two characters face. For while Teardrop seems to feel as though he has nothing to lose in pursuing vengeance (except maybe a patina of honour), Ree seems to feel as though she has lost enough already.

The absence of Ree's vengeance becomes all the more visible to the audience in the very last scene of the movie. Earlier in the film, Teardrop had said to Ree, "Even if you find out, you can't ever let me know who killed him. Knowing that would just mean I'd be toes up myself pretty soon." The way in which he says this suggests that revenge is presumed, not just by him and others but seemingly by the very nature of things (that is, by the offense itself, by the culture of masculinity, by the norms of the drug trade, and so on). Finally then, just prior to Ree reassuring Sonny that she "ain't goin' anywhere," Teardrop, in a rare moment of calm, plays Jessup's old banjo on the front porch for Ree and her siblings. He finishes playing, and then quietly and simply tells Ree, "Jessup – I know who." At that moment, both Ree and the audience know that he will now pursue a vengeance for his brother's death that he himself will not survive, suggesting two further turns of the cycle of vengeance. Ree valiantly and subtly tries to dissuade him by enlisting him in a future with the family, saying of the banjo that she holds out for him, "You should have this." But Teardrop declines her invitation to a shared future of interdependence. "Oh, no, you," he says starts haltingly, "Why don't you keep it here for me?" Reading the look on Ree's face as she tries to contain her fright, the audience knows that Ree knows what he will do. Teardrop then walks off to get in his truck, and Ree goes on to deliver her consummate declaration of dependence: "I'd lost without the weight of you two on my back. I ain't goin' anywhere."

Again, what is striking in this scene, as in the earlier face-off between Teardrop and the sheriff, is the difference registered by Ree's face and Teardrop's posture, the difference between subjectivity recognized and sovereignty asserted, between vengeance refused and vengeance personified. Teardrop's full embrace of vengeance is matched by Ree's abstention from it. Since she offers no words on the subject of vengeance in the scene, we are left to read her facial reactions to Teardrop's vengeful intent which is as plainly intelligible as Ree's very different intent to preserve what is left of her family without vengeance.

In the moment when she turns from Teardrop back to her siblings in order to assert her choice of inheritance, it is clear that Ree's choice represents the two ideas at the heart of this film: a negotiated freedom situated amidst relations of dependence, and a refusal of vengeance through an affirmation of vulnerability. Ree's double refusal of autonomy and vengeance, together with her embrace of care and dependence as she tries to nurture belonging, offer a powerful illustration of the idea that "Precariousness implies living socially, that is, the fact that one's life is always in some sense in the hands of the other."[29] Where Ree consistently negotiates her own and her family's fate with others as she tries to claim her father's hands, Teardrop refuses to accept that his or his brother's life might be in the hands of anyone else.

Given Ree's double affirmation of vulnerability and declaration of dependence, we can see *Winter's Bone* as something of an antidote or counterbalance to what Wendy Brown calls "liberal solipsism – the radical de-contextualization of the subject characteristic of liberal discourse that is key to the fictional sovereign individualism of liberalism."[30] *Winter's Bone* shows a full array of unchosen circumstances and structures, mostly rooted in family, that Ree must negotiate – her father's choices, her mother's choices/illness, her family's turn to crime as a response to economic crisis, the casual patriarchy that persists in contemporary society. Contrary to the claims of liberal common sense, we are not "free" in any kind of frictionless way. Rather, we must contend with and negotiate a set of relations, meanings, and circumstances that precede and exceed us: the paradox of freedom – we are free, but not completely. We find ourselves in a social, historical, cultural, and political context not of our own choosing, and some of the most significant choices we face involve how we negotiate with the unchosen.

Conclusion: The Unchosen and the Politics of Subjectivity

> I am already up against a world I never chose when I exercise my agency.
>
> (Judith Butler, "Interview with Judith Butler")[1]

That the pursuit of freedom and vengeance in American movies continues unabated suggests that American individualism remains a compelling mythology underpinned by an exaggerated belief in liberal freedom. Among the more favoured and familiar products of Hollywood are movies focused on heroic characters claiming the freedom to exact murderous revenge. Some of these are among the most celebrated films ever made – including *The Godfather*, *Unforgiven*, and *Gladiator* – while other more recent examples, such the *Taken* films (*1*, *2* and *3*), are simply popular. In turn, the popularity of a film like *Wild*,[2] based on the memoir of Cheryl Strayed, echoes *Into the Wild* and shows the continuing appeal of cinematic narratives focused on fearless individuals willing to strike out on completely their own in the wilderness. This form of liberal individualism in the American imagination nevertheless remains haunted by the unchosen. For what this myth obscures are the ways in which individuals are always already subjects, seeking independence in a social world inescapably built on dependence and necessarily exercising their free choice in circumstances not of their own choosing.

In his perceptive study of nineteenth-century American society, culture, and government, *Democracy in America*, Alexis de Tocqueville discerned a peculiarly strong voluntarist strain of individualism. Political theorist Jack Turner credits Tocqueville with having diagnosed American individualism as a "systematized self-delusion," such that "At the individual's heart is a will to see the world in a self-congratulatory way, to construe one's achievements as entirely self-authored, to interpret accidental privileges as just deserts."[3] Other theorists in recent years have detected similar notes of self-congratulation and self-authorship in the aspiration to sovereignty. Such sovereign individualism is at once all too familiar yet at the same time restricted in the public imagination, including some and excluding others. *Wild*, for instance, is a notable exception to the solitary adventure narrative in that the individualist-adventurer protagonists have most often been white men, whereas *Wild* brings a white woman into the tradition.

Films participating in an individualistic ideology can effectively reproduce both egoistic aspirations to sovereignty and disavowals of the unchosen conditions, norms, and circumstances that condition action. *Into the Wild*, for instance, is a vivid and striking example of this kind of disavowal. The prevalence and persistence of such hyper-individualistic tendencies attests to the importance of de-centring discursive practices of individualism and focusing instead on subjectivity and dependence. While American liberal common-sense individualism, as expressed in movies and politics alike, often remains blind to the unchosen relations and forces that make subjectivity and dependence inevitable, this lack of vision can be challenged discursively and cinematically, telling stories and offering modes of perception that assist in acknowledging that subjects are never sovereign but always dependent upon unchosen conditions, relationships, and norms that precede and exceed them.

American individualism tends to sustain the perception that we as individuals are single-handedly responsible for our achievements, but we are not.[4] We are situated in unchosen relations, contexts, norms, institutions, organizations, and the like. We are reliant on these rather than completely autonomous. The critique of individualistic sovereignty applies to the achievement of identity no less than material achievements. For not only are we not singularly responsible for ourselves and our achievements, we are not even singular. We are multiple, for subjects contain a multiplicity of identities.[5] As opposed to the idea that each one of us has "one true self," the language of subjectivity reminds us that subjects have multiple identities. For instance, your neighbour may be a businesswoman as well as a running enthusiast, a daughter, a spouse, or a sports fan. Among the multiple identities are not only those that subjects claim for themselves but also those that are unchosen, those thrust or written upon them by others, by norms, by institutions, and so forth. These are not diametrically opposed to, or separated from, one another but rather they are aspects of the dialectic of subject formation.

While the familiar individualistic lens tends to focus on identity as a matter of agency and choice, a significant aspect of identity derives from the unchosen. Consider identity as having two sides – one personal and the other social or cultural, one chosen and the other unchosen. Identity, then, is not only what you identify as, but also what you are identified as, not only how you see yourself, but how others and how larger society and culture sees you in light of categories that precede and exceed us. Freedom, then, consists not merely in crafting your own personal identity (liberalism's freely chosen "life plan"), but also in negotiating with the pre-existing, unchosen elements of your social/cultural identity. For instance, in terms of race, sex, gender, nationality, and so on, the meanings associated with those identity categories (e.g. "What does blackness mean?" or "What does it mean to be a man/woman/transperson?") are constructed not solely by individuals but rather through cultural and political discourses that precede and exceed any single individual. What this social construction of identity categories means for individual subjects is that they must fashion their identity through negotiation with the unchosen. Apprehending this negotiation can help to shift our idea from the free and sovereign individual to the situated subject.

The unchosen includes more than social and cultural identity categories. It also includes ontological conditions, such as vulnerability, precariousness, relationality, and grievability, which are inflected by particular social and political circumstances and institutions. That is, the unchosen entails political ontology as well as identity. It is not just that as subjects we are all always already "given over to others, to norms, to social and political organizations," but it is also that those very norms and organisations often "have developed historically in order to maximize precariousness for some and minimize precariousness for others."[6] It follows from this differential precariousness that, for instance, some losses are grieved publicly while others are not, as not all lives are understood to count in the same way.

One of the most powerful and historically injurious ways in which precariousness has been unevenly distributed is along lines of race. Throughout this book, all of the films, with the important exception of *The Three Burials of Melquiades Estrada*, have focused on white Americans, men and women, including Chris McCandless, Jimmy Markum, Dave Boyle, Sean Devine, Wendy, and Ree Dolly. Such a focus serves as a reminder of the whiteness of mainstream Hollywood films, which in turn says much about the presumed whiteness of the American individual and the privileges s/he enjoys. Still, as evidenced in *Three Burials*, those who are not white are often not afforded the privilege of individuality, are not recognized as subjects but instead must struggle to achieve a measure of recognition that their lives count, that they matter. Whereas grieving Melquiades Estrada publicly and respectfully required difficult and tortuous struggle in that film, grievability is easily and seamlessly accorded to Chris McCandless in *Into the Wild*. The final scenes of the latter movie are presented with such a reverential tone (and with a final shot that echoes the ascension of his soul) that the audience is practically forced to mourn the white man McCandless. The presumed grievability of a young, white male further illustrates the way in which that film eschews an engagement with the unchosen side of subjectivity.

While a politics of representation is one familiar response to this kind of disequilibrium, a politics of subjectivity, highlighting the ways in which every subject is enabled and constrained (though differentially) by social circumstances and forces, is more fertile. By highlighting the relations (social as well as institutional, cultural, and so forth) within which subjects are constituted, a politics of subjectivity challenges the entrenched, and even unconscious, autonomous individualism that has become normalized.[7] As a counterpoint to the politics of identity and representation, consider a film that addresses very directly the challenges and struggles of a marginalized subject, a subject who does not count, and moreover, addresses that subject precisely through the lens of subjectivity and grievability. *Fruitvale Station*[8] is a feature film "based on a true story" that calls attention not just to the death of a "young black man," Oscar Grant, at the hands of the police, but more significantly to his life. Grant was shot while being detained on the Fruitvale Station subway platform in Oakland, California on New Year's Eve 2009. Though the film was released about a year before the police brutality events and protests associated with the deaths of Michael Brown in Ferguson, Missouri, and Eric Garner in New York City, *Fruitvale Station* has received renewed attention in light of those events, and has played a part in placing Oscar Grant in the regrettable company of similar others, including Trayvon Martin and Tamir Rice. The deaths of these young men are a terrible indication of the systematic way in which the lives of people of colour are not only not valued in the United States, but are not even regarded as lives. This kind of normative devaluation of whole segments of the population speaks to the very personal costs associated with the structural effects of racist power.

While many Americans celebrate the election of President Barack Obama and anniversaries of the Civil Rights movement as evidence that racism is a thing of the past, the legal, desegregated coexistence of multiple races and cultures in the contemporary United States unfortunately does not attest to an achievement of full equality. One of the obstacles to full equality lies in the public and shared perceptions of whose lives matter, and thus the Twitter hashtag "#blacklivesmattter" has become a rallying cry for those who seek to make black lives not just grievable but valuable. In fact, as Judith Butler reminds us, "Part of the very problem of contemporary political life is that not everyone counts as a subject. Multiculturalism tends to presuppose already constituted communities, already established subjects, when what is at stake are communities not quite recognized as such, subjects who are living, but not yet regarded as 'lives.'"[9]

Fruitvale Station is a film that intervenes in this cultural politics of subjectivity and grievability quite self-consciously. It enlists its audience in the broader, political work of transforming perceptions not just of the category "young black men" but of particular lives, such that these persons can be recognized as full subjects with multiple identities, with a life rather than a single identity marked by a stereotyped caricature. Speaking of Oscar Grant, writer and director Ryan Coogler said, "I wanted the audience to get to know this guy, to get attached so that when the situation that happens to him happens, it's not just like you read it in the paper, you know what I mean? When you know somebody as a human being, you know that life means something."[10] Coogler's statement resonates with the politics of grievability and subjectivity, displaying an understanding of the dialectic of the universal and particular captured in the contrast of two statements "black lives matter" and "all lives matter,"[11] insisting on both while acknowledging the work needed to make the former a reality.

The film achieves its goal of making Oscar Grant grievable and making his life count more broadly by presenting Oscar in a very ordinary way throughout a single day as the bearer of multiple identities. Using this "day in the life" narrative structure, *Fruitvale* follows Oscar throughout the day leading up to his death and shows him in a variety of different relationships, and thus through different identities that constitute his subjectivity: a young black man, yes, but also a boyfriend, a father, a son, an employee, a seller of weed, and a former convict. While none of what the audience sees of Oscar this day preceding his death is especially strange, it is in other ways very strange given the cultural and racist perceptions of young black men in the media and society. The film's portrayal of an Oscar with multiple identities directly refutes the kind of "schematic racism, anti-black racism [that] figures black people through a certain lens and filter, one that can quite easily construe a black person, or another racial minority, who is walking toward us as someone who is potentially, or actually, threatening, or is considered, in his very being, a threat."[12]

Fruitvale's challenge to these racist figurations is apparent from its very first scene. The film opens with actual mobile-phone video footage of Oscar's shooting, but then flashes back 24 hours to the previous night, where we see Oscar in bed with his girlfriend, Sophina. After a brief argument about Oscar's infidelity, the two are beginning to move toward "make-up sex," when they are interrupted with a young girl's voice saying "Daddy?" and knocking on the door. Oscar first hides a bag of weed in the closet and then answers the door, and the camera cuts

The Unchosen and the Politics of Subjectivity

to a shot of a sleepy little girl in her pajamas rubbing her eyes. When Oscar asks tenderly, "What's up?" and she replies, "I can't sleep," he scoops her up in his arms, brings her into the room, and gently says, "Wanna sleep in here with Mommy and Daddy?" The shot of the three of them in bed soon after fades to black, followed by a shot overlooking early-morning Oakland and San Francisco. In this first scene of the film, Oscar is already seen to be more than just a stereotype, for while there is reference to infidelity and selling drugs, he is the furthest thing from an absent or violent father. This interplay between the complex reality of Oscar's subjectivity and the stereotypical perceptions of a "young black man" continues through the rest of the film. The picture thus intervenes in the cultural politics of race by showing Oscar to be a fully human subject whose life matters and who is worthy of grief.

If the unchosen makes life precarious and individual sovereignty impossible, then apprehending the unchosen elicits the need to rethink freedom and refuse vengeance. In many American films – including *Into the Wild* and *Mystic River* – characters and narratives refuse to acknowledge the limits of sovereign individualism. Other contemporary feature films – including *The Three Burials of Melquiades Estrada*, *Wendy and Lucy*, *Winter's Bone*, and *Fruitvale Station* – help to bring the unchosen into view, offering dramatic portrayals of the limits of the chosen and the power of the unchosen. The latter group, each in its own way, contributes to the effort to reconsider freedom and refuse revenge by attending to the precarious lives of minorities and marginalized persons – that is, staying with and attending to the subjectivities of women, immigrants, undocumented workers, itinerant labourers, poor and working class persons, and persons struggling with and for their families. As we have seen, these films acknowledge the importance of our dependent relations with others – but they do more than that. They also highlight the particular difficulties that specific subjects encounter as they try to preserve their relations with others: Pete with Melquiades, Melquiades with his home, Wendy with Lucy, Ree with her family and their home, and Oscar with his girlfriend and daughter, among others. These films can help audiences to perceive these protagonists as subjects, in spite of the larger social and political conditions that prevent or obscure such perception. These particular challenges for these particular subjects point, finally, toward a constitutive paradox at the heart of the politics of subjectivity.

Subjectivity is in one sense existential, for it is always already given and universal to the very nature of social beings. Judith Butler's insights into vulnerability and precariousness illustrate this clearly. In another sense, however, subjectivity names a challenge – indeed, a political problem. In particular, it challenges existing liberal democratic norms that self-evidently proclaim equality while overlooking the historical, social, cultural, economic, and political forces and factors that produce inequality. One key political problem is that subjectivity is denied to specific populations because the distribution of recognition of subjects is not as universal as liberal principles profess but rather uneven and unequal.

The paradox of marginalized subjectivity, then, is that although we are all subjects, subjected to the unchosen, some of us are not socially and culturally recognized or counted as subjects. Even as they are in many ways not counted or considered full subjects by the dominant cultural norms of perception, marginal subjects are daily more aware of their own subjection than are most normalized liberal individuals – those individuals with "a publicly recognized self,"[13] if you will. The reason is that marginalized and minority subjects are more often aware of confronting and negotiating the unchosen, where the unchosen appears in the form of identity categories that precede and exceed individuals and frame their social appearance.

This unevenness of recognition has been noted by political theorists for many years; it is a cornerstone of critiques of identity politics and the politics of recognition, and points toward a politics of subjectivity. Recall, for instance, an insight mentioned earlier in reference to *Three Burials* – namely, Patchen Markell's critique of the politics of recognition, wherein he points toward an "alternative diagnosis of relations of social and political subordination, which sees them not as systematic failures by some to recognize others' identities, but as ways of patterning and arranging the world that allow some people and groups to enjoy a semblance of sovereign agency at others' expense."[14] The emphasis on "ways of patterning and arranging the world" here shifts our attention to the role of institutions and practices in producing subjectivity rather than just presuming a subject's identity that is unrecognized. A further problem with the politics of recognition highlighted by Markell is that identity is never a fait accompli, but rather an ongoing product of our actions and our relations with others. Similarly, subjectivity is not a given but rather a political achievement – whether presumed, denied, or achieved through struggle.

Films that complicate our common-sense ideas of freedom and vengeance, and their conventional association with individualism and sovereignty, participate in a cultural politics of film and subjectivity. They do important work to elucidate cinematically an alternative to the dominant individualistic view, the normative individualistic ontology. As an alternative, Judith Butler evokes the idea of "a new bodily ontology, one that implies the rethinking of precariousness, vulnerability, injurability, interdependency, exposure, bodily persistence, desire, work, and the claims of language and social belonging."[15] The intimate and personal potential of film is well suited to conveying such an ontology. The cultural politics of subjectivity finds a powerful ally in movies that effectively convey the ways in which we are bodies that are always already given over to relations with others and acting in conditions not of our own choosing.

Notes

Introduction

1. Judith Butler, "Interview with Judith Butler," *Believer* (May 2003), p. 53.
2. See Anne Norton, *Republic of Signs: Liberal Theory and American Popular Culture* (Chicago: University of Chicago Press, 1993).
3. Mark Lilla, "The Tea Party Jacobins," *New York Review of Books*, May 27, 2010.
4. Clint Eastwood, dir. *Mystic River*, motion picture on DVD (USA: Warner Bros, 2003).
5. Wendy Brown, "American Nightmare: Neoliberalism, Neoconservatism, and Democracy," *Political Theory* 34:6 (2006), p. 18.
6. Kelly Reichardt, dir. *Wendy and Lucy*, motion picture on DVD (USA: Oscilloscope, 2008).
7. Debra Granik, dir. and wr. *Winter's Bone*, motion picture on DVD (USA: Lionsgate, 2010).
8. Brown, "American Nightmare."
9. Alexis de Tocqueville, *Democracy in America* [1835/1840] trans. George Lawrence (New York: Perennial Classics, 1988).
10. Ibid., p. 287.
11. Ibid., p. 508.
12. Hannah Arendt, *The Human Condition* (Chicago: University of Chicago Press, 1958).
13. See John Stuart Mill, *On Liberty* [1859] (Indianapolis, IN: Hackett, 1978).
14. To be fair, it should be noted that men are more often represented in the position of the free individual than women. This betrays the durable legacy of male privilege. Similarly, the free individual is most often racially coded, privileged or presumed as white, rather than black, Latino, Asian, or mixed race.
15. See, for instance, Slavoj Žižek, "Occupy Wall Street: What Is to Be Done Next?" *Guardian*, April 24, 2012. Available at www.theguardian.com/commentisfree/cifamerica/2012/apr/24/occupy-wall-street-what-is-to-be-done-next (accessed 22 June 2015).
16. Judith Butler, *Frames of War* (New York: Verso, 2009), p. 31.
17. Michel Foucault, "The Ethics of the Concern for Self as a Practice of Freedom," in Paul Rabinow (ed.), *Ethics: Subjectivity and Truth* (New York: The New Press, 1997), p. 167.
18. See, for instance, Judith Butler's publications: *Precarious Life: The Powers of Mourning and Violence* (New York: Verso, 2004); *Giving an Account of Oneself* (New York: Fordham University Press, 2005); and *Frames of War* (New York: Verso, 2009). See also Patchen Markell, *Bound by Recognition* (Princeton: Princeton University Press, 2003); and Lauren Berlant, *Cruel Optimism* (Durham, NC: Duke University Press, 2011).
19. Butler, *Frames*, p. 23.
20. Jeffrey Nealon, and Susan Searls Giroux, *The Theory Toolbox: Critical Concepts for the Humanities, Arts, and Social Sciences* (Lanham, MD: Rowman & Littlefield, 2003).
21. De Tocqueville, *Democracy*, p. 506.

22 See Amitai Etzioni, *The New Golden Rule: Community and Morality in a Democratic Society* (New York: Basic Books, 1996); and Michael Sandel, *Liberalism and the Limits of Justice*, second edition (New York: Cambridge University Press, 1998).
23 Robert E. Watkins, "Politics In Medias Res: Power that Precedes and Exceeds in Burke and Foucault," *History of the Human Sciences* 23 (2) (2010), pp. 1–19.
24 Sean Penn, dir. and wr. *Into the Wild*, motion picture on DVD (USA: Paramount Vantage, 2007).
25 Tommy Lee Jones, dir. *The Three Burials of Melquiades Estrada*, motion picture on DVD (USA: Sony Pictures, 2006).
26 Brown, "American Nightmare."
27 Roger Ebert, "Reflections After 25 Years At the Movies," *Time*, April 12, 1992. Available at www.rogerebert.com/rogers-journal/reflections-after-25-years-at-the-movies, (accessed July 4, 2015).
28 Anne Norton, *95 Theses on Politics, Culture, and Method* (New Haven, CT: Yale University Press, 2004).
29 See Michael Rogin, *Ronald Reagan, the Movie* (Berkeley, CA: University of California Press, 1987).
30 George J. Church, "Go Ahead – Make My Day," *Time*, March 25, 1985. Available at http://content.time.com/time/magazine/article/0,9171,964091,00.html (accessed July 4, 2015).
31 Michael Rogin, "'Make My Day!': Spectacle as Amnesia in Imperial Politics," *Representations* 29 (Winter 1990), p. 103.
32 Norton, *95 Theses*, p. 8.
33 Ibid., p. 12.
34 Raymond Williams, "Culture is Ordinary," in Jim McGuigan (ed.), *Raymond Williams on Culture and Society: Essential Writings* (Thousand Oaks, CA: Sage Publications, 1958).
35 Norton, *95 Theses*.
36 Ibid., p. 2.
37 Samuel A. Chambers, "Cultural Politics and the Practice of Fugitive Theory," *Contemporary Political Theory* 5 (2006), pp. 9–32.
38 Samuel A. Chambers, *The Queer Politics of Television* (London: I.B.Tauris, 2009), p. 8.
39 Ibid., p. xiii.
40 Douglas Kellner, *Cultural Studies, Identity and Politics Between the Modern and the Postmodern* (New York: Routledge, 1995).
41 Douglas Kellner and Michael Ryan, *Camera Politica: The Politics and Ideology of Contemporary Hollywood Film* (Bloomington, IN: Indiana University Press, 1988).
42 See Terry K. Aladjem, *The Culture of Vengeance and the Fate of American Justice* (New York: Cambridge University Press, 2008).
43 Henry Giroux, "Breaking into the Movies: Pedagogy and the Politics of Film." *JAC* 21 (3) (2001), p. 595.
44 Ibid., p. 585.
45 Ibid., p. 588. I do, however, find Giroux's approach to be limited in one respect. As a political theorist, I part ways with him when it comes to the character and expectations of the public conversation that opens up with this kind of film analysis. Since Giroux is especially invested in developing what he calls a critical practice of public pedagogy, he

examines what films teach their audiences. To be sure, such teaching is not formal – or even conscious. Culture works more subtly than that, as he acknowledges. Still, he sees movies as affording "a pedagogical space for addressing how a society views itself and the public world of power, events, politics, and institutions" (Ibid., p. 591). As a public part of culture, movies do constitute a space in which a polity can reflect and interrogate itself, much as Greek tragedy did for ancient Athens. Giroux also pursues his pedagogical project with an eye toward educating students to be more literate and critical in their movie-viewing. While I agree that film, and media generally, demand new and better forms of literacy in democratic publics, I find cultural politics to be a more fruitful frame than pedagogy for thinking about the opportunities afforded by film's interventions in public discourse, setting up an expectation of contestation and openness without guarantees of learning.

46 See Oliver Stone and Zachary Sklar (eds), *JFK: The Book of the Film* (New York: Applause Books, 1992). See the following as representative examples of critical reaction (all reprinted in Stone and Sklar): John Margolis, "*JFK* Movie and Book Attempt to Rewrite History"; George Lardner Jr., "On the Set: Dallas in Wonderland"; George Lardner Jr., "Or Just a Sloppy Mess?"; Richard Zoglin, "More Shots in Dealey Plaza"; Robert Sam Anson, "The Shooting of JFK."
47 Frank Beaver, *Oliver Stone: Wakeup Cinema*, Twayne's Filmmakers Series (New York: Twayne Publishers, 1994), p. 161.
48 Robert Burgoyne, "Modernism and the Narrative of Nation in JFK," in Vivian Sobchack (ed.), *The Persistence of History* (New York: Routledge, 1996), p. 124.
49 Barbie Zelizer, *Covering the Body: The Kennedy Assassination, the Media, and the Shaping of Collective Memory* (Chicago: University of Chicago Press, 1992), p. 201.
50 Chambers, "Cultural Politics," p. 5.
51 Hayden White, "The Modernist Event," in Sobchack, *Persistence*, 1996.
52 Ibid., p. 18.
53 Bilge Ebiri, "A Creation Myth for the Sixties: Does Oliver Stone's *JFK* Still Hold Up?" *Vulture*, November 22, 2013. Available at www.vulture.com/2013/11/does-oliver-stone-jfk-still-hold-up.html (accessed 8 June 2015).
54 Included among the many articles that conveyed such arguments/sentiments are: Anthony Lewis, "*JFK*," *New York Times*, 9 January 9, 1992; Bernard Weinraub, "Valenti Calls 'J.F.K.' 'Hoax' and 'Smear,'" *New York Times*, 2 April 2, 1992 (about Motion Picture Association of America president Jack Valenti's condemnation of the movie); *Chicago Tribune*, "Editorial," December 26, 1991; Brent Staples, "History by Default: The Blame Transcends Oliver Stone," *New York Times*, 25 December, 1991; Kenneth Auchincloss, Ginny Carroll, and Maggie Malone, "Twisted History," *Newsweek*, December 23, 1991 – all reprinted in Stone and Sklar, *JFK*.
55 John Hanc, "Students Seek the Truth in the JFK Case," *New York Times*, December 26, 1991, in Stone and Sklar, *JFK*, p. 317.
56 Norton, *95 Theses*, p. 47.
57 Kellner and Ryan, *Camera Politica*, p. 95.
58 See James Monaco, *How to Read a Film*, revised edition (New York: Oxford University Press, 1981).

59 See Jefferson Morley, "The Political Rorschach Test," *Los Angeles Times*, December 8, 1991, in Stone and Sklar, *JFK* (New York: Applause Books, 1992), 231–4, where he writes: "In the spring of 1964, one-third of Americans believed Lee Harvey Oswald acted in concert with others. Within two years, the figure had doubled. Every poll taken over the last quarter century has shown between 60% and 80% of the public favoring a conspiratorial explanation."

60 For the *Washington Post* poll, see Auchincloss et al., "Twisted History," cited by Janet Staiger, "Cinematic Shots: The Narration of Violence," in Sobchack, *Persistence*; for the NBC poll results, see Zelizer, *Covering*, pp. 209, 264, n. 60.

Chapter 1

1 All these texts have the added ideological allure of being "true stories" of actual individuals striking out on their own, seemingly making them all the more compelling as model representations of critical individualism.
2 Mill, *On Liberty*, p. 67.
3 Karl Marx, *The Eighteenth Brumaire of Louis Bonaparte [1852]* (New York: International Publishers, 1963), p. 15.
4 Jodi Dean, "Introduction: The Interface of Political Theory and Cultural Studies," in Jodi Dean (ed.), *Cultural Studies and Political Theory* (Ithaca, NY: Cornell University Press, 2000), p. 4.
5 Nealon and Giroux, *Toolbox*, pp. 68–9.
6 Norton, *Signs*, p. 4.
7 Michel Foucault, "Truth and Power," in Colin Gordon (ed.), *Power/Knowledge: Selected Interviews and Other Writings, 1972–1977* (New York: Pantheon, 1980), pp. 109–33.
8 Peter Schjeldhal quoted in Sandford Schwartz, "An Eye on the Tremors." *New York Review of Books*, March 12, 2009, p. 33.
9 Norton, *Signs*, p. 1.
10 Sheldon Wolin, *Politics and Vision*, expanded edition (Princeton, NJ: Princeton University Press, 2004), p. 280.
11 Michel Foucault, "Truth and Power," in James D. Faubion (ed.), *Power* (New York: The New Press, 2000), pp. 111–33.
12 Foucault, "Concern for Self," p. 292.
13 Michel Foucault, "The Subject and Power," in James D. Faubion (ed.), *Power* (New York: The New Press, 2000), p. 343.
14 Mill, *On Liberty*, p. 57.
15 Anne Norton, "Liberalism's Leap of Faith," in Bonnie Honig and David R. Mapel (eds), *Skepticism, Individuality, and Freedom* (Minneapolis, MN: University of Minnesota Press, 2002), p. 234.
16 Mill, *On Liberty*, p. 54.
17 Ibid., pp. 56–7.
18 Norton, *Signs*, p. 159.
19 Ibid. Similarly but with different conceptual language, Samuel Chambers has written that "the philosophical problem of anthropocentrism remains intimately bound up with

the idea of a given subject that precedes language, and then comes to make use of it as a tool or object." See Samuel A. Chambers, *The Lessons of Rancière* (New York: Oxford University Press, 2013).

20 Mill, *On Liberty*, p. 67.
21 Richard E. Flathman, *Reflecitons of a Would-Be Anarchist: Ideals and Institutions of Liberalism* (Minneapolis, MN: University of Minnesota Press, 1998), p. 14.
22 Richard E. Flathman, *Willful Liberalism: Voluntarism and Individuality in Political Theory and Practice* (Ithaca, NY: Cornell University Press, 1992), p. 50.
23 Ibid., p. 14.
24 Flathman, *Reflections*, p. 15.
25 Watkins, "Politics In Medias Res."
26 Foucault, "Concern for Self," p. 291.
27 Ibid.
28 Judith Butler, *The Psychic Life of Power: Theories in Subjection* (Stanford, CA: Stanford University Press, 1997), p. 83.
29 Norton, *Signs*, p. 160.
30 Jon Krakauer, *Into the Wild* (New York: Anchor Books, 2007).
31 Ibid., p. 163.
32 Ibid., p. 189.
33 Norton, *Signs*, p. 4.
34 Mill, *On Liberty*, p. 67.
35 Ibid., p. 56.
36 Krakauer, *Into the Wild*, p. 23.
37 Norton, "Leap of Faith," p. 236.
38 Norton, *Signs*, p. 4.
39 Ibid.
40 Ibid., p. 3.
41 Penn, *Into the Wild*.
42 Ibid.
43 Thanks to Sam Chambers for pointing out this resonance.
44 Krakauer, *Into the Wild*, p. 111.
45 Ronald Beiner, "The Fetish of Individuality: Richard Flathman's Willfully Liberal Politics," in Honig and Mapel, *Skepticism*, p. 117.
46 After that unplanned trip to Mexico down the Colorado River, the film presents a scene of McCandless trying to re-enter the country even though he does not have a passport or any other proof of his identity or citizenship, since he burned the contents of his wallet at the start of his epic adventure. The film shows him being able to re-enter after a gentle warning from the immigration officer handling him. This is a rather striking indication of the privilege (chiefly racial) that McCandless enjoys, for if he were not white it is unlikely that he would have been admitted to the US without proper documentation. And yet, the film's characterization of him offers no suggestion that he was aware of such privilege, and, given his antipathy toward thinking about the complexity of social norms and cultural relations, it should not be surprising that he is unaware of his privilege.

47 Krakauer, *Into the Wild*, p. 174.
48 Ibid., p. 196.
49 Watkins, "Politics In Medias Res."
50 Edmund Burke, *Reflections on the French Revolution* [1790]. *Select Works of Edmund Burke: A New Imprint of the Payne Edition*, vol. 2 (Indianapolis, IN: Liberty Fund, 1999), p. 182.
51 Norton, "Leap of Faith," p. 237.
52 Ibid., p. 236.
53 Norton, *Signs*, p. 160.
54 Norton, "Leap of Faith," pp. 234–5.
55 Norton, *95 Theses*, pp. 63–4.
56 Judith Butler, "The Question of Social Transformation," in Judith Butler, *Undoing Gender* (New York: Routledge, 2004).
57 Krakauer, *Into the Wild*, p. 198.
58 Burke, *Reflections*, p. 122.
59 Norton, *95 Theses*, p. 55.
60 Michel Foucault, "Sex, Power, and the Politics of Identity," in Paul Rabinow (ed.), *Ethics: Subjectivity and Truth* (New York: The New Press, 1997), p. 167.
61 Norton, *Signs*, p. 174.

Chapter 2

1 Michael Oakeshott, "Introduction to Leviathan," in Michael Oakeshott, *Rationalism in Politics and Other Essays*, expanded edition (Indianapolis, IN: Liberty Fund, 1991), p. 225.
2 Judith Butler, *Giving an Account of Oneself* (New York: Fordham University Press, 2005), p. 35.
3 Judith Butler, *Precarious Life: The Powers of Mourning and Violence* (New York: Verso, 2004), pp. 19, 29.
4 Ibid., pp. 22–3.
5 Butler, *Account*, pp. 33, 75.
6 Butler, *Precarious Life*, p. xii.
7 Ibid., p. 20.
8 Ibid., p. 27.
9 Ibid., p. xiv.
10 Ibid., p. 23.
11 Ibid., p. 28.
12 Butler, *Account*, p. 64.
13 Butler, *Psychic*, p. 20.
14 Butler, "Interview."
15 Butler, *Psychic*, p. 20.
16 Ibid., p. 195.
17 Ibid.
18 Butler, *Precarious Life*, p. 20.

19 Butler, "Interview."
20 Butler, *Precarious Life*, p. 26.
21 Butler, *Account*, p. 75.
22 Butler, *Precarious Life*, pp. 19, 23, 29, 31; *Account*, pp. 33, 101.
23 Butler, *Precarious Life*, pp. 22–3.
24 Ibid., p. 27.
25 Wolin, *Politics*, p. 218.
26 Butler, *Precarious Life*, p. 30.
27 Ibid., p. 25.
28 See Butler, *Account*, pp. 77, 78–9.
29 See Butler, *Psychic*, pp. 2–6.
30 Butler, *Precarious Life*, p. 20.
31 Ibid., p. 31.
32 Stephen K. White, "As the World Turns: Ontology and Politics in Judith Butler," *Polity* 32 (Winter) 1999, pp. 155–77. Butler discusses her concept of the "desire to desire" in *The Psychic Life of Power* (1997), and in some ways the concept is similar to the positive potential entailed in that aspect of vulnerability understood as a kind of openness to enriching connection with others.
33 Judith Butler, "For a Careful Reading," in Seyla Benhabib, et al. (eds), *Feminist Contentions: A Philosophical Exchange* (New York: Routledge, 1995), p. 133.
34 Butler, *Precarious Life*, p. 43.
35 Ibid., p. 43.
36 Ibid., p. 29.
37 Ibid., p. xii.
38 Butler, "Interview."
39 The 1992 revisionist Western that Eastwood starred in and directed, *Unforgiven*, is often hailed as a sharp turning point in his long association with vengeance, extending from the famed 'Man-with-No-Name' in the Spaghetti Westerns to the infamous vigilante cop Dirty Harry. In 1994, one critic summarized Eastwood's career screen persona in this way: "In movie after movie, whether as a cowboy or as a police detective, whether acting within the law or as a vigilante, the Eastwood character used force with no compunction in order to ensure that the innocent were saved and the guilty punished." As key to his argument that Eastwood had "gone PC," the same critic cites *Unforgiven* as "a full-scale act of contrition, a repudiation and dismantling of the whole legendary, masculine character type of which, for this generation, Eastwood himself had become the leading icon" (see Richard Grenier, "Clint Eastwood Goes PC," *Commentary* 97 March 1994). Yet, despite its alleged revision of the Western mythology, in the end *Unforgiven* still delivers the vengeful goods to its audience. Consider that at the end of the film, Eastwood's character, William Munny, dispenses the long-awaited, murderous comeuppance to the menacing, tyrannical sheriff, played by Gene Hackman. However reluctantly Eastwood's character executes this act of vengeance, the audience still revels in the destruction of the villainous sheriff, as teasing, passive reluctance is finally overcome by the hero, making the film only a slight revision of the vigilante ethos that Eastwood had cultivated on screen for decades.

40 Early in the film, the adult Dave draws the suspicion of the audience by returning home from a bar late one night with bruised hands, blood on his clothes, and a wound in his abdomen – suspicious because this occurs on the same night as the murder of Jimmy's daughter, Katie. Dave tells his wife that someone tried to mug him and he fought back and may have killed the mugger. Later, in a rare moment of lucidity, Dave says "It makes you feel alone – hurting somebody." Dave's statement reveals the truth of violence as a betrayal of the very vulnerability that Butler identifies with our social existence. Thus – in contrast to Jimmy's deliberate, self-righteous vengeance – Dave's vengeance is figured as the impulsive response of a damaged man-child, and produces a belated recognition of vulnerability.
41 Butler, "Interview."
42 Ibid.
43 Ibid.
44 Butler, *Account*, p. 100.
45 Butler, *Precarious Life*, p. 30.
46 Butler, "Interview."
47 Butler, *Precarious Life*, p. 25.
48 Ibid., p. 20.
49 Butler, "Interview."
50 Contrast with Robert Kagan's near-mythical celebration of the US's hard-headed Hobbesian worldview of necessary dominance in contrast to Europe's naïve, Kantian view of paradisiacal interdependence. Butler's view resonates more with the Kantian vision of cosmopolitan interdependence, not as a symptom of weakness but as a recognition of the reality of a vulnerability that cannot be willed away or dominated (see Robert Kagan, *Of Paradise and Power: America and Europe in the New World Order* (New York: Knopf, 2003).
51 Butler, *Precarious Life*, p. 27.
52 Ibid., p. 48.
53 Adriana Cavarero, "Politicizing Theory," *Political Theory* 30, August 2002, p. 512.
54 Butler, *Precarious Life*, pp. 48–9.
55 Butler, *Account*, p. 33.
56 Butler, *Precarious Life*, p. 20.
57 Ibid., p. 45.
58 Ibid.

Chapter 3

1 Butler, *Frames*, p. 23.
2 Jim Kitses, *Horizons West* (Bloomington, IN: Indiana University Press, 1969), p. 11.
3 Robert Pippin, *Hollywood Westerns and American Myth* (New Haven, CT: Yale University Press, 2010), p. 141.
4 Jane Tompkins, *West of Everything: The Inner Life of Westerns* (New York: Oxford University Press, 1992), p. 27.
5 By subvert, I mean undermining from within rather than completely overthrowing or destroying, as Samuel Chambers suggests: "This conceptualisation of subversion calls

up the Latin etymology of the word, *subvertere* – to turn from below [...] On this account [...] the agency involved in a subversive act or a subversive reading appears from inside the system it attempts to overturn" (Chambers, *Queer Politics*, p. 107).
6 Jim Kitses, "Days of the Dead," *Sight & Sound*, 16 (April 2006), p. 14.
7 Ibid., p. 18.
8 In using the term "political ontology," I draw upon the work of Patchen Markell, who has argued for "an engaged, interpretive approach to ontological issues, which folds ontology back into history and practice rather than serving as its ground, and which stakes the persuasiveness of an ontological perspective on its capacity to illuminate a range of different concrete circumstances" (Patchen Markell, "Ontology, Recognition, and Politics: A Reply," *Polity* 38 (1), 2006, p. 30.
9 Butler, *Precarious Life*, p. 26.
10 In *Precarious Life*, Judith Butler argues that rather than being "privatizing," grief "furnishes a sense of political community of a complex order, and it does this first of all by bringing to the fore the relational ties that have implications for theorizing fundamental dependency and ethical responsibility." (Ibid., p. 22.)
11 See Butler, *Frames*.
12 Markell, *Bound*, p. 5.
13 Hannah Arendt, quoted in Ibid., p. 13.
14 David Lusted, *The Western* (London: Pearson, 2003), p. 261.
15 Philip French, Review of *The Three Burials of Melquiades Estrada*, *Observer*, 2 April, 2006.
16 Lee Clark Mitchell, *Westerns: Making the Man in Fiction and Film* (Chicago: University of Chicago Press, 1996), p. 226.
17 Markell, *Bound*, p. 180.
18 Ibid, p. 11.
19 Ibid., p. 12.
20 Markell, *Bound*, p. 180.
21 Ibid., p. 63.
22 Frederic Jameson, quoted in Mitchell, *Westerns*, p. 20.
23 Kitses, "Days," p. 14.
24 Markell, *Bound*, p. 10.
25 Kitses, "Days," p. 17.
26 Ibid., p. 17.
27 Markell, *Bound*, p. 14.
28 Kitses, "Days," p. 18.
29 Markell, *Bound*, p. 14.
30 Ibid., p. 180.
31 Ibid., p. 181.
32 Tompkins, *Everything*, p. 228.
33 Butler, *Frames*, p. 14.
34 Butler, *Precarious Life*, p. 32.
35 Butler, *Frames*, p. 38.
36 Ibid., p. 1.

37 Markell, *Bound*, p. 5.
38 Butler, *Frames*, p. 42.
39 Ibid., p. 44.
40 Ibid.
41 Ibid.
42 Butler, *Precarious Life*, p. 26.
43 Butler, *Frames*, p. 3.
44 Ibid., p. 52.
45 Butler, *Precarious Life*, p. 26.
46 Butler, *Frames*, p. 15.
47 Tompkins, *Everything*, p. 45.
48 Butler, *Frames*, p. 14.
49 Ibid., p. 43.
50 Ibid., p. 23.

Chapter 4

1 Lauren Berlant, *Cruel Optimism* (Durham, N.C.: Duke University Press, 2011).
2 Steven Cohan and Ina Rae Hark (eds), *The Road Movie Book* (New York: Routledge, 1997), p. 1.
3 Berlant, *Optimism*, p. 4.
4 Ibid., p. 201.
5 Ibid., p. 10.
6 Berlant does, however, mention the director of *Wendy and Lucy*, Kelly Reichardt, and the director of *Winter's Bone*, Debra Granik, as being among "other writer-directors of this heavily atmospheric witnessing mode of contemporary capitalist fraying" that is characteristic of the cinema of precarity. See Lauren Berlant, "Nearly Utopian, Nearly Normal: Post-Fordist Affect in *La Promesse* and *Rosetta*," *Public Culture* 19, 2 (2007), p. 295 n. 30.
7 Cf. Patchen Markell's account of political ontology: "This is an engaged, interpretive approach to ontological issues, which folds ontology back into history and practice rather than serving as ground" (Markell, "Ontology," p. 30). Part of what I take this to mean is that political ontology names those conditions or circumstances in which politics takes place, and if these conditions are folded back into history and practice rather than grounding them, then the ambiguity of the circumstance, the ambivalence of the condition is essential to making the ontology political. In other words, the political character of ontology derives from the way in which actions are conditioned but not determined by unchosen circumstances – and not merely in whether or not the ontology is recognized, acknowledged, or apprehended but rather in leaving open alternate possibilities for action, attachment v. injury, violence v. non-violence.
8 Nicholas Ridout and Rebecca Schneider, "Precarity and Performance," *TDR: The Drama Review*, vol. 56, no. 4 (2012), pp. 5–9.
9 Berlant, *Optimism*, p. 192.

10 Andrew Ross, *Nice Work if You Can Get It: Life and Labor in Precarious Times* (New York: New York University Press, 2009), p. 34.
11 Rob Horning, "Precarity and 'affective resistance'," Marginal Utility blog, The New Inquiry website, February 14, 2012. Available at http://thenewinquiry.com/blogs/marginal-utility/precarity-and-affective-resistance/ (accessed 14 June 2015).
12 Wendy Brown, *Edgework* (Princeton, NJ: Princeton University Press, 2005), p. 42.
13 Mill, *On Liberty*, p. 56.
14 Brown, *Edgework*, pp. 42–3.
15 Brett Neilson and Ned Rossiter, "From Precarity to Precariousness and Back Again: Labour, Life and Unstable Networks," *Fibreculture Journal* 5 (2005). Available at http://five.fibreculturejournal.org/fcj-022-from-precarity-to-precariousness-and-back-again-labour-life-and-unstable-networks/ (accessed 14 June 2015).
16 It is not, however, yet true in a political sense in terms of class politics. While some have come to use the term "precariat," a neologism combining precarity and proletariat to describe (or try to bring into being) the collective class of precarious workers in contemporary capitalism, I want to resist that usage here, chiefly because I do not find these films making claims for the existence of a coherent precarious class, but also because precariat names more of an aspiration than reality at this point.
17 Note that Reichardt, in her interview with Gus Van Sant in *Bomb*, as well as Rick Groen in the *Globe and Mail*, and Jonathan Raban in the *New York Review of Books* all describe Wendy's situation as a "predicament." See Gus Van Sant, "Kelly Reichardt," *Bomb* 105, 2008 (available at http://bombsite.com/issues/105/articles/3182 [accessed 14 June 2015]); Rick Groen, "Why We Should Care about Wendy, and All the Wendys," review in the *Globe and Mail*, February 5, 2009 (available at www.theglobeandmail.com/arts/why-we-should-care-about-wendy-and-all-the-wendys/article1148540/ [accessed 14 June 2015]); and Jonathan Raban, "Metronatural America," *New York Review of Books*, March 26, 2009.
18 Van Sant, "Kelly Reichardt."
19 Groen, "Why We Should."
20 Berlant, *Optimism*, p. 10.
21 Ibid., p. 196.
22 *Wendy and Lucy* is not as pronounced as some films in its "slowness," for on average the length of shots is not excessively long. Rather, the "slowness" of *Wendy and Lucy* lies more in its observational mood, and it does share many of the characteristics of slow film that Sukhdev Sandhu describes: films considered slow cinema "opt for ambient noises or field recordings rather than bombastic sound design, embrace subdued visual schemes that require the viewer's eye to do more work, and evoke a sense of mystery that springs from the landscapes and local customs they depict more than it does from generic convention." Sukhdev Sandhu, "'Slow Cinema' Fights Back Against Bourne's Supremacy," *Guardian*, 9 March, 2012. Available at www.guardian.co.uk/film/2012/mar/09/slow-cinema-fights-bournes-supremacy (accessed 14 June 2015).
23 In fact, at the very start of the film in a touch of foreshadowing, the audience's first sight of Wendy is of her walking in the woods, whistling to herself and calling after Lucy.

24 The camera even reverses the usual left-to-right tracking in times of heightened anxiety and stress for Wendy, such as when she's walking back to the petrol station after being verbally accosted by a homeless man at night in the woods as she's trying to sleep. (Thanks to Mitch Arnold for pointing out this reverse tracking.)

25 As Zack Furness notes, "The automobile resides at the core of the post-World War II American dream and it functions as both the literal and symbolic centrepiece of a narrative equating individual mobility with personal freedom." But the automobile is not without its ideological contradictions as an expression of freedom: "Even in its earliest uses, the term automobility refers less to a form of transportation than an ideologically and symbolically loaded cultural phenomenon." See Zack Furness, *One Less Car: Bicycling and the Politics of Automobility* (Philadelphia, PA: Temple University Press, 2010), pp. 8 and 6 respectively.

26 His name is never revealed to the audience, and even in the film's end credits he is simply identified as "Security Guard."

27 Berlant, *Optimism*, p. 199.

28 Ibid., p. 8.

29 Interestingly, one prominent way in which the social imagery of "staying afloat" or "going under water" has penetrated US public consciousness of late is through the housing crisis. And in a move that bridges the personal and structural once more, what more "ordinary crisis" is there than the housing crisis?

30 Berlant, *Optimism*, p. 3.

31 Ibid., p. 10.

32 It is a striking commentary on precarity to contrast the meaning of Alaska in *Wendy and Lucy* with the symbolism of Alaska for Chris McCandless in the film *Into the Wild*. Whereas for McCandless, Alaska represents a space of total freedom from artificial society through immersion in a pure nature, *Wendy and Lucy* emplots Alaska in a very different narrative about the last frontier. For Wendy the goal is just economic survival, whereas for McCandless the goal is purely psychological and spiritual.

33 Ridout and Schneider, "Precarity," p. 5.

34 Mark Fisher, "Precarious Dystopias: *The Hunger Games*, *In Time*, and *Never Let Me Go*," *Film Quarterly*, vol. 65, no. 4 (2012), p. 33.

35 Thanks to Smita Rahman for pointing out the possible suggestion of stability in a "perpetual present," in contrast to a rapidly disappearing present vanishing into an uncertain and insecure future.

36 Berlant, *Optimism*, p. 196.

37 Van Sant, "Kelly Reichardt."

38 Wendy is caught by a teenage do-gooder of a stock clerk, who gives voice to the naïve ideology of personal responsibility: "If a person can't afford dog food, they shouldn't have a dog." Further, when he tries to explain to his manager in front of Wendy why they should call the police on her, he gives voice to a naïve liberalism stripped of power: "the rules apply to everyone equally […] Food is not the issue. It's about setting an example."

39 Berlant, *Optimism*, p. 192.

40 Cf. "Conditions do not 'act' in the way that individual agents do, but no agent acts without them. They are presupposed in what we do, but it would be a mistake to personify them as if they acted in place of us" (Butler, *Precarious Life*, p. 11).
41 Kelly Reichardt, quoted in Laura Winters, "'Wendy and Lucy' Filmmaker Kelly Reichardt Eyes the Frayed Edge of Social Fabric," *Washington Post*, 25 January, 2009. Available at http://www.washingtonpost.com/wp-dyn/content/article/2009/01/23/AR2009012300851.html (accessed 14 June 2015).
42 Berlant, *Optimism*, p. 201.
43 There is no trace of the moral revelation, victimization, or even pathos that characterize the "melodramatic mode." See Linda Williams, "Melodrama Revised," in Nick Browne (ed.), *Refiguring American Film Genres: History and Theory* (Berkeley, CA: University of California Press, 1998), pp. 42–88.
44 Wendy is taken away to jail by the police in a squad car, while Lucy remains tied to bike rack in front of the grocery store. When Wendy gets out of jail by paying a $50 fine hours later, Lucy is no longer where she left her.
45 During her second night in town without her car, Wendy beds down in the woods after looking for Lucy there. Later in the night, she's awakened by a man searching through her things. He proceeds to rant and ramble about the attitude of the people in town and how he hates them. He seems perhaps mentally ill and possibly dangerous, but he does not harm Wendy. She is very scared though, and once he leaves, she immediately walks, and walks and walks back to the petrol-station bathroom that she has used before to find refuge. This is a key instance where the camera tracks her right to left, indicating her stress.
46 It is not clear what Holly's relationship to him is.
47 In keeping with the reticence of precarity cinema as well as the features of slow cinema, her humming of this tune is the only music in the film.
48 Kelly Reichardt, quoted in Winters, "'Wendy and Lucy' Filmmaker."
49 Ibid.
50 Brown, *Edgework*, p. 44.

Chapter 5

1 Burke, *Reflections*, p. 3.
2 Erin Trahan, "Telling a Backwoods Tale with Chilling Accuracy," *Boston Globe*, 13 June 2010. Available at www.boston.com/ae/movies/articles/2010/06/13/winters_bone_director_strived_for_authenticity_in_cast_script_set/?page=full (accessed 15 June 2015).
3 Chambers, *Queer Politics*.
4 See Chambers' chapter on *Buffy the Vampire Slayer* in *Queer Politics* for an illuminating discussion of how that show participates in the politics of family, de-centring the traditional "sanguinuptial" family and positing a radically different form of family. By contrast, my concern here is not with the various possible forms that family can take, but rather with what the politics of a subject's negotiation among families looks like under severe economic conditions. My analysis takes Ree's family as it is, traditional but broken, in order to examine the politics of her subjectivity as situated in, and formed by, family.

5 Chambers, *Queer Politics*, p. 156.
6 Kennan Ferguson, *All in the Family: On Community and Incommensurability* (Durham, NC: Duke University Press, 2012), p. 7.
7 Ibid., p. 10.
8 Ibid.
9 Kennan Ferguson, "Reply to Dean's Review of All in the Family: On Community and Incommensurability," *Contemporary Political Theory* 13, no. 3 (2014), p. 314.
10 Ferguson, *All in the Family*, p. 7.
11 Many thanks go to Elizabeth Haas for pointing out Ree's relationship to multiple families.
12 Ty Burr, Review of *Winter's Bone*, Boston Globe. 18 June 2010. Available at www.boston.com/ae/movies/articles/2010/06/18/on_quest_to_find_her_father_mountain_girl_is_tower_of_strength_in_winters_bone/ (accessed 16 June 2015).
13 See Butler, *Undoing Gender*, pp. 217ff.
14 Burke, *Reflections*, p. 122.
15 David Bromwich, *A Choice of Inheritance* (Cambridge, MA: Harvard University Press, 1989).
16 Ibid., p. i.
17 Watkins, "Politics In Medias Res."
18 Stephen K. White, *Edmund Burke: Modernity, Politics, and Aesthetics*, New Edition (Lanham, MD: Rowman & Littlefield, 2002), p. 6.
19 Burke, *Reflections*, p. 193.
20 Uday Mehta, *Liberalism and Empire: A Study in Nineteenth Century British Liberal Thought* (Chicago: University of Chicago Press, 1999), p. 148.
21 Burke, *Reflections*, p. 122.
22 White, *Edmund Burke*, p. 55.
23 Note that Berlant's approach to the family in *Cruel Optimism* departs from Ferguson's in *All in the Family*, though not perhaps as much as it may appear at first glance. While Berlant examines the social forces and economic pressures that shape the affective environment in which the "tattered family" struggles to survive these days, Ferguson, in a recent critical exchange with Jodi Dean on his book, seems to eschew forces external to families. For instance, he characterizes his disagreement with Dean in this way: "Another way to conceptualize Dean's disagreement with me might be: whereas Dean holds that politics should (and does) determine the framework of everyday life, I hold that everyday life should (and does) determine the political" (Ferguson, "Dean's Review," p. 315). Further, he writes, "Whereas in the first model, the family forms either a refuge from politics or an effect of power, in the second the family comprises the location where we first, and most strongly, strive for attachment and independence, collectivity and self-expression." (Ibid., p. 314). This dichotomy is too restrictive, and it seems to overlook the interrelations between families and larger social, political, and economic contexts. For example, we can instead read Ree's choice of inheritance as a response that not only is shaped by crisis but also itself reshapes crisis, in that she does not respond in ways typical of, or normative for, her context – either fleeing her family for the army or falling in with the easy money of the drug trade. Further, the film does not present Ree

as a paragon of moral virtue but rather as very ordinary subject of desires and norms, even though she is remarkably strong and resolute. To his credit, Ferguson even goes on to note later that we ought not "neglect how macropolitics forms and constrains" (Ibid., p. 315). And he is much closer than most commentators to someone like Berlant in viewing politics "located across registers of interpersonality, theology, affect, tradition, judgment and care" (Ibid., p. 314). Still, though his book attends well enough to the way in which affect and norms form bridges between structures and agency, this defence by Ferguson underplays the significant interaction between families and contexts.
24 Berlant, *Optimism*, p. 168.
25 Ibid., p. 19.
26 Ibid., p. 169.
27 Ibid.
28 Ibid., p. 166.
29 Butler, *Frames*, p. 14.
30 Wendy Brown, *States of Injury* (Princeton, NJ: Princeton University Press, 1995), pp. 22–3.

Conclusion

1 Butler, "Interview," p. 53.
2 Jean-Marc Vallée, dir. *Wild*, motion picture on DVD (USA: 20th Century Fox 2015).
3 Jack Turner, *Awakening to Race: Individualism and Social Consciousness in America* (Chicago: University of Chicago Press, 2012), p. 25.
4 As a telling example, recall the attention and controversy in 2012 when President Obama criticized the notion of self-made wealth. In a speech in Roanoke, Virginia during his campaign for a second term, Obama said, "If you were successful, somebody along the line gave you some help. There was a great teacher somewhere in your life. Somebody helped to create this unbelievable American system that we have that allowed you to thrive. Somebody invested in roads and bridges. If you've got a business, you didn't build that. Somebody else made that happen" (quoted in Aaron Blake, "Obama's 'You Didn't Build That' Problem," *Washington Post*. June 18, 2012. Available at http://www.washingtonpost.com/blogs/the-fix/post/obamas-you-didnt-build-that-problem/2012/07/18/gJQAJxyotW_blog.html [accessed June 22, 2015]). The President was rhetorically echoing a criticism launched a few months earlier by Elizabeth Warren during her campaign for the US Senate from Massachusetts. To a small group of supporters, she said very directly, "There is nobody in this country who got rich on his own. Nobody" (quoted in Lucy Madison, "Elizabeth Warren: 'There is Nobody in This Country Who Got Rich on His Own,'" CBS News, September 22, 2011. Available at www.cbsnews.com/news/elizabeth-warren-there-is-nobody-in-this-country-who-got-rich-on-his-own/ [accessed 22 June 2015]).
5 See Norton, *95 Theses*, p. 47.
6 Butler, *Frames*, pp. 2–3.

7 I see such a politics of subjectivity as complementing the politics of norms that Samuel Chambers identifies as a challenge to the politics of identity and representation in his study of "queer television." See Chambers, *Queer Politics*.
8 Ryan Coogler, dir. and wr. *Fruitvale Station*, motion picture on DVD (USA: Weinstein Company, 2013).
9 Butler, *Frames*, pp. 31–2.
10 Ryan Coogler quoted in Joe Rhodes, "A Man's Death, A Career's Birth," *New York Times*, 23 June 2013. Available at www.nytimes.com/2013/06/30/movies/a-bay-area-killing-inspires-fruitvale-station.html?ref=movies&_r=0 (accessed 22 June 2015).
11 See George Yancey and Judith Butler, "What's Wrong with 'All Lives Matter'?" *New York Times*, Opinionator blog, January 13, 2015.
12 Judith Butler quoted in Ibid.
13 Ibid.
14 Markell, *Bound*, p. 5.
15 Butler, *Frames*, pp. 2–3.

Bibliography

Aladjem, Terry K. *The Culture of Vengeance and the Fate of American Justice* (New York: Cambridge University Press, 2008).
Albert, Michael, "JFK and US," *Z Magazine*, February 1992. In Stone and Sklar, *JFK: The Book of the Film*.
Anson, Robert Sam, "The Shooting of JFK," *Esquire*, November 1991. In Stone and Sklar, *JFK: The Book of the Film*.
Arendt, Hannah, *The Human Condition* (Chicago: University of Chicago Press, 1958).
Auchincloss, Kenneth, Ginny Carroll, and Maggie Malone, "Twisted History," *Newsweek*, December 23, 1991.
Beaver, Frank, *Oliver Stone: Wakeup Cinema*, Twayne's Filmmakers Series (New York: Twayne Publishers, 1994).
Beiner, Ronald, "The Fetish of Individuality: Richard Flathman's Willfully Liberal Politics," in Bonnie Honig and David R. Mapel (eds), *Skepticism, Individuality, and Freedom* (Minneapolis, MN: University of Minnesota Press, 2002), pp. 111–26.
Berardi, Franco, *Precarious Rhapsody: Semiocapitalism and the Pathologies of the Post-alpha Generation* (London: Minor Compositions, 2009).
Berlant, Lauren, *Cruel Optimism* (Durham, NC: Duke University Press, 2011).
——"Nearly Utopian, Nearly Normal: Post-Fordist Affect in *La Promesse* and *Rosetta*," *Public Culture* 19, 2 (2007), pp. 273–301.
Blake, Aaron, "Obama's 'You Didn't Build That' Problem," *Washington Post*, June 18, 2012. Available at http://www.washingtonpost.com/blogs/the-fix/post/obamas-you-didnt-build-that-problem/2012/07/18/gJQAJxyotW_blog.html (accessed 22 June, 2015).
Bromwich, David, *A Choice of Inheritance* (Cambridge, MA: Harvard University Press, 1989).
Brown, Wendy, *States of Injury* (Princeton, NJ: Princeton University Press, 1995).
——*Edgework* (Princeton, NJ: Princeton University Press, 2005).
——"American Nightmare: Neoliberalism, Neoconservatism, and Democracy," *Political Theory* 34:6 (2006), pp. 690–714.
Burgoyne, Robert, "Modernism and the Narrative of Nation in *JFK*," in Vivian Sobchack (ed.), *The Persistence of History* (New York: Routledge, 1996).
Burke, Edmund, *Reflections on the French Revolution* [1790]. *Select Works of Edmund Burke: A New Imprint of the Payne Edition*, vol. 2 (Indianapolis, IN: Liberty Fund, 1999).
Burr, Ty, Review of *Winter's Bone*, *Boston Globe*. June 18, 2010. Available at www.boston.com/ae/movies/articles/2010/06/18/on_quest_to_find_her_father_mountain_girl_is_tower_of_strength_in_winters_bone/ (accessed 16 June, 2015).
Butler, Judith, "For a Careful Reading," in Seyla Benhabib et. al. (eds), *Feminist Contentions: A Philosophical Exchange* (New York: Routledge, 1995).

Bibliography

——*The Psychic Life of Power: Theories in Subjection* (Stanford, CA: Stanford University Press, 1997).
——"Interview with Judith Butler," *Believer*, May 2003.
——*Precarious Life: The Powers of Mourning and Violence* (New York: Verso, 2004).
——"The Question of Social Transformation," in Judith Butler, *Undoing Gender*.
——*Undoing Gender* (New York: Routledge, 2004).
——*Giving an Account of Oneself* (New York: Fordham University Press, 2005).
——*Frames of War* (New York: Verso, 2009).
Cavarero, Adriana, "Politicizing Theory," *Political Theory* 30 (August 2002), pp. 506–32.
Chambers, Samuel A. 2006. "Cultural Politics and the Practice of Fugitive Theory," *Contemporary Political Theory* 5 (2006): 9–32.
—— *The Queer Politics of Television* (London: I.B.Tauris, 2009).
—— *The Lessons of Rancière* (New York: Oxford University Press, 2013).
Chicago Tribune "Editorial." December 26, 1991. In Stone and Sklar, *JFK: The Book of the Film*.
Cohan, Steven and Ina Rae Hark (eds), *The Road Movie Book* (New York: Routledge, 1997).
Coogler, Ryan, dir. and wr. *Fruitvale Station*, motion picure on DVD (USA: Weinstein Company, 2013).
de Tocqueville, Alexis, *Democracy in America* [1835/1840] trans. George Lawrence (New York: Perennial Classics, 1988).
Dean, Jodi "Introduction: The Interface of Political Theory and Cultural Studies," in Jodi Dean (ed.), *Cultural Studies and Political Theory* (Ithaca, NY: Cornell University Press, 2000).
Deleuze, Gilles, *Empiricism and Subjectivity: An Essay on Hume's Theory of Human Nature*, translated and introduced by Constantin V. Boundas (New York: Columbia University Press, 1991).
Eastwood, Clint, dir. *Mystic River*, motion picture on DVD (USA: Warner Bros, 2003).
Ebert, Roger, "Reflections After 25 Years At the Movies," *Time*, April 12, 1992. Available at www.rogerebert.com/rogers-journal/reflections-after-25-years-at-the-movies (accessed July 4, 2015)
Ebiri, Bilge, "A Creation Myth for the Sixties: Does Oliver Stone's *JFK* Still Hold Up?" *Vulture*, November 22, 2013. Available at www.vulture.com/2013/11/does-oliver-stone-jfk-still-hold-up.html (accessed June 8, 2015).
Etzioni, Amitai, *The New Golden Rule: Community and Morality in a Democratic Society* (New York: Basic Books, 1996).
Ferguson, Kennan, *All in the Family: On Community and Incommensurability* (Durham, NC: Duke University Press, 2012).
——"Reply to Dean's Review of *All in the Family: On Community and Incommensurability*," *Contemporary Political Theory* 13, no. 3 (2014), pp. 312–16.
Fisher, Mark, "Precarious Dystopias: *The Hunger Games*, *In Time*, and *Never Let Me Go*," *Film Quarterly*, vol. 65, no. 4 (2012), pp. 27–33.
Flathman, R.E., *Willful Liberalism: Voluntarism and Individuality in Political Theory and Practice* (Ithaca, NY: Cornell University Press, 1992).

Bibliography

——*Reflections of a Would-Be Anarchist: Ideals and Institutions of Liberalism* (Minneapolis, MN: University of Minnesota Press, 1998).

Foucault, Michel, "The History of Sexuality," in Colin Gordon (ed.), *Power/Knowledge: Selected Interviews and Other Writings, 1972–1977* (New York: Pantheon, 1980), pp. 183–93.

——"Truth and Power," in Gordon, *Power/Knowledge*, pp. 109–33.

——"Sex, Power, and the Politics of Identity," in Paul Rabinow (ed.), *Ethics: Subjectivity and Truth* (New York: The New Press, 1997), pp. 163–74.

——"The Ethics of the Concern for Self as a Practice of Freedom," in Rabinow, *Ethics*, pp. 281–301.

——"The Subject and Power," in James D. Faubion (ed.), *Power* (New York: The New Press, 2000), pp. 326–48.

——"Truth and Power," in Faubion, *Power*, pp. 111–33.

French, Philip, Review of *The Three Burials of Melquiades Estrada*, *Observer*, 2 April, 2006.

Furness, Zack, *One Less Car: Bicycling and the Politics of Automobility* (Philadelphia, PA: Temple University Press, 2010).

Gardels, Nathan and Leila Conners, "Splinters to the Brain," *New Perspectives Quarterly* 9 (Spring 1992).

Gilbert, Elizabeth, *The Last American Man* (New York: Penguin, 2002).

Giroux, Henry, "Breaking into the Movies: Pedagogy and the Politics of Film," *JAC* 21 (3) (2001), pp. 583–98.

Gitlin, Todd, "The Stoning of Oliver," *Image Magazine, San Francisco Examiner*, February 16, 1992. In Stone and Sklar, *JFK: The Book of the Film*.

Gramsci, Antonio, *Selections from the Prison Notebooks*, edited and translated by Quentin Hoare and Geoffrey Nowell Smith (New York: International Publishers, 1971).

Granik, Debra, dir. & wr. *Winter's Bone*, motion picture on DVD (USA: Lionsgate, 2010).

Green, Philip, "Hunkered in the Bunker," *Nation*, May 18, 1992. In Stone and Sklar, *JFK: The Book of the Film*.

Grenier, Richard, "Clint Eastwood Goes PC," *Commentary* 97 (March 1994).

Groen, Rick, "Why We Should Care about Wendy, and All the Wendys," review in the *Globe and Mail*, 5 February, 2009. Available at www.theglobeandmail.com/arts/why-we-should-care-about-wendy-and-all-the-wendys/article1148540/ (accessed June 14, 2015).

Hanc, John, "Students Seek the Truth in the JFK Case," *New York Times*, December 26, 1991. In Stone and Sklar, *JFK: The Book of the Film*.

Hayden, Tom, "Shadows on the American Storybook," *Los Angeles Times*, January 8, 1992. In Stone and Sklar, *JFK: The Book of the Film*.

Herman, Edward S. and Noam Chomsky, *Manufacturing Consent: The Political Economy of the Mass Media* (New York: Pantheon Books, 1988).

Horning, Rob, "Precarity and 'affective resistance,'" Marginal Utility Blog, The New Inquiry website, 14 February, 2012. Available at http://thenewinquiry.com/blogs/marginal-utility/precarity-and-affective-resistance/ (accessed June 14, 2015).

Jones, Tommy Lee, dir. *The Three Burials of Melquiades Estrada*, motion picture on DVD (USA: Sony Pictures, 2006).

Bibliography

Kagan, Robert, *Of Paradise and Power: America and Europe in the New World Order* (New York: Knopf, 2003).

Katz, Bob, "*JFK*: Is History That Which Gets Broadcast the Loudest?" *Chicago Tribune*, 20 December, 1991. In Stone and Sklar, *JFK: The Book of the Film*.

Kellner, Douglas, *Cultural Studies, Identity and Politics Between the Modern and the Postmodern* (New York: Routledge, 1995).

——and Michael Ryan, *Camera Politica: The Politics and Ideology of Contemporary Hollywood Film* (Bloomington, IN: Indiana University Press, 1988).

Kitses, Jim, *Horizons West* (Bloomington, IN: Indiana University Press, 1969).

——"Days of the Dead," *Sight & Sound* 16 (April 2006), pp. 14–18.

Krakauer, Jon, *Into the Wild* (New York: Anchor Books, 2007).

Laclau, Ernesto and Chantal Mouffe, *Hegemony and Socialist Strategy: Towards a Radical Democratic Politics* (New York: Verso, 1985).

Lardner Jr., George, "On the Set: Dallas in Wonderland," *Washington Post*, May 19, 1991. In Stone and Sklar, *JFK: The Book of the Film*.

——"Or Just a Sloppy Mess?" *Washington Post*, June 2, 1991. In Stone and Sklar, *JFK: The Book of the Film*.

Lewis, Anthony, "*JFK*," *New York Times*, January 9, 1992. In Stone and Sklar, *JFK: The Book of the Film*.

Lilla, Mark, "The Tea Party Jacobins," *New York Review of Books*, May 27, 2010.

Lusted, David, *The Western* (London: Pearson, 2003).

Lustick, Ian S., *Unsettled States, Disputed Lands: Britain and Ireland, France and Algeria, Israel and the West Bank-Gaza* (Ithaca, NY: Cornell University Press, 1993).

Mackey-Kallis, Susan, *Oliver Stone's America: "Dreaming the Myth Outward,"* (Boulder, CO: Westview Press, 1996).

Madison, Lucy, "Elizabeth Warren: 'There is Nobody in This Country Who Got Rich on His Own,'" CBS News, 22 September, 2011. Available at www.cbsnews.com/news/elizabeth-warren-there-is-nobody-in-this-country-who-got-rich-on-his-own/ (accessed June 22, 2015).

Margolis, John, "*JFK* Movie and Book Attempt to Rewrite History," *Dallas Morning News*, May 14, 1991. In Stone and Sklar, *JFK: The Book of the Film*.

Markell, Patchen, *Bound by Recognition* (Princeton, NJ: Princeton University Press, 2003).

——"Ontology, Recognition, and Politics: A Reply," *Polity* 38 (1) (2006), pp. 28–39.

Marx, Karl, *The Eighteenth Brumaire of Louis Bonaparte [1852]* (New York: International Publishers, 1963).

Mehta, Uday, *Liberalism and Empire: A Study in Nineteenth Century British Liberal Thought* (Chicago: University of Chicago Press, 1999).

Mill, John Stuart, *On Liberty* [1859] (Indianapolis, IN: Hackett, 1978).

Mitchell, Lee Clark, *Westerns: Making the Man in Fiction and Film* (Chicago: University of Chicago Press, 1996).

Monaco, James, *How to Read a Film*, revised edition (New York: Oxford University Press, 1981).

Morley, Jefferson, "The Political Rorschach Test," *Los Angeles Times*, 8 December, 1991. In Oliver Stone and Zachary Sklar, *JFK: The Book of the Film*, pp. 231–4.

Bibliography

Nealon, Jeffrey and Susan Searls Giroux, *The Theory Toolbox: Critical Concepts for the Humanities, Arts, and Social Sciences* (Lanham, MD: Rowman & Littlefield, 2003).

Neilson, Brett and Ned Rossiter, "From Precarity to Precariousness and Back Again: Labour, Life and Unstable Networks," *Fibreculture Journal* 5 (2005). Available at http://five.fibreculturejournal.org/fcj-022-from-precarity-to-precariousness-and-back-again-labour-life-and-unstable-networks/ (accessed June 14, 2015).

Norton, Anne, *Republic of Signs: Liberal Theory and American Popular Culture* (Chicago: University of Chicago Press, 1993).

——"Liberalism's Leap of Faith," in Bonnie Honig and David R. Mapel (eds), *Skepticism, Individuality, and Freedom* (Minneapolis, MN: University of Minnesota Press, 2002), pp. 231–43.

——*95 Theses on Politics, Culture, and Method* (New Haven: Yale University Press, 2004).

Oakeshott, Michael, "Introduction to *Leviathan*," in Michael Oakeshott, *Rationalism in Politics and Other Essays*, expanded edition (Foreword by Timothy Fuller) (Indianapolis, IN: Liberty Fund. 1991).

O'Byrne, James, "The Garrison Probe: The Story Hollywood Won't Tell," *Times-Picayune*, December 15, 1991. In Stone and Sklar, *JFK: The Book of the Film*.

O'Hehir, Andrew, "*JFK*: Tragedy into Farce," *San Francisco Weekly*, December 18, 1991. In Stone and Sklar, *JFK: The Book of the Film*.

Panagia, Davide, "Why Film Matters to Political Theory," *Contemporary Political Theory* 12 (1) (2013), pp. 2–25.

Parenti, Michael, "Morte D'Arthur," *Nation*, March 9, 1992. In Stone and Sklar, *JFK: The Book of the Film*.

——*Dirty Truths: Reflections on Politics, Media, Ideology, Conspiracy, Ethnic Life, and Class Power* (San Francisco, CA: City Lights Books, 1996).

Penn, Sean, dir & wr. *Into the Wild*, motion picture on DVD (USA: Paramount Vantage, 2006).

Pippin, Robert, *Hollywood Westerns and American Myth* (New Haven, CT: Yale University Press, 2010).

Raban, Jonathan, "Metronatural America," *New York Review of Books*, March 26, 2009.

Rancière, Jacques, *The Politics of Aesthetics: The Distribution of the Sensible*, translated by Gabriel Rockhill (New York: Continuum, 2004).

Reichardt, Kelly, dir. *Wendy and Lucy*, motion picture on DVD (USA: Oscilloscope, 2008).

Rhodes, Joe, "A Man's Death, A Career's Birth," *New York Times*, June 23, 2013. Available at www.nytimes.com/2013/06/30/movies/a-bay-area-killing-inspires-fruitvale-station.html?ref=movies&_r=0 (accessed June 22, 2015).

Ridout, Nicholas and Rebecca Schneider, "Precarity and Performance," *TDR: The Drama Review*, vol. 56, no. 4 (2012), pp. 5–9.

Rogin, Michael, *Ronald Reagan, the Movie* (Berkeley, CA: University of California Press, 1987).

——"'Make My Day!': Spectacle as Amnesia in Imperial Politics," *Representations* 29 (Winter 1990), pp. 99–123.

Ross, Andrew, *Nice Work if You Can Get It: Life and Labor in Precarious Times* (New York: New York University Press, 2009).

Bibliography

Sandel, Michael, *Liberalism and the Limits of Justice*, second edition (New York: Cambridge University Press, 1998).

Sandhu, Sukhdev, "'Slow Cinema' Fights Back Against Bourne's Supremacy," *Guardian*, March 9, 2012. Available at www.guardian.co.uk/film/2012/mar/09/slow-cinema-fights-bournes-supremacy (accessed June 14, 2015).

Schwartz, Sandford, "An Eye on the Tremors," *New York Review of Books*, March 12, 2009.

Staiger, Janet, "Cinematic Shots: The Narration of Violence," in Sobchack, *Persistence*.

Staples, Brent, "History by Default: The Blame Transcends Oliver Stone," *New York Times*, December 25, 1991. In Stone and Sklar, *JFK: The Book of the Film*.

Stone, Oliver and Zachary Sklar (eds), *JFK: The Book of the Film* (New York: Applause Books, 1992).

—— "*JFK*: The Documented Screenplay," in Stone and Sklar, *JFK: The Book of the Film*.

Tompkins, Jane, *West of Everything: The Inner Life of Westerns* (New York: Oxford University Press, 1992).

Trahan, Erin, "Telling a Backwoods Tale with Chilling Accuracy," *Boston Globe*, June 13, 2010. Available at www.boston.com/ae/movies/articles/2010/06/13/winters_bone_director_strived_for_authenticity_in_cast_script_set/?page=full (accessed June 15, 2015).

Turner, Jack, *Awakening to Race: Individualism and Social Consciousness in America* (Chicago: University of Chicago Press, 2012).

Van Sant, Gus, "Kelly Reichardt," *Bomb* 105, 2008. Available at http://bombsite.com/issues/105/articles/3182 (accessed June 14, 2015).

Watkins, Robert E. "Politics In Medias Res: Power that Precedes and Exceeds in Burke and Foucault," *History of the Human Sciences* 23 (2) (2010), pp. 1–19.

Weinraub, Bernard, "Valenti Calls 'J.F.K.' 'Hoax' and 'Smear,'" *New York Times*, April 2, 1992. In Stone and Sklar, *JFK: The Book of the Film*.

White, Hayden, "The Modernist Event," in Sobchack, *Persistence*.

—— "As the World Turns: Ontology and Politics in Judith Butler," *Polity* 32 (Winter 1999), pp. 155–177.

White, Stephen K. *Edmund Burke: Modernity, Politics, and Aesthetics*, New Edition (Lanham, MD: Rowman & Littlefield, 2002).

Wicker, Tom, "Does JFK Conspire Against Reason?" *New York Times*, December 15, 1991. In Stone and Sklar, *JFK: The Book of the Film*.

Williams, Linda, "Melodrama Revised," in Nick Browne (ed.), *Refiguring American Film Genres: History and Theory* (Berkeley, CA: University of California Press, 1998), pp. 42–88.

Williams, Raymond, "Culture is Ordinary," in Jim McGuigan (ed.), *Raymond Williams on Culture and Society: Essential Writings* (Thousand Oaks, CA: Sage Publications, 1958).

Winters, Laura, "'Wendy and Lucy' Filmmaker Kelly Reichardt Eyes the Frayed Edge of Social Fabric," *Washington Post*, January 25, 2009. Available at http://www.washingtonpost.com/wp-dyn/content/article/2009/01/23/AR2009012300851.html (accessed June 15, 2015).

Wolin, Sheldon, *Politics and Vision*, expanded edition (Princeton, NJ: Princeton University Press, 2004).

Yancey, George and Judith Butler, "What's Wrong with 'All Lives Matter'?" *New York Times*, Opinionator Blog, January 13, 2015.

Bibliography

Zelizer, Barbie, *Covering the Body: The Kennedy Assassination, the Media, and the Shaping of Collective Memory* (Chicago: University of Chicago Press, 1992).

Žižek, Slavoj, "Occupy Wall Street: What is to be done next?" *Guardian*, April 24, 2012. Available at www.theguardian.com/commentisfree/cifamerica/2012/apr/24/occupy-wall-street-what-is-to-be-done-next (accessed June 22, 2015).

Zoglin, Richard, "More Shots in Dealey Plaza," *Time*, June 10, 1991. In Stone and Sklar, *JFK: The Book of the Film*.

Index

Alaska, 39, 43, 85, 90, 95–96, 149n.32
All in the Family (Ferguson), 110
Arriaga, Guillermo, 66
autonomy, 1–2, 12, 25, 31–32, 51–53, 63, 79, 85, 100, 112; and automobility, 93

Berlant, Lauren, 84, 86–87, 92, 94–95, 97, 99–100, 102, 119, 123–4, 151n.23; *Cruel Optimism*, 87
Bodies that Matter 50 (*see also* Butler)
Bring Me the Head of Alfredo Garcia (Peckinpah), 69
Bromwich, David, 120
Brown, Wendy, 3, 10, 22, 89, 103–4, 129
Burke, Edmund, 44, 47, 105, 120–23
Butler, Judith, 6–7, 32, 46, 49–64, 65, 78–82, 112, 130, 133, 135–36, 144n.32, 145n.40, 146n.10, 150n.40

Camera Politica (Kellner and Ryan), 14
Cavarero, Adriana, 63
Chambers, Samuel A., 13, 18, 109, 141n.19, 145n.5, 150n.4, 153n.7
choice of inheritance, 47, 120–23, 125, 128, 151n.23
cinema of precarity, 86, 90, 92, 97, 99–100, 123, 147n.6
circumstances, 25, 76, 108, 129, 130, 147n.7
Coogler, Ryan, 134
Cruel Optimism (Berlant), 87
cultural politics, 9, 12–15, 18, 134–36, 139n.45
cultural studies, 7, 11, 14–15, 25–26

Dean, Jodi, 26
dependence, 30, 32–33, 38, 42–44, 76, 84, 89, 91, 99, 105–06, 109–11; declaration of, 113, 119, 120, 123, 128
de Tocqueville, Alexis, 4, 7, 130
"Dirty Harry", 12, 144n.39
Dirty Harry, 15

Eastwood, Clint, 12, 15, 50, 57, 112, 144n.39
Ebert, Roger, 10
Ebiri, Bilge, 19–20
Emerson, Ralph Waldo, 4

family, 33, 66, 68, 73, 79, 97, 100–01, 104, 105–29, 150n.4, 151n.23; the unchosen and, 108–10
Ferguson, Kennan, 110–12, 151n.23
Fisher, Mark, 97
Flathman, Richard, 26, 31–32, 37, 41
Foucault, Michel, 6–7, 25–26, 28, 32, 44, 48
Frames of War, 65, 77 (*see also* Butler)
freedom, 1–10, 12–15, 27, 29, 38, 42, 48, 84–85, 106, 129, 132, 149n.25; neoliberal, 89, 99, 104; power and, 6, 28, 30, 32, 48; pure, 39; vengeance and, 2, 8–9, 14, 105, 108, 110, 112–13, 125, 130, 135
Freud, Sigmund, 30
Fruitvale Station 133–35 (*see also* Coogler)
Furness, Zack, 129n.25

Giroux, Henry, 15
Giving an Account of Oneself, 51, 59 (*see also* Butler)
Granik, Debra, 106, 147n.6 (*see also Winter's Bone*)
Grant, Oscar, 133–35
grievability, 65–83, 132–34

Hobbes, Thomas, 49, 52–53, 145n.50

independence, 7–8, 10, 34, 87, 111, 126
individualism, 1–10, 19, 35, 63, 89; hyper-, 40–42; liberal, 6–9, 24–25, 36–37, 48, 108, 130; sovereign, 3, 7, 9, 83, 129, 131, 135
inheritance, 44–47, 114, 120–23
Into the Wild 9, 24–48, 84–85, 130–32, 149n.32 (*see also* Penn)

JFK (Stone), 15–23
Jones, Tommy Lee, 66

Kellner, Douglas, 14
Kitses, Jim, 66, 74–76
Krakauer, Jon, 24, 33–36, 40, 43–44, 46

liberalism, 1–2, 4, 9, 26–48, 86, 89, 129
Lilla, Mark, 1
Lusted, David, 69

Index

Markell, Patchen, 67, 70, 72–76, 136, 147n.7
Marx, Karl, 25
McCandless, Christopher, 26, 28–29, 33–48, 85, 106, 132, 142n.46, 149n.32
Mehta, Uday Singh, 121
Mill, John Stuart, 6, 24, 27–32, 36, 39 (*see also* On Liberty)
Mitchell, Lee Clark, 69
Mystic River 3, 9, 49, 50, 54, 56, 57, 58, 61, 105, 112, 135 (*see also* Eastwood)

Nealon, Jeffrey, 26
negotiation, 3, 8, 25, 27, 31, 42, 45–48, 84–85, 91–92; family, 110–12, 120, 129, 132
neoliberalism, 8–9, 86–89, 99–100, 104
Nietzsche, Friedrich, 26, 30–31, 45
norms, 52, 56, 77–78, 92, 99–100, 131–32, 151n.23, 153n7
Norton, Anne, 12, 21, 26–27, 29–32, 34, 37–38, 40, 44–45, 47

Oakeshott, Michael, 49
On Liberty 6, 24 (*see also* Mill)
otherness, 68–74

Peckinpah, Sam, 69 (*see also* Bring Me The Head of Alfredo Garcia)
Penn, Sean 24, 35, 55 (*see also* Into the Wild)
political ontology, 49, 67–68, 72, 74–75, 81–83, 86, 146n.8, 147n.7
political theory, 7, 13, 25, 50–53, 62, 108–10
politics of recognition, 67–68, 72, 74–76, 81, 136
power, 3, 6–10, 14–15, 33, 35–36, 42, 46–48; Butler and, 51–52, 62, 64; Foucault and, 7, 26, 28, 32; freedom and, 6, 28, 30, 32, 48; sovereign, 78–79,
Precarious Life 50, 52, 77, 146n.10 (*see also* Butler)
precariousness, 7, 14, 49, 63, 67–68, 79, 81–83, 129, 132
precarity, 84–104, 123–24, 148n.16, 149n.32; cinema of, 86, 90, 92, 97, 99–100, 123, 147n.6
The Psychic Life of Power 50–52, 63, 144n.32 (*see also* Butler)

Reagan, Ronald, 11,
Reichardt, Kelly, 84–5, 91–93, 97, 99–100, 102–04, 147n.6, 148n.17
Rogin, Michael, 12
Romanticism, 24, 28–29
Ryan, Michael, 14

Schjeldhal, Peter, 27
Searls Giroux, Susan, 26
slow cinema, 92, 148n.22
Stone, Oliver, 16–22
subject/subjectivity, 2–4, 6–10, 15, 52, 55, 67, 105, 108–10, 119–21, 126, 131–137; familial, 111–13; liberal, 24–27, 34–35, 40, 44–45, 47; neoliberal, 89, 104

Thoreau, Henry David, 4
The Three Burials of Melquiades Estrada 10, 65–83
Tompkins, Jane, 66, 82

the unchosen, 3–10, 25–26, 44–48, 53, 85–86, 91, 123, 130–36, 147n.7; family, 108–12, 114–15, 129
unfreedom, 5–6, 104

Vedder, Eddie, 24, 36, 40, 42
vengeance, 2, 9, 15, 49–64, 67, 76–77, 81–83, 125–6; freedom and, 2, 8–9, 14, 105, 108, 110, 112–13, 125, 130, 135
vulnerability, 49–64, 71, 75–76, 80, 117, 128–29, 144n.32, 145n.40, 145n.50

Walden (Thoreau), 4, 24, 39
Wendy and Lucy 3, 10, 84–104, 106 (*see also* Reichardt)
White, Stephen K., 121–23
Winter's Bone 3, 10, 105–129 (*see also* Granik)
Wolin, Sheldon, 28, 53

Zelizer, Barbie, 18
Žižek, Slavoj, 5–6

www.ingramcontent.com/pod-product-compliance
Lightning Source LLC
Chambersburg PA
CBHW052049300426
44117CB00012B/2035